Preparing Our Country
for the
21st Century

The Official Transcript of the
United We Stand America Conference

D1506423

Foreword by
ROSS PEROT

HarperPerennial
A Division of HarperCollins*Publishers*

ALBRIGHT COLLEGE LIBRARY

PREPARING OUR COUNTRY FOR THE 21ST CENTURY. Copyright © 1995 by United We Stand America, Inc. All rights reserved. Printed in the United States of America. No part of this book may be used or reproduced in any manner whatsoever without written permission except in the case of brief quotations embodied in critical articles and reviews. For information address HarperCollins Publishers, Inc., 10 East 53rd Street, New York, NY 10022.

HarperCollins books may be purchased for educational, business, or sales promotional use. For information please write: Special Markets Department, HarperCollins Publishers, Inc., 10 East 53rd Street, New York, NY 10022.

ISBN 0-06-095183-4

95 96 97 98 99 ❖/HC 10 9 8 7 6 5 4 3 2

973.928
U58 UP

246943

18.00

This book is dedicated to the thousands of individuals from all over America who sacrificed their time and money to attend this historic conference. The weekend's activities could not have been successful without their dedication to becoming better educated on the issues in the hope of making our country a better place for future generations.

What people said about the conference

"[Conference attendees and those whom they represent] are the people who think our political system and parties have failed in their basic mission of channeling the people's commands to the organs of government. Millions of others who share that view have quit voting, have stopped following public affairs and have turned their backs on the responsibilities of citizenship.

"The Perot people share that disillusionment but instead of dropping out, they have stepped up their civic involvement. They have been moved to take action on their own to repair what they think is wrong.

"For that reason alone, they deserve admiration...

"The attention that prominent Republicans and Democrats lavished on them last weekend was not misplaced. It was, if anything, a necessary plea from the political establishment to the people who may help save the system of self-government from the corrosive cynicism that is undermining it."

David Broder
Washington Post, August 16, 1995

"The Dallas meeting of Ross Perot's United We Stand...was a 19th century sort of event, an echo of an era before electronic entertainments and big-time professional sports and other modern amusements, when self-improvements and social improvement were pastimes and rhetoric was central to both. The Dallas event was in part a recrudescence of the Chautauqua movement of adult education organized around visiting lecturers."

George F. Will
Washington Post, August 17, 1995

"There was no escaping the feeling on the floor hall...that something on the order of a national political convention was under way."

Drummond Ayers
New York Times, August 12, 1995

"The people who came to Dallas showed themselves to be thoughtful and serious. They do have strong views—devoted to granting more power to the states and geared to a revolution in American government. They are as ready to respond to the Rev. Jesse Jackson as to House Speaker Newt Gingrich.

"United We Stand America must be taken seriously. Even if it never forms a national party, its members are starting third parties on the state level. And, of course, United We Stand America voters will be critical, if not decisive, in presidential elections."

Lee Cullum
The Dallas Morning News, August 16, 1995

"The atmosphere (at the UWSA Conference) was as much a civics class as political rally. A few thousand earnest attendees sat for ten and twelve hour days in straight-backed chairs taking notes on the speeches, preparing for the workshops to be held on the final day. They were a skeptical audience but not a cynical one...

"While the candidates hope to leave Dallas with new supporters for next year's campaign, the Perot people seemed more interested in what they could do to force more immediate change in Washington."

Margaret Warner
The MacNeil/Lehrer NewsHour, August 14, 1995

"You [UWSA members] had a sense of urgency—and weren't satisfied with business as usual...I read the other day that you're the fly in the ointment. We need more flies. You're making a difference."

Bob Dole, Senate Majority Leader
The Washington Times, August 13, 1995

"We've got to take the politics out of it and get the problems solved, and that's what I want to do. I'm here because hopefully we can learn some things. That's what this is all about."

Ernest Owen, UWSA member
The Baltimore Sun, August 12, 1995

"The racket of voices and the crush of crowds on the floor of the party conventions defeat all but the loudest or most eloquent speakers. Here, by contrast, the hall was quiet, the attendees in their seats, listening intently and often taking notes—for nine hours one day, eight hours the next.

"Editorial writers who trashed the politicians for 'heading obsequiously to Dallas' should ask those politicians how often they can find 4,000 people who will actually listen closely to their ideas and arguments for a half-hour or more.

"These folks are avid consumers of political news and information—which, in selfish terms, is reason alone for journalists to treat them with respect."

David Broder
The Washington Post, August 15, 1995

"The thing we have to keep focused on is how do we best reform the Congress. If Ross Perot can accomplish that by getting into the political arena, so that he can maintain focus on the critical issues during a campaign and get them enacted and commitments from the candidate, I would support that. If he determines that he could accomplish the same thing by sitting on the sidelines...that would suit me fine also. Ross Perot as president per se is not my personal objective, nor do I believe it is his. It is how can we best effect the reforms that we need in order to move our country forward. And at this point I think we have to wait and see how well the Republicans and the Democrats respond to this conference."

Fred Everett, UWSA member
United Press International, August 13, 1995

"There are enough people in this auditorium to change the nation. You can give us the balanced-budget amendment if you can get the lobbyists out of D.C. You can give us Medicare reform if you get the lobbyists out of D.C. There are enough people here to go back to the nation and do that."

Congresswoman Linda Smith (Washington, 3rd District)
The Washington Times, August 13, 1995

"I've heard a lot of what I hoped I'd hear when I signed up to come down here. Just about everybody has talked about balancing the budget and controlling the power of lobbyists and cleaning up Washington—all the things important to us. But they can't be all things to all people. We've got to talk about this, think on it. Then we'll see where we'll go."

John Schutzbach, UWSA member
New York Times, August 13, 1995

"They [the conference attendees] were energized by this whole thing...I mean they are skeptical of government but they haven't become cynical enough to be turned off yet, and—the fact that they would travel to Dallas for this kind of gathering—these are people who go home at night and watch C-Span. They viewed this as a chance to see all these people live and in color. There was one woman I talked to who said 'this is the greatest educational experience one could ever have.'"

Scott Thurm, *San Jose Mercury News* reporter
Inside Politics, August 14, 1995

"The plane tickets were a strain. I work by the hour. I punch a clock. I worked until 1:00 AM Friday morning and got on a plane at 7:00 AM to be here for a 10:00 AM meeting. I got two hours sleep Friday morning. But is was worth it. This is the turning point. This meeting will be looked at as the turning point in American politics for the 20th century."

Ed Neil, UWSA member
NPR Weekend Edition, August 13, 1995

Table of Contents

The Issues

GOVERNMENT REFORM

GOVERNMENT SPENDING AND TAXES

Political Party Leaders

Presidential Candidates

Ross Perot
Preparing Our Country for the 21st Century

─────────────

Foreword

Ross Perot

From August 11 – 13, 1995, United We Stand America hosted an historic event in Dallas, Texas. *Preparing Our Country for the 21st Century*, a three-day conference about the issues affecting the lives of all Americans, was attended by concerned citizens from across the United States. This meeting was covered by more than 1,000 representatives of the television, radio, and print media from the United States and 24 countries.

The conference was unique in that it brought together national policy experts, leaders of the Democratic and Republican parties, and ten Republican presidential candidates. For the first two days, 36 speakers presented real solutions to critical problems facing our country. This discussion took place in a shared forum of bipartisan cooperation. The speakers received an ample amount of time to express their views. Each was kind enough to allow his or her remarks to be reproduced in this book.

Workshops were held on the third day of the conference. Everyone in attendance had an opportunity to express an opinion on a variety of topics. Experts from various disciplines and backgrounds moderated lively debates. These sessions revealed an interesting crosscurrent of ideas, as well as unique insights into some of the more challenging questions of the day. Any elected official who has doubted the level of interest and concern that hard-working Americans have for the future of this great country need only to have visited the workshops to put those doubts to rest.

This book is composed of three sections: The Issues, Political Party Leaders, and Presidential Candidates. The Issues section is divided into five areas of discussion – Government Reform, Government Spending and Taxes, Jobs, Social Issues, and Foreign Policy. These topics were addressed by nineteen speakers representing both the public and private sectors. The speakers included current and former members of the Senate and House of Representatives, a sitting Governor, and highly respected independent policy experts.

The second section of the book includes speeches by the leaders of the Republican and Democratic Parties, including a representative from the White House. The party leaders were asked to address the question of what their party planned to do to prepare America for the 21st century.

The last section presents the speeches by the Republican Party candidates for President of the United States. Each candidate was asked to give his vision of America in the 21st century, and what specifically would be required to meet these goals.

This conference was also unique in that the members of the audience paid their own expenses to travel to Dallas to take part in a weekend dedicated to helping America. They did not attend for any personal gain or recognition. They came to listen and learn. They came to participate in interactive workshops, where they shared their ideas concerning the federal budget; campaign and lobbying reform; foreign trade agreements; job creation; health care, Medicare, and Medicaid reform; immigration; Social Security reform; term limits; initiative and referendum; tax reform; and welfare reform.

Their goal was to help find solutions to problems. In looking for these solutions, their only filter was, "Is it good for America?" The only motivation of the participants was to leave a better future for their children and grandchildren, and to make the 21st century the greatest in our country's history.

United We Stand America sought to achieve three goals with this conference. First, we wanted to create an environment for political leaders and citizens to come together to discuss the serious problems facing our nation and to explore the possible solutions – an environ-ment beyond the influence of the special interests. Second, we wanted to create an environment where the focus would be on issues and not personalities – a place where sound bites would be replaced with thoughtful discussion; a place where bipartisan bickering would be overcome by positive consensus. Third, we hoped the weekend, and this book, would lead to a better-informed electorate willing to look beyond themselves to what is best for America. We believe that we succeeded in these objectives.

Welcome

Ron Kirk
Mayor of Dallas

As the mayor of the host city, I am pleased to welcome you to Dallas. This is an exciting and historic event – one that will focus on the critical issues that face our nation as we approach the 1996 elections and the 21st century. It is an opportunity for the citizens of this great country to become better informed and more involved.

Thomas Jefferson once said, "The spirit of American Democracy depends on an informed electorate." I believe the activities scheduled for this weekend fulfill that quotation.

As a representative of local government, I recognize the importance and responsibility of developing local solutions to national issues. I share in the hope to move power from special interests in Washington to hometown America. At this level of government we can hear and respond to the hopes and fears of our citizens. This is a great place and time to begin that effort.

The next three days offer the opportunity to look beyond simple sound bites that prevail in our current political system and to learn about the critical issues that face our cities, states, and country. For example, it is one thing to hold out the promise of a flat tax; it is another to explain its impact on businesses and families. It is important to discuss improving Medicare and Social Security, if it can be done without frightening our senior citizens. We must talk about shifting government focus from the distant and centralized, but only if local governments and citizens are prepared to assume the responsibility for improvement. These are the types of questions that will be addressed this weekend.

Let us recognize and respect our differences of beliefs and opinions. We must realize that we each hope and work for a better America as we all move toward the 21st century.

Thank you for coming to Dallas. Thank you for bringing your questions, intensity, and commitment to this event.

Mr. Perot, on behalf of the City of Dallas, I would like to thank United We Stand America and you for giving the City of Dallas the opportunity to host this event.

Ross Perot

Preparing Our Country for the 21st Century

Opening Remarks to the Conference

Welcome. It is great to be with you. Please have a seat. I wanted to bring this young lady who just sang the National Anthem out here to remind everybody across America that we have come together for three days to make sure that her generation and her children can live the American dream just as we have.

The doctors told LeAnn Rimes' parents that they could not have a child. The parents prayed and they had this beautiful daughter.

Obviously, she is their pearl.

God gave LeAnn another gift – a wonderful voice. I want everybody in America to understand LeAnn has never had a voice lesson. Isn't that incredible when you consider her talent?

As we face and grapple with the problems we have to solve to assure a great future for our country, keep all of our children very much in your thoughts; and I know you all agree that no matter what it takes, we will get the job done for them.

Thank you, LeAnn.

This three-day program is dedicated to a real American hero.

Major Richard Meadows is a man who actually lived the role of James Bond in the movies.

Dick Meadows died two weeks ago.

In my judgment our children have the wrong heroes today. Everybody knows who the rock and roll stars are. Everybody knows who the professional athletes are. We know who everybody is that has done something obscene, but we ignore the people who do incredible things.

We have a very knowledgeable audience here. I would like for everybody who knows who Edwin Armstrong was to raise their hands.

This is the man who harnessed the airwaves, made radio possible, and made it possible for us to take this meeting not only across the nation but across the world. He is a real hero.

How many people in this audience know who Jack Kilby is?

He lives in Dallas. I see him at Dickey's Barbecue. He is the man that holds the basic patent on the integrated circuit.

Without the integrated circuit there would be no space program, no space stations and no satellites.

We are transmitting this program all over the world by satellite.

He changed the world.

These should be our children's heroes.

I can put this in perspective with a story.

I had the privilege of introducing Colonel Bull Simons to John Wayne one night. Big tears came into John Wayne's eyes, and he was a man that did not cry easily. He said, "Colonel, you are in real life the role that I only play in the movies."

In our country everybody's favorite fighter pilot is Tom Cruise, a movie actor in *Top Gun*. He can't fly.

Major Dick Meadows is a legendary hero and few people know who he was. We will honor him today.

To explain how important Dick Meadows has been to our country, there was a dinner in Washington after the Berlin Wall came down to honor the heroes of the Cold War. Guess which hero of the Cold War was invited to introduce the President of the United States? Major Dick Meadows, a man you have probably never heard of.

I would like to read the introduction that was given to Major Meadows – before he introduced the President.

Major Dick Meadows' service to our country spans the entire Cold War. Every person here in uniform tonight either knows him personally or knows of his legendary record. He has lived Patrick

Henry's words since 1947 when he joined the Army.

He fought in Korea.

He fought for over three years in Laos and Vietnam.

He led the first team into Son Tay prison. They flew in a helicopter 35 miles behind enemy lines over the most heavily defended city in the history of warfare.

The helicopter had to crash-land into the compound. Dick was on that helicopter. He and his team took the initiative. Unfortunately, the Vietnamese had moved the prisoners from the camp, but the raid was a textbook success.

The only person injured on that raid had a broken ankle caused by a fire extinguisher on the helicopter that hit him in the ankle.

This was Dick Meadows' signature – do the impossible and have no casualties.

He is one of the founders of the Delta Team.

Although retired, Dick Meadows was sent into Tehran in advance of the effort to rescue our 52 hostages.

Imagine going in alone, having to slip in.

He had to buy cars and trucks and arrange all sorts of things. He was going to create explosions and other distractions as the team landed. The team had problems because of a sand storm and had to cancel the mission.

They left Dick Meadows' picture in an abandoned helicopter in Iran, which put his life in even greater danger.

Dick had to get out of Iran on his own. He did.

When the Panama attack occurred, he was already on the ground before our troops arrived. His son, Mark, in the great Meadows tradition, parachuted onto the airport and led the team that captured the airport.

Dick Meadows epitomizes the courage that all of the heroes and their families in the audience represent.

Patrick Henry must be looking down from heaven smiling as he hears about Dick Meadows.

Ladies and gentlemen, it is my privilege to introduce Major Richard Meadows.

Then Major Meadows introduced the President of the United States and here are President George Bush's words: "I have been introduced by kings, heads of state, members of Congress, and leaders of every kind from all around the world, but I don't believe I have ever been more honored in my life than I am tonight to be introduced by Major Richard Meadows."

He turned to Dick and said, "Thank you very, very much, sir."

That tells you what Dick Meadows did for us.

This is a country where ordinary people do extraordinary things. We will make that very clear during this weekend. That is the magic of America. Everything we are doing is to keep this country a place where some young person who is a nobody from nowhere, but has a dream, is only limited by his or her willingness to work and prepare himself or herself to make that dream come true. That is what our country is all about.

I want to thank the members of United We Stand America and every person who has taken the time to come here today.

Good, honest, hard-working people have traveled all across the country from all fifty states at their own expense, spending their hard-earned money to get here.

To the best of my knowledge there has never been an event where so many people have come together to study and learn the details about the issues that will determine the future of this great country.

Many of them had to sacrifice to be here.

Again and again people ask me, "Who are all these people?"

Let me tell you who they are.

These are people who work hard, play by the rules, and live in the center of the field of ethical behavior.

They love this great country.

They are willing to make whatever sacrifices are necessary to make sure that the 21st century is the greatest in its history. They will pass a better country on to their children.

I have every confidence that those who fought and won the Revolution – those who died in combat in all our wars and paid the ultimate price – are looking down on this group today smiling because they realize that true patriotism is alive and well in the U.S.A. as we enter the 21st century.

This meeting could be called a Joe Friday meeting. Those attending want "just the facts, ma'am."

It will be devoted to the issues and the facts.

I would like to thank everyone who is speaking on the issues for participating in this conference.

At a time when civility and dignified behavior seem to be disappearing in our country, I ask every person in this audience to treat every speaker with dignity and respect.

Let's set a new standard for how people act. Let's assume you disagree with what a speaker is saying. Let's just sit there in a nice dignified, quiet way. We do not need any booing, shouting or other disruptive behavior. Thank you very much.

For the next three days we are going to be talking about serious problems we have to deal with now. We cannot keep putting them off.

If we do not solve these problems in a timely manner, literally millions of people will suffer for decades in this great country. In our legislative process, we tend to deal with problems one at a time, as if they were separate and unrelated, when in fact all of these problems are pieces of a complex puzzle. They all must fit together in order for the country to work. Please keep all of this in perspective as we go from one headache to another. You could say, "I'm getting depressed."

Just remember the song from *Annie* – "Tomorrow, tomorrow, I love you tomorrow, you're only a day away." Those of you who lived in the Depression know that was the mood of the nation at that time.

We are the luckiest people in the world because we just happen to live in the country that hundreds of millions of people would give anything to come to.

Today as we discuss the problems that we must solve, please keep in mind that dealing with these problems is insignificant compared to the problems that our ancestors faced and solved.

They came from all over the world in sailing ships.

They populated this great country in covered wagons. You would not want to take that trip – no roads, no shock absorbers, no McDonald's, no Dairy Queen. They hunted for food.

The pioneer's creed tells their story – "The coward never started, the weak died on the way, and only the strong survived."

We have the strong in this meeting today, and we will survive.

What was the reward for the people who made these sacrifices?

Their reward was to get to fight the Revolution. And they won it.

They survived the Civil War and reunited our country.

They survived the Depression and built an even better, stronger country.

They fought and won World War I and World War II, the two greatest wars in the history of man.

They faced every challenge that came along. They realized problems do not go away. If you do not solve problems, they get worse.

The problems we have to deal with today are simple compared to the ones I just mentioned.

Every problem we have to deal with today has been created as a result of our self-indulgence, our divisiveness, and our lack of active participation in government.

It is human nature to blame others for our problems. We would like to blame those we elect to office, but the final blame must be accepted by us, the owners of the country, because we elected them.

We are the problem. These are our problems. We own this country, we must solve these problems by reasserting ourselves and making sure that the people we elect do face these problems.

Millions of ordinary people own this country and it is the vote of the ordinary citizen that determines who gets elected, not the special interest money.

If we are so well informed that we cannot be manipulated by all the campaign tricks, then an intelligent vote will assure the future of our country.

Political campaigns have deteriorated into name-calling, propaganda, dirty tricks, blaming the other party, spin control, and whatever else they can come up with that is unrelated to dealing with issues.

An emotional statement such as "I really care about you" gets votes. You would think that even Forrest Gump would say, "Well, what are you going to do about it?"

Political campaigns are like a magic act now. Now you see it; now you don't. You see it during the election, and then you don't see it anymore. Campaigns also divide our country.

We have asked every speaker to explain how to solve these problems and not use negative techniques. Starting today I hope that every American and every member of Congress will pledge to work together as one team to solve our problems. If we will, nothing can stop us.

In our organization there is only one filter that everything must go through – "Is it good for our country?"

Wait a minute, isn't there a "what's in it for me" filter?

No. Throw that filter away if it exists in any organization that is involved with the issues of our country, and we will give our filter – is it good for our country – to both parties.

Look at the great country our ancestors left us. Think about their sacrifices. Look at your children and grandchildren. Should we burden them with our problems that we have created? No!

Shouldn't we leave them an even better country in the 21st century than we inherited?

We have been free so long, we take it for granted. As we face and deal with these problems, never forget that freedom is precious, freedom is very fragile.

We have been rich so long, we just assume it is our birthright. As you all know, it's not.

After we have put our country's house back in order, it is very important for the young people here to remember enough from this experience not to repeat it in the 21st century. As you study history and civics, you will see that history does tend to repeat itself. Don't let this happen again. If you do, you will have to clean up the mess again.

History also teaches us that in order to have a free society endure, it must rest on a strong moral, ethical base and that every citizen must take full responsibility for his or her own actions.

Someone asked me a few minutes ago, "Why did you have the Boy Scouts here?"

To remind everybody, "Be prepared."

To remind everybody to do a good turn daily – that is the best social program ever invented in the history of man. Help your neighbor. Nothing will ever replace that.

We know we cannot count on others to solve problems for us and that we must stay involved and get these problems solved.

I can summarize everything I have said today with Thomas Jefferson's words: "Whenever the people are well informed, they can be trusted with their own government."

Thank you.

The Issues

Government Reform

Senator
David Boren

Making Government More Responsive to the People

ROSS PEROT: Our first speaker is former Senator David Boren from Oklahoma.

Senator David Boren was born in Washington, D.C. He was raised in Seminole, Oklahoma, and he attended high school there.

He graduated in the top 1 percent of his class at Yale University in 1963. In recognition of his outstanding academic record, he was selected for membership in Phi Beta Kappa.

He was named a Rhodes Scholar and earned a master's degree in politics, philosophy and economics from Oxford University in England in 1965.

In 1968, Mr. Boren obtained a law degree from the University of Oklahoma College of Law, where he received the Bledsoe Prize as the outstanding graduate.

He was elected to the Oklahoma State Legislature in 1968, where he co-authored a bill that established the statewide system of vocational technical schools.

As Governor of Oklahoma from 1975 - 1979, he promoted a number of key educational initiatives.

Governor Boren was elected to the United States Senate in 1979. He served on a number of key committees, including the Finance Committee and the Agriculture Committee. He was the longest-serving Chairman of the Senate Select Committee on Intelligence, and he was Co-chairman of the Joint Committee on the Organization of Congress. He was the author of the National Security Education Act in 1992.

Senator Boren retired from the Senate in 1994, and he now serves as the President of the University of Oklahoma. In 1985, he founded the Oklahoma Foundation for Excellence in Education. Since 1988, he has served as a member of the Yale University Board of Trustees. In 1993, he was presented the Henry Yost Award as Education Advocate of the Year by the American Association of University Professors.

Senator Boren's wife, Molly, is a former lawyer, judge and English teacher. She has been very active in Oklahoma education and arts projects. They have two children – Carrie, a graduate of Yale University, and David, a student at Texas Christian University.

Senator Boren is uniquely qualified to assess the need for making government more responsible to the people.

Senator Boren, it is an honor to have you here today.

T hank you very much. Thank you, Ross Perot. It is a privilege to be with all of you in what is truly a unique gathering of American citizens to come together to grapple with the problems that face us and to try to form a national agenda that will turn our country around. And I suppose it is appropriate that this very large and unique gathering would occur here in Texas. Texas prides itself on doing things that are a little bigger and a little different than anyplace else in the country.

How many here are from Texas? [Applause] Well, that is quite a group. I have to tell you that I am proud of my own Texas roots, my great-great-grandfather came to Texas with Stephen F. Austin, my great-grandfather was here during the Texas Republic and was Land Commissioner. I am a member of the Sons of the Representatives of Texas and then our family was able to realize the dream of every Texas family. We were able to go to Oklahoma to live.

Seriously, when it was known that I was going to come to this conference a lot of people questioned me, some people questioned me in the media, they said, "Why are you going to Dallas to participate in the conference that United We Stand America and Ross Perot have organized to talk about the issues?" I told them, "I want to be with this group of people from across the country to thank them, because when

I was a Senator I attempted to pass campaign finance reform for nine straight years to reduce the influence of PACs and special interest money in American politics."

I also said, "I want to go to thank them, because I pleaded with our President, and with my colleagues, and with the Democratic Party not to pass a budget with just the votes of our own party. We need a budget that is an American budget that we can all stand behind – one that will truly reduce the deficit. United We Stand America tried to make that happen."

You helped me and you stood with me. I would like to come and thank you again because you wrote the cards and the letters and some of you came to Washington to walk the corridors when we were trying to pass the bill to close the revolving door of our own government.

But why have we come here today? I come, like you, as a citizen. Have we come to cheer either Ross Perot or this political movement or other candidates of other parties that will be speaking? Have we come simply to have a rally and to cheer? It is appropriate to have rallies, but they rarely change the course of events in a country.

No, we have come for some higher purpose than that.

Have we come simply to see a good fight between the Republicans and the Democrats and the various candidates that will be here – to take pleasure in watching them score points against each other?

No, we have all seen enough of that. That is America's problem; that is not America's solution.

No, we have come here because we do not take America for granted, because as Ross Perot just said, we realize all that has been given to us by our parents and grandparents and all who came before. We realize that we have been a part of a unique nation. For all of 200 years each succeeding generation has added something of its own sacrifice to what has been given to them and has passed on an enhanced opportunity to the generation that has followed.

We realize that our country, in many ways, is challenged; that we are, in many ways, in trouble; and that some people are in doubt as to whether we can pass along our opportunities to the next generation. We are here because we are determined that we will not pass on a diminished America to our children and to our grandchildren.

About a year ago, as Ross said, I decided to leave the Senate and to go home to the University of Oklahoma to accept an invitation to be

President of that great institution. I did not leave public life or public office because I was disillusioned with public service. I honored public service. I honored the efforts of many sincere men and women who served in public offices, and who want to render a real service to their country. But I believe, also, that public service is not about power; public service is about where you can do the most good. And I decided that at this point in my life, I could do more good by trying to touch the lives of the next generation. Whatever else we do in this country and whatever else we decide on any other issue, if we fail to effectively educate and mentor and nurture and pass our values on to the next generation, we will lose it all.

After I got to the university, I decided I did not want to just sit in the President's office and be an administrator, I wanted to teach, because I remembered all those teachers that had made a difference in my own life. I decided that I wanted to teach the freshman government class, and I taught that class to about 150 freshmen this last semester.

Something happened as I was preparing for my first lecture that also influenced me to want to be here with you today. I asked myself, "How do these young people who I am going to teach – these young people who will hear my very first lecture – how do they feel about their government?" I tried to think back about how I felt about our government at the time that I was a freshman in a government class a few years before. In researching for that first lecture, I ran across a poll that had been conducted by *Time*. The very same question had been asked every 10 years for the past 40 years, "Do you usually trust your government to do what is right?"

In 1964, about the time that I was a freshman in a college government class, 76 percent of the young people said that they trusted their government. I saw the polling results in 1984, and it said that 44 percent of the people in the country trusted their country. I saw the polling data in 1994, and it said that 19 percent of the American people at that time trusted their government. And just before the election, it fell all the way down to 14 percent.

I realized as I walked into that classroom what had happened to our country between the time that I was a freshman in a government class and those students that entered my class this fall. I realized that we had to stop fooling ourselves. Government will always be criticized for decisions and political leaders will always be criticized, but to go from having a 76 percent confidence rating down to 19 percent is not normal; it is not natural, and we cannot accept it. We must not accept it in this country. Those rights that are written in the Constitution are only as secure as we make them by our own love, concern and care for our political system. We must invest ourselves. Others started this country, others wrote the Constitution, others cared for it, others tended to the political process, but now it is ours. We are the trustees. We must not fail in our duty to keep this country alive and strong and vital.

So what must we do to rebuild the lost trust, to reweave the fabric of our society, to bring ourselves together, to give people once again that sense that the government is theirs? First of all, we must continue to fight for the basic reforms of the political institutions of this country.

A poll this morning reflects the fact that 62 percent of the people feel that the two-party system has failed us. Why do people feel as they do?

First of all, they feel it because they feel that Washington really has very little to do with them; that they cannot reach it; that it does not listen to them; and that it does not belong to them anymore. They look at the statistics. They look at the fact that in 1950 there were 1,000 lawyers in Washington, D.C. Today there are 63,000 lawyers in Washington, D.C., more per capita than any other city in the world.

They look at the fact that many of those lawyers have circulated in and out of government – like 51 percent of our trade negotiators have done over the past few years. They work for our government for a few years, and then they go to work for foreign governments and foreign interests against the very government that paid their salaries and whose offices they held.

A few years ago there were Democrats in the majority in Congress, and they did not want to close the revolving door, because so many members of Congress and their staff members also go out the revolving door into the same situation. And guess what? It is not on the agenda – again. The parties have changed, but the same opportunities show that the political establishment still wants to protect itself. We must insist that it go back on the political agenda of this country.

I have often been called upon to give commencement addresses to high school students, and I have urged them to go into government. I still would, because we need our best and brightest and our most caring to occupy the public offices of this country. I urge them to think about running for office. But I leave something out, and perhaps I am not being completely truthful. I do not say to them, "If you want to go to the Congress of the United States, if you want to be a Governor, or if you want to be a United States Senator, not only should you prepare and educate yourself and learn as much as you can so that you will have talent and wise ideas to share with your country; but you must also figure out how you are going to raise the $5 million that it takes to win one of those elections."

At the commencement addresses, I do not ask them, "Are you going to talk the political action committees – who have given more than half of all the campaign money to more than half of all the people now sitting in the Congress – into supporting you, a newcomer, instead of giving the money to the people who are already there and giving money to the people who specialize and impact their own interests more closely? How are you going to deal with the political action committees that gave eight to one to incumbents over challengers?"

How are you going to tell young people that they have to fight those kinds of odds to get into our political system? How are you going to tell them that the government belongs to them when so much control and influence is being wielded in that way? All I can say is that we have waited too long. How long are we going to wait? Are we going to wait until it takes $10 million, or are we going to wait until 80 percent or 90 percent or all of the members of Congress get most of their money from PACs? We have waited too long. We will send a message that we will wait no longer.

Let me say, I did receive some welcome news this week. I am told that a bipartisan effort is underway to reintroduce some of the legislation which I and others and you worked on so hard – campaign finance reform. Senator McCain, a Republican, and Senator Feingold, a Democrat, are planning to join together to reintroduce that bill. This time let us pass it, and let us help them do it.

We have waited too long in terms of restoring confidence to establish an independent ethics commission that will judge our public officials instead of believing that they could be impartial judges in their own cases. So, political reform – reform of the basic political institutions of this country so that people will see that the government really is ours, that it really will listen to us, that we really can have impact – is absolutely essential. That is number one.

Number two, if we intend to rebuild the trust between the people and our government, if we intend to rebuild the social and political fabric of this country, we must also realize that something else has been going on in this country. The very same polling data polled by the Kettering Foundation – the same data that showed people's trust in the federal government was at an all-time low – found something else. It found more people today are involved as volunteers in their local communities; foster grandparents taking the time to mentor young people who do not have family members of their own to do it, people tutoring children, and people forming community groups.

What is really happening all across this country is a virtual renaissance of citizens' involvement again in solving our problems. People may not think they can impact Washington as much as they would like, but people have not stopped caring. They decided to get involved at the state level, at the local level, and through private groups to make a difference in this country.

If we are going to fashion solutions to our problems – whether it is strengthening our educational system, reducing the level of crime and violence in our society, putting people to work who are no longer working or accepting jobs from the government – then many of the solutions, along with the creativity and the vitality to implement the solutions, will come from the grass roots.

People say to me, "Senator, how does it feel to have left the center of action in our country?" I say to them, "I did not leave it when I left Washington. I came home to the center of action where we are going to save this country and turn it around, and head it on the right track again."

Our message to our leaders and to those in Washington is this: have faith in us as people; have faith in our commitment to our country; have faith in our ability to understand the issues; have faith in our creativity; have faith in our willingness to work right in our home communities to turn them around and to get the job done; get out of our way and return some of the financial resources to us so that we can do the job of revitalizing America ourselves.

We need basic political reform. We need further decentralization of the political process. Above all, we need bipartisanship.

The greatest frustration and disappointment that I have had as a member of the Senate, and the factor that probably influenced me more than any other single item – other than my positive desire to go home and make a difference in working with educating young people – was the frustration of seeing the growing party polarization in Washington, trying to work with it every day, and trying to overcome it so that we can solve our problems.

When I first came to the Senate almost 17 years ago, there was an unwritten rule: members of Congress of either party did not campaign against each other. Oh, yes, they could campaign for their own parties when there was an open seat, but they did not go out and campaign against each other. Now, they not only campaign against each other; they take notes against each other; they plot against each other; and then they attempt to sit down and work around a committee table to solve the nation's problems. It will not work. It cannot work.

When I first came to the Senate, we did not have caucus meetings every single week, meetings where all the Democrats go to one room and all the Republicans go to another room to separately create their own partisan agendas. Very often each party tries to figure out how they can offer an amendment on the floor to embarrass the other party – something that will make the other look bad or immoral, or make them look like they do not care about poor people or young people, for example. The accused other party spends time trying to figure out a way not to be embarrassed by the amendment, and then turns around and attempts to embarrass the other side. So many times I wanted to stand up in one of those meetings and say, "Couldn't we put something else on the caucus meetings other than trying to score points on the other political party just as they are trying to score points against us? Why can't we focus the agenda on the need for change?"

We did not need the poll in the morning papers to tell us that the two-party system was in jeopardy. I do not really celebrate that news because I think for most of our history it has served us well. Countries that become too fragmented with multiple parties have problems.

We have all seen what has happened in both parties when they become polarized and members begin to feel unwelcome. The people cannot work together in the center of the country – in the center of the political spectrum – to hammer out a consensus, to hammer out solutions. When the majority of members do not feel productive, they quit going to party meetings and the two parties become controlled by the extreme elements. So more and more people in the country are feeling left out of the political process, forced with the choice of the lesser of the evils.

The two-party system can still survive, but it will only survive if the members of those two parties stop trying to score points on each other. They need to reach across the aisle, join hands, include all of us, and help all of us work together to solve the problems of this country.

It is not too late to do it, but they must do it soon if the party system is to survive as we now know it. The vast majority of the American people are not forever going to sit by with 76 or 80 or 85 percent distrust in their own government and just continue to select between the lesser of evils. We want choices that will set our country on the right path, and we must have those choices.

Why not, for a change, go back to the old rule where members of Congress do not campaign against each other, where they try to form relationships of stability and respect so they can work together? This would be better than having every Tuesday devoted to meetings where only Republicans get in one room and only Democrats get in the other and each talks negatively about the other. Why do we not have a meeting at least every other Tuesday, where the leaders of the two parties get together to see if they can work on a common agenda. Before Congress starts, why don't we have a bipartisan meeting of the leadership and find some things that we could agree upon? There are some fundamental goals that the two parties hold in common. They could agree to work on those items first to hammer out a solution.

Think what we could do for this country if we encouraged the political leadership all across the spectrum to come together to form an agenda that focuses upon those basic problems, those important and fundamental problems that have to be solved if we are going to prepare our country for the next century. That is what we need.

We need to say to our leaders, "Stop concentrating on those highly emotional issues which divide us and find those fundamental principles we must value to prepare all of us as Americans for the next century. That is the agenda that we want as Americans." Let us concentrate on the fundamentals. Very briefly, I will list them.

Let's concentrate on public education, because we know if we do not train our children, then we do not pass on our skills and values to the next generation; those skills and values will die with us. Let's remember that most of our children are always going to be in the public schools. It may be tempting, but let us not fool ourselves into believing that just because some programs simply take a few children from the public schools that we are providing quality education for all the children of this country.

We must strengthen our public schools; we must strengthen them and do it from the grass roots for the next generation in this country. We must internationalize our curriculum. We must prepare our children to speak the languages of other countries and to understand other cultures so that they will be able to react politically and economically with other people in the marketplace of the world. Education is fundamental. If we spent half as much time talking about trying to educate the next generation as we spent on some of the more marginal issues that confront us, we would be a long way down the road as a country.

And second, no one has done more than this group – and I would have to say more than Ross Perot did in the last election – to focus attention on the fact that we must get our budget under control. When you look at what has happened in just 10 years, we have moved from 30 percent of our budget being automatic – beyond our control – to now, within five years, a projection that 72 percent of all the spending in this country will be interest on the debt or automatic entitlement spending. We will no longer be able to set our priorities.

Within 10 years, it is projected that all the private savings of this country will be used just to pay the interest on the national debt. When those two things have happened, we will have lost control of our destiny as Americans. We must never let that happen.

Third, we must reform the tax system. We will never lead the world economically in the next century if we stick with a tax system that penalizes the investment and savings needed to create jobs and productivity, while at the same time encouraging the consumption that causes us to live beyond our means.

Let's talk about the fundamentals: education, budget and taxes. Let's talk about welfare reform. We will never be a whole and a healthy society ever again as long as we have millions of people who have no reason to get out of bed in the morning because we send them a check through the mail for doing nothing.

Let us tell our elected officials in Washington and our candidates for President, "Do not underestimate our intelligence." We know that in the short run it is cheaper to send someone a check through the mail for doing nothing, than it is

- To train that person for a job;
- To help that person find a job;
- To provide day care or transportation to get that person to a job;
- Or, if no private jobs are available, to provide public works projects that are valuable and needed in communities to put those people to work.

Yes, we know it will cost in the short run; but we are willing to pay the cost because we know that if we do not do it, in the long run we will bankrupt this country, both morally and economically.

Fifth, we will all be held accountable at this moment in history if we dodge our international responsibilities. I know that my friend Senator Nunn will be talking to you later about that subject. We are given a unique moment in history, a moment in which the world is not divided into superpower camps facing each other. Think about how long it has been since that has happened.

When I was Chairman of the Intelligence Committee, we saw then the danger of the spread of weapons of mass destruction – including chemical weapons and biological weapons – to those nations of the world that threaten the public peace and to terrorist groups.

We saw that problem as the greatest threat facing the United States. And yet, even though we have a world that is not divided in the superpower confrontation, we need to take the lead in stopping the spread of these kinds of weapons – even through the use of force, if that is what it takes. We must not wait any longer to exercise that leadership, or we will be held accountable by the generations that will follow us.

If our parties will just come together, form an agenda, focus on the things that really matter, and not allow ourselves to be distracted or divided by emotional issues, America will once again move in the right direction.

Some of us, perhaps, will never come to closure on our dream; but let's look at the fundamentals. If we just spend half as much time talking about education, budget, tax policy, welfare reform, and foreign policy as we spend on some of the more sensational issues today, we would be doing our country a great service and we wouldn't have 76 percent of our people saying that they lack trust in their own government.

A few months ago, on April 19th, we were all reminded – and those of us in Oklahoma were especially reminded – about what really counts in our lives. In the moment when that powerful explosion ripped through the Murrah Federal Building – leaving many dead, hundreds of others wounded, families separated, children killed, and other children orphaned – we realized something about ourselves as a people that I hope we will not forget. We saw pictures of that African-American fireman and rescue worker holding that small white child. We saw pictures of that Hispanic citizen holding in his arms an American Indian woman who was weeping. And in that moment – no one asked as they reached out to help, to render assistance, to render medical care, to care for the family members left behind – no one stopped to say, "Are you a Republican or a Democrat, a liberal or con-servative; what race do you belong to; what is your religion; pardon me, where do you stand on some of these issues that we argue about so heatedly in the coffee shop?"

We reached out with love and understanding, and we realized that we were one American people. We realized that the things which unite us are so much more fundamental than the things that divide us: the value of human life, the importance of family, the importance of the rule of law and living in a society where you can get up and go to your job and about your business each day without fear. It brought so much into focus.

So we begin this conference. Many others will follow me: leaders of the political parties, candidates for President of the United States, experts in various fields, and passionate advocates of different points of view on issues in this country. I challenge all of those who will follow – and I urge you not just to be an audience but to be participants in this process of challenging those that will come to this podium – to tell us how they will bring people together.

I urge you to ask them these questions:

- How will they help to focus us on what is truly lasting and impor-tant to our future?
- How will they dampen the flames of those emotional issues that divide us and divert our attention?
- How will they appeal to our best instincts?
- How will they appeal to our willingness to sacrifice for the com-mon good?

Americans are not angry because they hate their country or their government. Americans are frustrated because they love their country so much they want it to be all that it can be.

To those who will follow me at this podium and to those who would ask you that they be our leaders, we say, "Do not appeal to our fears, do not appeal to our prejudices, do not appeal to our selfishness. Instead, seek the common ground, and bind us together around goals worthy of our best effort."

To our leaders we make three appeals: Bring us together; bring us together; bring us together.

Thank you very, very much.

ALBRIGHT COLLEGE LIBRARY 246943

Congresswoman Linda Smith and Congressman Sam Brownback

Campaign Finance Reform and Lobbying Reform

ROSS PEROT: Congresswoman Linda Smith represents the Third District from the state of Washington. She was elected to the House of Representatives in 1994, and she is the first person in the history of that state to qualify for the general election ballot as a write-in candidate.

She was born in 1950 in La Junta, Colorado. She operated a tax consulting business for 14 years.

She was elected to the Washington State House in 1983 in a special election, and she was reelected in 1984 and 1986. She was elected to the state senate in 1987 and reelected in 1988 and 1992.

She is one of the few freshmen members of Congress to chair a subcommittee – the Small Business Subcommittee on Taxation and Finance. She is a member of the Resources Committee.

Congresswoman Smith and her husband, Vern, have two children and five grandchildren.

Congressman Sam Brownback is a Republican first-term Congressman from Topeka, Kansas. He has taken a lead role among the members of the freshman class in reducing the size and intrusiveness of the federal government.

He grew up on a farm near Parker, Kansas. He was Student Council President at Prairie View High School. He was also State President and a national officer of the FFA.

Congressman Brownback graduated from Kansas State University where he was Student Body President. After graduation, he worked at the Kansas State University radio station as a broadcaster for farmers.

He received his law degree from the University of Kansas. He then became a partner in a law firm in Manhattan, Kansas. He also taught agricultural law at Kansas State. He served as city attorney in both Ogden, Kansas, and Leonardville, Kansas.

He served as Secretary of Agriculture for the state of Kansas.

Congressman Brownback serves on the House Budget Committee, International Relations Committee, and Small Business Administration Committee.

He and his wife, Mary, have three children.

The topic of Congresswoman Smith and Congressman Brownback's talk today is the Freshman Clean Government Act.

Let us welcome them both.

CONGRESSWOMAN SMITH: This is one of the most exciting days of my life because I see people who care more about clean government than they do about politics, and I thank you for that.

You know this time last year I was a woman getting out of politics. I was on a weekend trip with my husband saying, "No more." I came back on Labor Day of last year resolved that Congress would not change, and I was getting out. I arrived to a grassroots effort, and in two weeks the people of Washington wrote me in on the ballot and I was sent to Congress within a few weeks of that. I did not run for election.

I want to tell you that I was not only shocked, but I was sent with a mandate from my people to do the same thing that I had done in Washington State with grassroots organizations – clean up politics. In Washington State just two years earlier, the people and I passed a

Clean Government Act. That Clean Government Act returned power to the people of Washington.

You see, what had happened in Washington is the same thing that has happened all over our nation. The candidates were relying less and less on individual contributions, and they were turning to deep-pocketed PACs. It was an alarming trend that the people of Washington were not willing to tolerate.

So, by 1992 they responded decisively by voting for a Campaign Reform Act that I had drafted. It significantly reduced special interest control over Washington state politics. It eliminated gifts and severely limited the type of junk mail that you get in an election paid for by your tax dollars. During this last year, the incumbents who would not go to the streets and campaign just decided to not run again. We ended up having grassroots politics putting in candidates who came off the streets all over Washington State. We had our own version of term limits in Washington. The chart below illustrates the impact of the Campaign Reform Act in the state of Washington.

Contributions and Spending Levels in Washington State
Before and After Campaign Reform Law (in millions)

Total Contributions

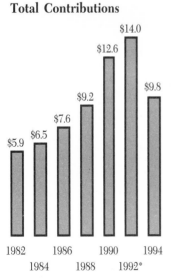

Total Spending

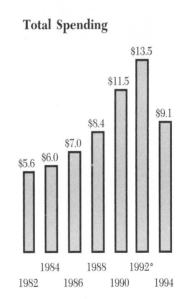

° Year Campaign Reform bill became law

What I want to tell you today is that I arrived in Washington, D.C., with 89 other freshmen. I was pleased to find out that they had all been sent with the same mandate – clean up Washington, D.C. We were to be a different Congress – a clean Congress, a group of idealists from the heartland of America. Most of us were grassroots politicians. We were not seasoned politicians, and we had our victories. Things were great. We did some things at first to reform Congress, but not for very long. In just a few days, we were enrolled in the School of Hard Knocks. The war machine that had been fueling for 40 years to block campaign finance fired up. It was looking for recruits, and it looked to the freshmen.

I watched my freshmen colleagues come up against a system that will just eat you up. It is like being thrown into a polluted lake. You either swim as hard as you can and keep your head above water, or you sink. And we are all survivors, so we were swimming. It was frightening.

These idealists – one by one – had to face something that they could not get around. Their opponents had been raising PAC money, and many of these challengers had to go with a big debt to Washington, D.C. These challengers ran against people like Speaker of the House Tom Foley, who had millions of special-interest dollars. Guess who was at the door to pay the debt? The special interests. Guess who was at the other door? Their new opponent, raising money from special interests.

These freshmen are not stupid. They are bold, but they are not stupid. They are not going to lay down their arms when someone else is holding the bazooka. So what I saw was good people pulled right into a system from which they could not escape.

This is the way it is in Washington, D.C., right now. I am not going to pull any punches – the only people who can change the special-interest stranglehold are in this room.

We arrived to fact-finding trips. The best way that I can explain this is to compare it to an addiction. You get there, and the first night on your schedule you are at all of these receptions. The members of Congress are there to raise money and the special interests are lined up to oblige. You go because it is part of your schedule. It is where you meet people. Then you go to another reception where another member is trying to pay his or her debt. And then another, and another.

I do not have fundraisers in D.C., but I did not have a debt.

A group of us have come together, and we are saying, "No more."

Sam Brownback and I are standing, and we are standing alone right now. One by one, members are starting to come to us, old-timers and newcomers, and saying, "You are right, you are right, you are right."

I want Sam Brownback to talk to you about his impressions of what it is like to arrive, and what it is like to face offers for trips around the world your first day after arriving in Washington, D.C.

I would like to introduce Sam Brownback to you.

CONGRESSMAN BROWNBACK: Thank you, Linda. I appreciate that. And I appreciate you folks and all you are doing to change the course of this country. It is imperative that we do it.

I have to give you one quick aside on Linda Smith. How many of you have seen the classic Jimmy Stewart movie of *Mr. Smith Goes to Washington*? This is the 1995 version: Mrs. Smith Goes To Washington, and she is doing a great job with it. That's right – we're just going to update that film and play it again.

I will tell you what I saw when I first came to Washington – a domestication process. A domestication process where they bring in new, fresh legislators and start to tame them with gifts and meals and trips – almost like a horse with a sugar cube. The special interests just kind of hold the rewards out and domesticate the members of Congress. They take the edges off of the members and take the grassroots ideas out of them that they brought from home. The system tells them, "No, you cannot do that," or "You have to be reasonable," or "That is too difficult."

Well, it is not too difficult. At this point in time we need to be reasonable about what we need to do for the future of our country and for our children. This system is being influenced by those special-interest, outside factors.

I am going to talk particularly about gifts. I am talking about trips and meals and just straight gifts that special interests give to people in Congress. You have got to ask yourself, "Well, why do they do that?" I am not saying that a Congressman is bought and sold for a gift, but it does influence the system. Otherwise, why did lobbyists fly Dan Rostenkowski to Palm Springs ten times during 1990 and 1991 and to Hawaii four times during that time period? They are trying to influence the system.

Why was I offered a nice clock by a large Fortune 500 company in this country after I was elected to Congress? You know, they did not offer one the year before when I was not in Congress. Maybe they just did not know me then and what a nice guy I am. I rather think they are trying to influence the system. The truth is, it does influence the system. People are not bought and sold there, but many are influenced by this corrupt system.

Three-fourths of the American people do not trust their government to do what is right most of the time. That is from a poll taken recently. It is too high. A big part of the reason they do not trust the system is they think it is bought and paid for. We have to change that. It is time to stop. It is time to just say no to gifts. Just say no, we do not need these things. We are paid a good salary. We can earn things just like everybody else. Just say no.

This is the essence of our bill, H.R. 2072. It is very simple. It is a very short bill – you just cannot accept trips, gifts, or meals from lobbyists or special-interest groups. That is pretty simple, pretty straightforward.

You know, I think it would be a good exercise to have Congressmen go out for a meal and go Dutch. They should have to pay for a "free lunch" every once in a while, see what that is like. I think it will also help Congress understand that there is no such thing as a free lunch when they are spending your taxpayer dollars.

These are simple reforms. They are needed reforms. We need massive change in Washington so that people can trust their representative government again.

Gil Gutknecht, from Minnesota, is one of the members of our freshman class – the new Third Party, as Newt Gingrich named it last night. Gil's grandmother has a saying that I think is awfully good. She says, "You know, if you always do what you've always done, you always get what you always got." When you think about it, if we keep on – in this system – always doing what we have always done, we are going to always get what we have always got. This is why we have to change the system.

We have made some important strides. We are not done yet, but we have made some good strides.

I want to tick off some of these because I think they are impressive. A lot of these measures were things that were championed by United We Stand America and by Ross Perot.

On the opening day we passed and authorized the first audit ever of the House of Representatives. The place has never been audited in its history. We found a system with two sets of books – a system that met the Congressmen's and Congresswomen's needs and desires, regardless of efficiency or economy. We found a system that in one 15-month time period could not account for $9.3 million. We found a system that Price Waterhouse would not "pass" because the validity of the records are so bad. That is what we found in the audit.

We also did some other things this group championed. You know the subsidized barbershop, the one that will not give Ross Perot a haircut? Well, we did away with that, by privatizing it.

You know what? We also had a House aesthetician. I do not know how many of you know what an aesthetician is, but it is a person who gives facials. We had one that was being subsidized by taxpayer dollars. You all know the last thing Congress needs is another facial; it needs a fire hose.

I do not know how many of you knew this, but we had daily buckets of ice delivered to our doors, as members of Congress. I do not know why. We have refrigerators; we can make ice. Maybe it dated back to a time period before there was refrigeration, so they delivered a bucket of ice. You know how much it costs? It costs a half a million dollars a year just to deliver ice to Congressmen's doors. That is ridiculous. So we kicked the bucket. We said, "Get it out of here. We are not going to do that anymore." That is what we ought to be doing.

And you know the junk mail that you get – the franked mail that is the taxpayer-financed communications that you get from your member of Congress? We cut that back by one-third, and I think it needs to be cut out altogether during election years. We made that progress. And committee staffs – we cut committee staffs by one-third, and we need to cut our personal staffs back, too. We are pushing to get that done.

We banned proxy voting so you cannot just have a chairman sitting in the committee and voting for all the members. We said, "You know what? We elected you guys, you go sit in a room and vote. We do not have the chairman there to do that." We also limited the committee chairman to six years. In other words, no more dictators being developed up in these committees over many years. Six years as a committee chairman, and that is it; you are done.

We applied to Congress all the laws as they applied to the rest of the land. Wasn't it about time that that happened?

Ladies and gentlemen, we have made some real changes under this new leadership and under this new Third Party of the freshman class. More dramatic reforms are needed. We need your help to get two things done. First, we must change the system by passing the Clean Congress Act. We have to have that, folks. We need your help.

And the second point – we have to get more of the power and control out of imperial Washington and back to the people. That is where it belongs; that is where the Constitution says it should be, and that is where it has to be. Otherwise, you are always going to have people willing to spend millions of dollars to influence billions of dollars in decisions by the government. The power must go out to the people.

We need to delimit Washington, make it smaller, more efficient, and more focused. It must be less intrusive and return to being a servant of the people and not their master.

Thank you.

Linda is now going to tell you how we are going to get these reforms done.

CONGRESSWOMAN SMITH: Well, what I would like to do is summarize for you the freshman plan. I want to tell you it is not easy, but it will change the culture of the political process.

First, we want to stop all Washington, D.C., fundraising – no money at all in Washington, D.C. This will do two things – stop some money and stop the influence. It will also give us a lot more time at night to do our work instead of going to fundraisers.

Second, and probably more important, I am going to tell you about something that happened to me three weeks ago that just literally made me sick at my stomach.

I was running the amendment to eliminate the tobacco subsidy. Sounds easy, doesn't it? You go to the lunchroom and there are tables of tobacco lobbyists and people there to work the bill. These people are lobbying for something the American people do not want. Then the day of the vote came; I lost by 13 votes. I looked at it and I thought, no way are there 230 votes from the tobacco states for the subsidy. The tobacco lobby won. We absolutely have to take them out of these halls. I do not think I should have to wonder whether I lost a vote because of a lobbyist's check.

You know, for too long the lobbyists have muddied up the welcome mat of Washington, D.C. Something has just gone terribly wrong. When you read on the front page of the paper that a luncheon is being sold at the White House for a hundred thousand dollars for Congressional races, and the voters are left out in the cold, something is definitely wrong.

I want to read a quote to you from Senator Wyche Fowler from Georgia in the book *Speaking Freely*, where all the lobbyists, or all of the ex-politicians, were able to say what they really thought about Washington, D.C. He says, "A brutal fact we all agonize over is that if you get two calls and one is from a constituent that wants to complain about the Veterans Administration mistreating her father and one is from somebody who is giving you a party and raises $10,000, you call back the contributor."

You know, PACs have demonstrated their ability to raise huge sums of money and their willingness to use it to buy influence. Voters just do not have that kind of money, and it has to change.

To illustrate that point, look at 1984. PACs gave $75 million. Last year it was $132 million. That money is not coming from your states, it is coming at receptions and fundraisers between votes. It is coming every night of the week that we are in Washington voting.

Now, who is getting the money? Primarily incumbents – incumbents, plain and simple. In the 1994 election, PACs favored incumbents four to one. And in fact, challengers received over 80 percent of their money from voters. It was merely 50 percent for incumbents. The chart on the next page shows the diversity in campaign contributions between incumbents and challengers.

PACs may have their place at the table, but they should be there with their ideas, not their money. The loudest voice that Congress hears has to be yours.

And finally, the bring-campaigns-home provisions do one thing plain and simple, they make the incumbents go home. Right now, they sit there and the money flows in. They do not have to go home.

The interesting thing about this, and the reason most of us support term limits, is we believe that the power that is in Washington, D.C., needs to be terminated. The Clean Congress Act does it. It returns candidates home. If I am sitting in Washington, D.C., and my opponent is at home raising money, and I cannot raise it in D.C., guess what is going to happen? I am going to go home. You are not going to see Tom Foley

1994 Campaign Contributions by Category

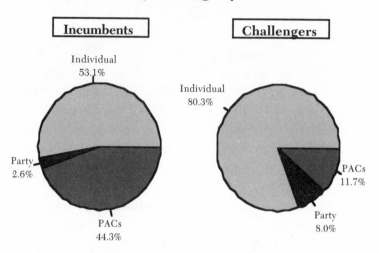

| Incumbents | Challengers |

Incumbents
Individual 53.1%
Party 2.6%
PACs 44.3%

Challengers
Individual 80.3%
PACs 11.7%
Party 8.0%

and others build houses in Washington, D.C., for long-term stays if they cannot raise money there. They are going to have to go home.

You know, I take this very seriously. About five years ago I started working on this issue in our state. It took me until 1992 to get it passed. It was not an easy thing to do. But I will tell you what it did. Candidates in the streets won last year. It dropped the spending on campaigns by a third. It took out those 15 top special interests that controlled most of the nation and most of the politics. It took them to their knees – took them mostly out – and it returned campaigns to the people. We literally have a new set of folks in Washington state politics, not the old-timers anymore.

In summary, we take PACs out of all federal elections. U.S. Representative Mel Levin confirms the impact PACs have. I want to read this to you. He is another former U.S. Representative. He said, "On the tax side, the appropriations side, the subsidy side and the expenditure side, decisions are clearly weighted and influenced by who has contributed to the candidates. The price that the public pays for this process, whether it's a subsidy, a tax, or appropriation, is quite high." Under H.R. 2072 we eliminate PAC-buying influence. We also say no federal candidate can take any money from anybody except someone in his or her state, and only reasonable small party contributions. We effectively eliminate the mass mailings in the election year by saying that 90 days before the primary and 90 days before the general election, no money is paid out of taxpayer money to fund these mailings. We tell the wealthy they can no longer put money up front and then raise it back from PACs after winning. Maybe under the Supreme Court you get to do that because of *Buckley v. Valeo*, but you just cannot pay yourself back. If you give it, you have given it. The advantage they have is brought way down.

The wealthy are losing traditionally in campaigns because people find it offensive for them to buy campaigns.

Now, Representative Brownback mentioned the part that we find the most objectionable. We will be eliminating totally all meals, all trips, all gifts – everything, no exceptions.

My mom used to say, "Linda Ann, if you're complaining and you're standing up, you can complain; but if you're sitting down, just shut up." And I have to say, "If you are willing to stand up with us and march forward, then stand up and clap; but just sit down and shut up if you are not." America has to have change and that means doers. You here are doers. That is why I paid my way and my husband's way and a couple of other people's way to be here, because I believe you are doers. And I am going to say something that makes people very uncomfortable, not just you, but everybody else. No more studies, no more commissions. We know what is right, let us call on our leaders to do it right now.

You know, the theme of this conference is Preparing Our Country for the 21st Century. If there is one thing that you can deliver, and there are enough people in this auditorium to change the nation, you can give us a Balanced Budget Amendment. You must get the lobbyists out of D.C. You can give us Medicare reform if you get the lobbyists out of D.C. There are enough people here to go back to the nation and do that. We have to pull out our mops and buckets and brooms to clean out the cobwebs and close the doors of Congress to the special interests.

Sam is going to tell you how we want you to help us. We came here with a plan, and we know we are just two lonely, kind of angry, kind of determined voices without you.

Thank you.

CONGRESSMAN BROWNBACK: Thanks, Linda. We need your help, ladies and gentlemen. You heard Newt Gingrich speak last night and Bob Dole speak this morning. These leaders are interested and willing to go ahead and put forward campaign finance reform and gift lobbying reform. They are willing to do it. They are absolutely willing to do it, but you have to push hard to get it up the priority list. They are willing to do it, but unless it becomes a priority, it competes with a whole lot of other interests. So we need your help.

You need to be able to talk to your radio talk show hosts and say, "Let's talk about campaign finance reform, let's talk about gift bans." Write a letter to the editor. You can do that. You can express your support for reform. We need to be able to do these things to influence this system and change it and clean the House.

We can do these sorts of things. You, this organization, United We Stand America, has put issues on the radar screen in Washington, D.C., before. You have done it on a lot of big issues. You can do it on this issue if you choose. We want you to make it an issue. We need you to make it an issue. This is something that is going to have to come from outside, from the grassroots into the system.

I want to finally say, on behalf of Congresswoman Smith and myself, thank you for the force that you are in American politics today – the force of renewal, the force of revival, the force which says, "Let us put the country first, and let us do what is right for the kids. We have to do it for the future of our country."

You have done that and Ross Perot has helped make those issues front and center – bringing renewal and revival to a renewed America that is going to be ever prosperous in the future if we make the right choices today. Help us. Help us pass H.R. 2072.

Thank you very much. God bless you all.

Congressman
Bob Inglis

Term Limits

ROSS PEROT: Our next speaker is Congressman Bob Inglis. Congressman Inglis represents the Fourth Congressional District of South Carolina. He grew up in Bluffton, South Carolina.

Congressman Inglis is a 1981 Phi Beta Kappa graduate of Duke University and a 1984 graduate of the University of Virginia Law School. He was elected to Congress in 1992.

Congressman Inglis has been at the forefront of the term limits debate. He wrote one of the two term limits bills in the Republican's Contract with America. He has pledged to limit his own term to three two-year terms.

True to his goal of abolishing Political Action Committees, Congressman Inglis has never accepted any contributions from a PAC. Congressman Inglis serves on the Budget and Judiciary Committees. He and his wife, Mary, have four children.

Congressman Inglis is with us this evening to talk about one of the more controversial subjects of reform in Congress – term limits. He will assess what we can realistically expect Congress to do in this area. I am sure you are going to find it very interesting.

Let's welcome Congressman Inglis from South Carolina.

Thank you. It is great to be with you. Mr. Perot, thank you for that introduction. Thank you for the opportunity to speak to you tonight. It really is a great honor.

When you are in Texas, you get reminded of a lot of Texan stories. I am reminded of the story of the child in Texas who met a stranger, and the child asked the stranger where he was from. The child's father, before the stranger could answer, gently rebuked the young guy and said, "Son, never do that. If a man is from Texas, he will tell you. If he is not, why embarrass him by asking?"

I want to start tonight by thanking the 25 million Americans in 22 states, many of whom are represented right here, who voted for term limits when they had the ballot opportunity. I also want to thank the thousands of grassroots activists and volunteers who worked at the state and local level to put those initiatives on the ballot and who made this issue come to the forefront of the modern political debate.

The bubble-up strategy on term limits is working – the idea of forcing the issue at the state and local level and bringing it to Washington. The incredible pressure that you have applied has helped bring the vote – the first-ever vote in the history of this country – to the floor of the House in March of this year.

The beauty of that vote is it now will create accountability for members of Congress, particularly in the states that voted for term limits in those ballot initiatives.

I also want to congratulate you on this remarkable national conference and the gathering of political leaders and activists from across the country. Congratulations also to those of you who have been brought into or, in some cases, brought back into the political process with the formation of United We Stand America.

Ross Perot's appeal to America has energized millions in this country who had grown completely disaffected from government. United We Stand America has given a voice to those who felt the gulf between the government and the governed was too great. As a bridge, United We Stand America has brought many into the national discussion who were lost when Americans checked out of politics and we began our failed experiment with a ruling political class.

Starting in 1992 and continuing in 1994, you sent that ruling political class a message: Americans intend to be back in charge. You and I know that term limits are the best way to make sure that ruling class does not come back.

I would like to be able to tell you that the new majority would some-how be immune from that problem, but it will not be. While I hope the philosophy of downsizing government holds on for a good, long time, the same individuals holding on for a good, long time will create the same problem we had before. That is why it is essential that we limit terms in office.

Just as we limit the President to two terms, and just as we limit most of the governors in this country to two terms in office, we must limit the terms of members of Congress and Senators in this country so that we can have a truly representative body.

Some would have you believe that there is no need for term limits now. They will point to a tremendous change in 1994 and say, "See, there it is, proof positive, an election can work as well as term limits. You can do at the ballot box what you can do in the Constitution."

But it is very important to make one observation to somebody who says that. The reelection rate in 1994 of those who wanted to come back was 90 percent. Let me repeat that incredible fact, 90 percent of the members of Congress who wanted to come back in 1994 came back.

We got some turnover. Some of it was because of high profile losses by incumbents, but most of it was because of retirements, not losses by virtue of challengers beating incumbents.

That reelection rate does not indicate that people love their own member of Congress. Although, I hope that the folks in South Carolina, at least in the fourth district, love the current speaker.

It does not indicate that people love their own member of Congress when they reelect him or her time and again. What it indicates is that the average member of Congress has an incredible incumbent advan-tage, starting with the fundraising, and going on in other ways.

We need campaign finance reform, and that would fix part of the problem. But the tremendous advantages of incumbency would still remain. Just as with the President and the governors, term limits are the best way to fix the problem of long-term incumbency and to make sure we can keep that closed sign on the professional politician's office.

Now, as you are aware, we suffered a little setback when the Supreme Court recently ruled that states cannot, by state action, limit the terms of federal officeholders. But I believe that the Supreme Court has actually inadvertently done us a great favor. Respecting the Court's opinion, as we must, it is now clear what we have to do. We have to pass a constitutional amendment to the U.S. Constitution calling for term limits.

The only way to do that is to start with a two-thirds vote in both houses of Congress amending the Constitution with the proposed amendment, and then it goes out for ratification by 38 states.

Now, I realize that is a little bit tough because asking members of Congress to vote for term limits is a little bit like asking the chickens to vote for Colonel Sanders. But before you despair, there is a chance that even the yard birds would choose a well-fed life in the Colonel's cages.

There is hope. In fact, we have every reason for hope because of the quantifiable progress that has happened in the last Congresses.

The chart below shows that in the 102nd Congress – the Congress elected in 1990 to serve from 1991 to 1992 – there were only 33 cosponsors of term limits legislation.

Congressional Support for Term Limits

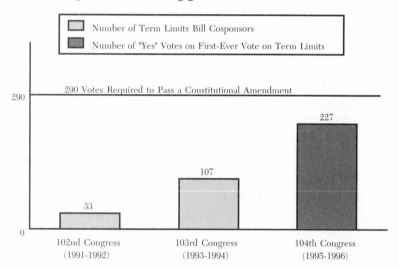

With your help, the 1992 elections brought in the 103rd Congress where we had 107 cosponsors of term limits legislation. There was not a vote because the ruling class refused to give us a vote, but we had 107 cosponsors.

Some of those are people like Tillie Fowler of Florida. Tillie and I were both elected in 1992. Our class is the one that took it to 107 cosponsors. Then because of your help at the polls in 1994, a number of key retirements, maybe a few indictments, and a couple of wins by key challengers, we got 227 votes for term limits, and it came to the floor for the first vote in the history of this country.

I have to tell you that I am happy with the progress you see, but there is a sense of urgency on my part and people like Tillie Fowler. You see, I propose that we limit members of Congress to six years; and, therefore, I am going to limit myself to six years in the House. Tillie Fowler is proposing an eight-year limit; and, therefore, she is going to limit herself to eight years in the House – none of this hanging around for 14 or 16 years in office and pushing for 12-year term limits. "How many years do you want to limit?" is an awkward question to answer if you are a member of Congress.

Therefore, I only have one more shot at this, one more term in order to see this happen, and I need your help.

A minute ago I told you that the Supreme Court decision had helped us to focus all of our effort on getting an amendment to the U.S. Constitution. We need 63 votes in the House of Representatives in order to propose that constitutional amendment.

It is hard to amend the United States Constitution. It should be, and it is. You have to start by getting that two-thirds vote in both the House and the Senate. That means we need 290 votes in the House and 67 votes in the Senate. After that, with your help, I think we will easily get the 38 states to ratify. All we need is 63 more votes in the House. When you consider how we have come from 33 cosponsors to 107 cosponsors to 227 votes in March, getting 63 more votes should not be that hard for Americans – Americans who desperately want to be back in charge of this process.

Let me make sure you know that this is not a crop that grows indigenously in Washington, D.C. You have to import term limits supporters to Washington. They just do not grow there. You have to import them from places like South Carolina, Florida, Texas, California, Wisconsin, and New York. And just to make sure you understand what we are up against, consider my selection for the most arrogant statement made on the floor of the House during the term limits debate. In response to the observation that the American people want term limits, a member of Congress actually said, "Sometimes the American people are simply wrong."

Apparently, he is wrong. I have to believe that it was this kind of member of Congress that a staff member of President Grant's cabinet long ago was thinking of when he said, "You can't use tact with a congressman. A congressman is a hog. You must take a stick and hit him on the snout."

Get ready because here comes the stick. Republicans, Democrats, and Independents all overwhelmingly support term limits.

Support for Term Limits
Among the American People

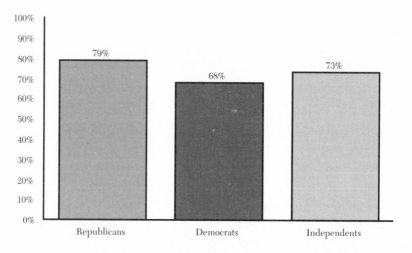

In March it did become a slightly more partisan issue with 227 votes – 83 percent of the Republicans voting yes, 82 percent of the Democrats voting no. But there is an important fact that Democrats in particular should notice. In a recent poll commissioned by Cleta Mitchell of Americans Back in Charge – the leading term limit group helping us with this endeavor – 78 percent of those who identified themselves as conservative Democrats supported term limits, and 54 percent of those said that a candidate's stand on term limits would be an important deciding factor in their vote for 1996. I can assure you that that block of conservative Democrats will be a very critical constituent in the 1996 election cycle.

Here is where we need your input. We need your help in figuring this out. We know what we have to do in order to get term limits. We have to amend the U.S. Constitution. The Supreme Court has made that clear to us. We know what we need in order to do it. We need 63 votes in the House. The question then is how to do it. What kind of term limits is the best? That is where we need your help and your input.

I would hope that in the breakout groups that you have tomorrow you would discuss which of the options would be the best for us to take up in the next Congress. Some people like a maximum of 12 years, allowing the states the flexibility to choose under that 12-year maximum limit. Some people like a uniform, nationwide 12-year limit. Others, like me, prefer a six-year limit in the House and still others an eight-year limit.

Optimal Term Limit For House Members: Opinions of American Voters

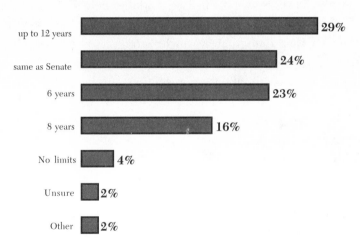

What I hope you will do is discuss that among yourselves tomorrow and communicate your conclusions to Russ Verney [Executive Director of United We Stand America]. Russ is doing an excellent job for you on behalf of your organization and is somebody that we count on as a critical member of this team to get term limits. We really do sincerely solicit your input through the breakout groups tomorrow. I hope that you will remain open to the consensus position that emerges on this matter.

Regardless of the final outcome of that process, I am going to limit myself to what I propose, three two-year terms in the House. But I believe that I have to remain open in this process to other proposals if you and others come to us with another proposal.

Americans want term limits. They want them to be real, but they will take term limits in a number of different flavors. The key here is to avoid the confusion that we could have had in the last vote in March without the help of Dick Armey, our very principled and helpful majority leader from the great state of Texas. I can tell you that the options would have proliferated to the point that our opponents would have had the opportunity to cast throwaway votes for one of the many versions of term limits on the floor while scheming to scuttle our cause. It might surprise you that that kind of thing happens in Washington, but it does happen there in these funny votes on the floor of the House.

It is my hope that we can agree on a consensus position, rally behind it, and then go out and find those 63 votes.

Now, the 63 votes, where shall we find them? Here I have saved the best for last. There is a special list that I am about to describe to you.

I believe that the greatest single strength of United We Stand America is your insistence on accountability; accountability in balancing the budget, accountability representing your people, accountability to the future of America. That is where that vote we had back in March becomes so very critical. Because that vote was included in the Contract With America, we now have accountability.

Some of the 63 votes will come from new members who replace retiring members who voted no. And then some will come from that very special list.

I mentioned earlier Cleta Mitchell of Americans Back in Charge. They have compiled a list, shown on the following page, of what they call the un-representative representatives. This is a very special list of people. There are 55, and let me remind you we only need 63. These are 55 members of Congress whose districts voted for term limits with ballot initiatives. When those members had the chance to vote on the floor of the House in March, they voted no, contrary to the will, the expressed will, of the people of their districts in those ballot initiatives.

The House Members Who Voted "No" on Term Limits
From Congressional Districts That Voted "Yes"

Member, State & District	Term Limits Vote in CD (Yes/No)	Year Elected	Years in Office
Harold Volkmer (MO-9)	80/20	76	18.5
Sam Gibbons (FL-11)	78/22	62	32.5
Corrine Brown (FL-3)	76/24	92	2.5
Karen Thurman (FL-5)	76/24	92	2.5
Ike Skelton (MO-4)	76/24	76	18.5
Joel Hefley (CO-5)	74/26 59/41	86	8.5
Jerry Lewis (CA-40)	72/28	78	16.5
Richard Gephardt (MO-3)	72/28	76	18.5
Harry Jonston (FL-19)	71/29	88	6.5
Alcee Hastings (FL-23)	71/29	92	2.5
Ed Paston (AZ-2)	70/30	91	3.5
Duncan Hunter (CA-52)	69/31	80	14.5
Michael Oxley (OH-4)	69/31	81	13.5
David Skaggs (CO-2)	68/32 49/51	86	8.5
David Dreier (CA-28)	68/32	80	14.5
Carrie Meek (FL-17)	68/32	92	2.5
Pat Williams (MT-AL)	67/33	78	16.5
Thomas Sawyer (OH-14)	67/33	86	8.5
Vic Fazio (CA-3)	66/34	78	16.5
George Brown, Jr. (CA-42)	66/34	72	22.5
William Clay, Sr. (MO-1)	66/34	68	26.5
Ron Wyden (OR-3)	66/34	80	14.5
Bob Filner (CA-50)	65/35	92	2.5
David Bonior (MI-10)	65/35	76	18.5
Norm Mineta (CA-15)	64/36	74	20.5
Zoe Lofgren (CA-16)	64/36	94	0.5
Tony Hall (OH-3)	64/36	78	16.5
Marcy Kaptur (OH-9)	64/36	82	12.5
Pat Schroeder (CO-1)	63/37 44/56	72	22.5
Matthew Martinez (CA-31)	63/37	82	12.5
Esteban Torres (CA-34)	63/37	82	12.5
Lynn Wolsey (CA-6)	62/38	92	2.5

Member, State & District	Term Limits Vote in CD (Yes/No)	Year Elected	Years in Office
Fortney (Pete) Stary (CA-13)	62/38	72	22.5
Tom Lantos (CA-12)	61/39	80	14.5
Anthony Beilenson (CA-24)	61/39	76	18.5
Bart Stupak (MI-1)	61/39	92	2.5
Sander Levin (MI-12)	61/39	82	12.5
Lynn Rivers (MI-13)	61/39	94	0.5
Robert Matsui (CA-5)	60/40	78	16.5
Howard Berman (CA-26)	60/40	82	12.5
John Dingell (MI-16)	60/40	55	39.5
Dale Kildee (MI-9)	59/41	76	18.5
George Miller (CA-7)	58/42	74	20.5
Blanche L. Lincoln (AR-1)	57/43	92	2.5
Sam Farr (CA-17)	57/43	93	1.5
Cal Dooley (CA-20)	57/43	90	4.5
Lucille Roybal-Allard (CA-33)	57/43	92	2.5
Xavier Beccerra (CA-30)	56/44	92	2.5
Earl Pomeroy (ND-AL)	56/44	92	2.5
Louis Stokes (OH-11)	56/44	68	26.5
Norm Dicks (WA-6)	56/44	76	18.5
Richard Neal (MA-2)	54/46	88	6.5
John Olver (MA-1)	52/48	91	3.5
Edward Markey (MA-7)	52/48	76	18.5
Gerry Studds (MA-10)	52/48	72	22.5

Republicans are noted in italics.

Those people need to hear from you. And if they do not hear you, their challengers definitely need to hear from you. On that, I'll tell you that I know a thing or two about challenge races. Having never run for office, I ran against a veteran incumbent in 1992 in a race that almost nobody thought we could win.

In fact, two weeks before the election, a major newspaper in my district did a front page story where they reported results of their poll that showed us 18 points behind two weeks out. Miraculously, nobody gave up. High school and college students stood in the rain holding our signs. Phoners kept phoning. Volunteers, including many dedicated, determined United We Stand America volunteers, kept volunteering. All kept praying.

At 8:30 on election night, the local media was expecting my concession speech. At 9:00 they were dancing at the incumbent's reelection headquarters. At 10:00 it started to turn around. At 11:15 the incumbent called to concede. We had won by 5,700 votes.

Davids still get Goliaths. Miracles still happen.

You have to believe, and you have to work hard. We can win on term limits. Americans can stay back in charge. All we need is 63 more votes. With your help we can get them.

Thank you very much.

The Issues

Government Spending and Taxes

Senator
Pete Domenici

The Need to Balance the Federal Budget

ROSS PEROT: *Senator Pete Domenici is the Chairman of the Senate Budget Committee. He is a leading authority on the steps necessary to balance the budget and pay the debt.*

Senator Domenici was born in 1932 in Albuquerque, New Mexico. His father was an Italian immigrant who owned a wholesale grocery business. Senator Domenici was one of five children.

He graduated from St. Mary's High School in Albuquerque, and earned a bachelor's degree in education from the University of New Mexico in 1954. Immediately after graduation, he joined the Albuquerque Dukes, a farm club of the Brooklyn Dodgers, where he was a pitcher for one season.

Senator Domenici then became a math teacher at Garfield Junior High School in Albuquerque. He earned his law degree from the University of Denver in 1958. After law school, he returned to Albuquerque and entered the private practice of law.

He married the former Nancy Burke in 1958. The Domenicis have eight children – six girls and two boys.

In 1967, Senator Domenici was elected Chairman of the Albuquerque Commission – the equivalent of being mayor of the city. In 1972, he was elected to the United States Senate – the first

Republican to serve as a Senator from New Mexico in 38 years.

Senator Domenici was elected to his fourth term in 1990, receiving 73 percent of the popular vote.

In addition to serving as Chairman of the Senate Budget Committee, Senator Domenici serves on the Appropriations Committee, the Energy and Natural Resources Committee, and the Senate Select Committee on Indian Affairs.

U.S. News & World Report stated that "Pete Domenici has a reputation for honesty and courage in fighting deficits."

The former Democratic Speaker of the House, Tom Foley, said, "Over the years, Senator Domenici has stood for doing something about deficit reduction. He has taken hard, tough positions. I have nothing but praise for him."

Senator Domenici has a particularly important message that affects every American. He will be speaking about the need to balance the federal budget.

Thank you for being with us today, Senator Domenici.

Hello, everybody. Thank you very, very much. Thank you, Ross, for that introduction. I do want you to know I was given a limited amount of time to speak, and I thought maybe you were going to use all my time!

But first I would like to tell you all a funny story, the kind that sets the framework for people that have to get up and talk a lot.

Out in the West, there was a rancher who got up one morning early, so he could go into town. There was a chill in the air, so he put on his warm coat as he walked out the back door. As he did so, he saw a baby bird that had fallen out of the tree, and was just sort of lying there, looking bad. He walked over to the bird and picked it up, and he said, "This warm coat might help." So he tucked it into his coat, to give a little warmth to the bird, and the bird reacted pretty well. So he said, "I must do something more for this bird." So he looked into the corral, and he saw a fresh cow dropping. And he said, "Well, now, that's warm," so he walked over and with his boot he made a little nest to put the bird in. As he stepped back, the bird started moving, and pretty soon put its head up and made a little noise. The rancher walked off exhilarated, thinking, "I've done something wonderful today." Little did he know the warmth would make that bird *really* chirp loud.

So the rancher left, and the bird chirped. A coyote that frequented the corral came along, and guess what happened? The chirping attracted him. So, he went over, he plucked up the bird, and he ate it.

Now there are three lessons that we learn from this: It is not always your enemies that get you into it; it is not always your friends that get you out of it; but most important, when you're in it up to your neck, keep your mouth shut!

I am in it up to my neck, but I am not going to keep my mouth shut. America needs a balanced budget. Republicans do not need a balanced budget, Democrats do not need a balanced budget, seniors do not need a balanced budget. Everyone in America needs a balanced budget.

My dear friends, our country has its origins in revolution and revolutionary ideas. I want to just give you a quotation to start my discussion today. This is a quotation about why the United States of America and all her people must do something about a government beset by fiscal irresponsibility such that we cannot say *no* to anything, and we cannot stop putting money into programs that we cannot afford. The quotation comes from professor Lawrence Tribe of Harvard: "Given the centrality of our revolutionary origins and of the precept that there should be no taxation without representation, it seems especially fitting in principle that we seek somehow to tie our hands so that we cannot spend our children's legacy."

That is why we need a constitutional amendment to balance the budget. This is the greatest nation on earth, with the most fantastic government any people on earth have ever lived under, with more opportunity, individual by individual, than any other system the world has ever known. In this country each generation has the great hope that they might live better than the previous generation. Parents and grandparents look at their children and grandchildren and say, "We want to give them a better America than we have."

But there can be no doubt that this can *never* happen if the United States of America continues to incur deficits of 200 to 300 billion dollars a year for as far as the eye can see. Because what deficits of this magnitude do to America today, and America tomorrow, and America in the future for our children, is to say, "We want to take away from you your economic birthright. We want to take it from you, to pay for things that we know we cannot afford. But we will not tell the people of our country that we cannot afford it."

This is a new era. We ought to put a new phrase in the lexicon of words that have to do with America's fiscal policy. It's a very simple one that all of you would say should be there: "What can we afford?" Often citizens will ask, "Will you do this for me? Will you do that? Can you get this grant for me?" Do you know that most members of Congress, and I include myself in this, very seldom are willing to answer that we cannot afford it, we just cannot afford it. The reason is that the government of the United States has put herself in a posture where, if any other government in America cannot pay for it, then the government in Washington will. We will pay for it.

As a result, we have a government so bloated and so far from the people that many people no longer even appreciate what the federal government does. They would prefer government closer to home, more responsive and more personal. The truth is that the federal government does not have the money to continue doing this, but instead is borrowing and borrowing and borrowing.

My friends, I wish and hope that before this year is out, Republicans and Democrats might yet get together to give America a balanced budget and, in doing so, get rid of the acrimony, hate and fear that we are stirring up among all our people.

Nobody in this land will understand what deficits are doing to our future, because they have been happening little by little over a long period of time. It's something like being put to death with lots of little tiny cuts whose cumulative effect is devastating. Because America is still a proud nation, a powerful nation, the economy is still the best in the world. But will it continue? There are many signs, friends, that it will not. And there are many facts that should frighten us.

First, one of the biggest problems for the United States of America is that our economy is not growing enough. As a result, the economic pie that is shared by Americans is not growing large enough for people to get a little more each year. One of the reasons is that our savings are being eaten up by the federal deficit. We have to borrow to finance a five-trillion-dollar debt. The more that government has to borrow, the less money there is available for American businesses, large and small, to invest and create new job opportunities. And, yes, the more we use up our savings to pay our government's bill, instead of making it available for investment for the next generation, the more we take away opportunity from the next generation.

Let me give you a couple of numbers. A child born today will pay more than $100,000 of his or her earnings just to pay interest on the debt that will accumulate in the next 18 years. Every man, woman and child in America today has a debt of $18,500, and it's growing astronomically.

At a town meeting in my state, I was asked by a very fine constituent, "Is it real, this debt? We are such a nice country, maybe those to whom we owe this money would forgive this debt." Well, as best I could, I tried to explain that we owe this money to many millions of people. There are Americans who bought our debt and have an IOU. There are banks that took the money of their depositors, and put it into the government in return for a commitment that the government would pay them back. There are many countries that own our debt. There are many insurance companies. And if America could not pay its debt, America's economy and the world's economy would be in shambles.

We have not reached that point, yet, and I do not mean to imply that it's right around the corner. But just as I said before, when it happens little by little over a long period of time, how will we know when it is here? There are some great economists who say, because we have incurred so much debt, we have taken five percent growth out of the American economy during the last eight or nine years. One percent equates to about 600,000 of the best jobs. So, we have probably denied ourselves three million jobs by using our economic resources to pay our bills instead of letting those resources be invested to provide us with good jobs and good things.

Interest rates are much higher than they ought to be, because America uses all of its savings to pay interest on its debt. If we achieve a balanced budget in seven years, we might have interest rates as low as three and a half to four percent. Just think of the amount of money that average Americans could keep in their pockets – if they were buying a refrigerator on credit or making payments on a house – if our interest rates were lower rather than distorted by our debt.

We can go on and on, but everything comes down to this: Do we have the courage, do we have the guts, or are we going to make excuses again that we cannot balance the budget? I know the seven-year plan that we offered is not perfect, but it will get us there. For all those who prefer to complain that we should not do this and we should not do that, I would like to ask them, "What would you do? How will you get America's fiscal house in order?" Then there are those who are saying, "But you cannot touch Medicare or Medicaid!" And yesterday we heard that we cannot touch infrastructure. I must tell you in all candor that I have had scores of citizens come to me worried about certain programs, and not one has volunteered to reduce in size or eliminate a program that helps them personally. That makes it tough. That's why this kind of assembly is truly worthwhile for America, because I do not believe you are doing that.

Now, I do not know how many minutes I have been talking, but I will tell you that for each minute, we have added $335,000 to the national debt, $20 million in every hour. And the first day you finish your assembly here, we will have incurred $482 million in additional debt. That cannot go on forever.

For those who were saying Medicare should be off the table, or are using some other kind of excuse to keep from reforming it, I want to make one thing very clear. Whether we have a balanced budget or not, Medicare is going broke. If we do not balance the budget, Medicare is going broke. If we balance the budget and do not change Medicare, then Medicare is still going broke. Some will tell you we should take the tax cuts off the table to save Medicare, but Medicare would still go broke. You see, Medicare will go broke until we decide either to put new resources into it by raising taxes, which nobody seems to want to do, or we reform the system. To keep Medicare solvent, the delivery of health care to seniors must be made more competitive, more cost-effective, and more efficient. Seniors must be given plenty of time to work into a choice between competitive systems, as is now beginning to happen across America today.

Now, I want to close, because I have a feeling that I am talking to the choir. I believe the United We Stand America people are for a balanced budget. I do not believe that you want to pit one program against another. I do not believe that you want to say, "Leave this program out!" Nor do I believe that you want us to back away from the goal when a group of Americans says, "Leave us alone!" But I would like to tell you emphatically that we can get a balanced budget, and it need not hurt very many people.

First, the budget of America is growing at 5 percent a year. To get it into balance, believe it or not, the federal budget can continue to grow at 3 percent a year. We must bring this budget under control to preserve this country for future generations. Why not let it grow at 3 percent instead of 5 percent without claiming that the world is falling in? Essentially, that is what we are proposing in our budget.

Now, let me suggest that this great country of ours needs people like you, and millions more like you, who have a deep conviction that America is a fantastic power for strength in the world, and offers more opportunity to more people than any country ever. And you believe we ought to fix those things which might ruin it. That is why you are here, and I compliment you for that.

I think there are two things that are required to keep America the land of opportunity, where we are not just free, but we are free with many opportunities to move ahead and succeed. There are two things that must be fixed in order to sustain these opportunities. One, put the word *affordable* back into the federal budget process. Ask, "What can we afford?" Then answer it against a balanced budget where we spend only as much as we take in. That's one.

The second is to get rid of an income tax system that has become extremely difficult to understand, unfair, crazy, inside out and upside down! Senator Nunn and I believe that we ought to approach the changes based on a singular principle, which I would like to share with you. We believe the American people ought to have an opportunity to save money and invest in America, without paying taxes on what they save and invest until they spend it. It's very simple. As an example, if you decide to save $10,000 and buy $2,000 worth of stock in a given year, instead of spending all of the money you earn that year, under our proposal you would deduct these invested amounts from your earnings and not pay any taxes on them. The savings pool, into which you have contributed for your future use, is also a contribution to America's growth and prosperity. So, we think you should not be taxed on this amount of savings until you withdraw it from the savings pool and spend it.

I close today by saying that in New Mexico, as in many states in America, there is concern about change, about not staying with the status quo. There is anxiety about making government smaller and more affordable, and about getting fraud or inefficiencies out of programs that honest people have come to rely on. I know that across our country and in my state people are anxious about the impact of these changes. But let me suggest that if we care about our future now, and our children's future later, there is no avoiding adult leadership and responsibility by saying, "Let's quit spending more than we take in. Let's balance the federal budget."

Thank you all very much.

Congressman
John Kasich

Options for Balancing the
Federal Budget

ROSS PEROT: Our next speaker is Congressman John Kasich from Ohio. Courageous, principled, and tenacious are words that accurately describe John Kasich. He has strong convictions and he is willing to fight for what he believes is right.

Congressman Kasich grew up in McKees Rocks, Pennsylvania. He graduated from the Ohio State University with a bachelor of arts degree.

He ran for the Ohio Senate in 1978 with little financial support. His door-to-door campaign defeated a two-term incumbent.

He ran for the U.S. House of Representatives in 1982. That year, he was the only Republican challenger to defeat a Democratic incumbent. For years as a member of the House Budget Committee, Congressman Kasich has worked to balance the budget, reduce government spending, and improve the cost-effectiveness of government agencies. Long before these steps of balancing the budget and cutting government spending became popular ideas, he waged a spirited but often lonely battle.

He was among the first to understand that we had been putting our country's future at risk by excess spending. He clearly understands that we must cut spending first, and he has aggressively presented specific bills to accomplish this goal.

He also serves on the House Armed Forces Committee, and has been instrumental in reforming Pentagon spending.

House Budget Committee Chairman Kasich is uniquely qualified for explaining our options for balancing the federal budget.

Thank you, Mr. Perot. First, I want to compliment all of you for being here. Dallas in August for anybody who does not live in Texas is pretty tough duty, isn't it?

I know that a lot of people who are here today gave up their vacations, took the money they would have spent sitting at a pool somewhere nice and cool, and instead decided to put America first. You came here because you believe that by participating aggressively in this country's government, each one of you can make a difference. You are right. And I want to thank you as a fellow American for being willing to come here and spend the time and the energy.

Let me just suggest to you that we have to do everything we can to preserve this great country. Compliment yourselves, your neighbors, for taking the time to come here and use your hard-earned money to give politicians a sense of what you think we should do. Applaud yourselves for participating in the American governing process.

As Mr. Perot said, I went to Congress in 1982, and in 1983 I joined the Armed Services Committee. It was a wonderful experience because the Armed Services Committee was a committee where people put the country first – almost no politics at all.

My mentor was a Democrat from Alabama by the name of Bill Nichols. My best friends were on both sides of the aisle, and they helped a young man who had ideas to make the Pentagon efficient. I believe that the constituents of my party ought not to be protected, or that somebody else's constituents should be the only ones affected – I think the whole darn kit and caboodle has got to be fixed. We should have no green eyeshades and we should not play favorites. Americans who do not have lobbyists representing them in Washington should not fair worse than those who do. That is what America is all about. Everybody should be treated equally.

It was great serving on the Armed Services Committee, but in 1989 I asked to be assigned to the Budget Committee. I remember Congressman Ralph Regula from Ohio called to tell me I had been selected to serve on the Budget Committee. I was so excited. I said, "Ralph, this is the best call I have had since I was asked to be on a Little League team when I was 12 years old. This is wonderful."

I went to my first Budget Committee meeting. It was the pits. The Republicans had become professional at attacking the Democrat plans. The Democrats' rhetoric was astounding and terrible as far as I was concerned. The committee members were arguing about two sets of plans, neither of which were really worth the paper they were printed on.

I was at Johnny's Gas Station, which is located right on the edge of my district in Westerville, and I was telling the proprietor about this. I said, "I got on the Budget Committee. I used to do well on Armed Services, but now I am on this committee. They are arguing over these documents, neither of them are very good. I do not understand the partisanship. This is just terrible."

As I filled up my Jeep and told Johnny this story, another guy walked around the car. He said, "You know, if things are so bad, John, what are you going to do about them?" And I didn't have an answer.

Later I was driving downtown in my Jeep thinking about this conversation. I got to my office, gathered my staff, and told them, "You know, this guy asked me a very good question. What am I going to do about it? Well, I'll tell you what I'm going to do about it. I'm going to write my own budget."

So, in 1989 five budgets were presented on the floor of the House – the Bush budget, the Democrat budget, two others, and the Kasich budget. Approximately 29 or 30 other brave souls decided to join me and vote for my budget.

Now, I received only 29 or 30 votes but that means there were 29 or 30 other people who thought my budget was pretty good. I figured if a kid like me can write a budget and get any votes at all, he was doing all right. So I stayed at it. It would have been unfair to the next generation not to slow the spending of government down and do something about it then.

So I came back in 1990 and offered another budget. This time there were four budgets offered, mine among them. That year I received 106 votes. The press came to me and said, "Why are you doing this, John? You cannot win." I said, "I'll tell you why I am doing it. It doesn't matter if I don't get any votes. I am doing the best I can to stand on principle to find out the kinds of things that I have to do – that we ought to do –

in this Congress. And if I have to be alone, so be it."

And the next year, I got 114 votes. I did a little better, and received more votes than President Bush had for his. I thought, "That's not bad."

In 1993 – after being a rebel in Congress fighting the B-2 bomber, deciding to clean up the entire operations of the government and sometimes having to oppose my own party – I was elected the ranking Republican on the Budget Committee. Just like Frank Sinatra used to say, "I did it my way," and it stunned everybody.

You should all know, particularly those who follow me, I am not a partisan person. I do what I do on principle. If I can work with Democrats, I am going to work with Democrats. If I have to tell it like it is, I am going to tell it like it is.

The President sent us a budget bill that had big taxes and big spending in it. I told my party it was not good enough to say no and just criticize. I told them when I would come home from college and criticize things, my dad would say to me, "John, that's fine. What are your ideas?" If I didn't have one, he shut me up pretty quickly.

I told my party that we cannot just oppose. We cannot just fight. We cannot just be negative. We must lay out our vision for how we would govern this country. And, thank goodness for Congressmen Bob Michel and Newt Gingrich pushing me forward and saying, "We are going to do it."

In 1993, we presented the Cut Spending First Budget to show how we could make deep cuts in the deficit without a tax increase. It was the alternative to President Clinton's budget, and it brought out people who wanted change in Washington.

Later that year, my friend, former Congressman Tim Penny, and I joined together to draft the Penny-Kasich budget. In it, we tried to cut one penny in spending from every dollar to save only $90 billion.

I should have brought my scroll here today. It would stretch from me to the front row of the audience with its list of all the lobbyists who said, "If you do this, if you cut one penny out of the dollar, American civilization will cease to exist as we know it." They lobbied against us. They beat us with scare tactics and delays, and we lost by six votes. But the Penny-Kasich vote was the sign of things to come.

In 1994, when we won the majority, I became the chairman of the House Budget Committee with this wonderful team of members, including Bob Franks and Bob Inglis. These wonderful people said,

"We are not just going to talk, we are going to get the job done. We are going to balance the budget over the next seven years. We are going to be held accountable, and we are going to hold you accountable."

We put a budget together. We did something that Ross Perot suggested in the Presidential campaign. Ross Perot was asked in 1992, "How are you going to balance the budget?" He said, "There are so many plans in Washington, so many instructions in so many darn drawers, all you have to do is pull them out and use them." Do you want to know something? He is absolutely right. The only thing it took to use those things was a little bit of guts, and the willingness to put America first, politics second – to put the next generation first, and the status quo out the door. And that is what we started to do.

To balance the budget over the next seven years, our philosophy was to put everything on the table, except for Social Security, because we made a promise. I believe the Republican majority has done a good job of keeping our promises. We kept the Contract With America. The most important thing was not what was in the Contract, but that we gave you a promise. We gave you our word, and we kept our word. That is what you want from politicians – straight talk.

Our philosophy is there are some things we could cut. There are some things we could eliminate. There are some things we could privatize. There are some things we could shift back to local government.

Do you know what the Contract was all about? It was about taking money, power and influence from the city of Washington, and giving it back to people where they live.

I want to talk to you about tax cuts. I had a reporter come up to me and say, "You know, John, the Perot people do not want tax cuts. They just want to balance the budget." I want to tell you what the two big pieces to the tax cut proposals are.

One is to reduce the capital gains tax. The capital gains tax cut is about every boy and girl in America being able to fly and live their dreams. Let me explain what I mean. You have a jug with prosperity in it and you want to pour that prosperity through a funnel. But if you have a tiny narrow stem on that funnel, what happens to that prosperity? It cannot get through the funnel, can it? The prosperity spills over and you lose a lot of it.

Capital gains is about giving people a reason to invest and take risks. It is not about anything for rich people. In fact, as I tell my liberal friends, the only people who hate the rich are the guilty rich. We want the rich people to take risks and invest because, when they take risks and invest, our kids get the jobs, then they become presidents of the companies and then the people who do the investing are working for us. That is the American Dream. That is what America is all about. Capital gains is about widening the funnel stem so we can pour as much prosperity and as many jobs as possible into bountiful America.

Let me tell you about the other part of the tax cut – family tax cuts.

Everybody wants to go around the world and construct dams and bridges. And we pay for it in the name of foreign aid. When we cut foreign aid, when we save money by cutting corporate welfare, why don't we give it to the family and let them spend it on their kids the way they know best, rather than the government deciding how to spend that money.

As we head into the 21st century, the institution in this country that needs to be reemphasized, underscored, rebuilt, and held up is the American family. I think we can all agree on that. Think of the problems that we could solve, think of the value problems that we could solve in this country if we could do nothing more than rebuild the American family.

In our budget plan, when you receive some of your money back in a capital gains cut or family tax relief, you are not sacrificing any of the goals that needed to be achieved in order to balance the budget. Only those who favor high government spending are opposed to tax cuts. Because – as I said in 1994 and in 1995, and my committee proved it this year – we can, in fact, balance the budget and give people tax relief at the same time. We are not just going to be supply-siders who cut taxes and hope for the best. We are what we call supply-side deficit hawks. Reduce taxes, reduce government, reduce overhead. You can accomplish both spending cuts and tax cuts because, when you reduce capital gains, you help grow the economy and help produce more revenue to help balance this budget.

What are you hearing about our budget plan? You are hearing from all the people who love power and influence and money in Washington. But we are trying to take it out of there. We are trying to downsize the federal government. We are trying to give you some of your money back and more of your power back so you can solve problems where you live. The people who live in Washington will do anything to protect the status quo and to prevent you from being empowered.

What do they do now? They talk about all the cuts. Let me give you some of the numbers. Total federal spending was $9.5 trillion over the last seven years. Let me put it in perspective. If Mr. Perot had started a business when Christ was on earth, if he lost a million dollars a day seven days a week, he would have to lose a million dollars a day seven days a week for the next 700 years to get to $1 trillion in debt.

Our national debt will be $5 trillion, and we spent $9.5 trillion over the last seven years. Over the next seven years, under the plan to balance the budget and give you some of your money back, we are going to go from $9.5 trillion in total federal spending to $12.1 trillion. You have not heard that before, have you? You thought we were going down. But you see, all we have to do to balance the budget in this country, to stop running deficits and then begin to pay off the debt, is to slowly but surely restrain the growth of federal spending.

How do I know it is true? I have a chart. How could I come here without a chart? I think Perot stole that idea from me. I had charts before Perot.

Let me tell you about welfare. Let me tell you about food stamps, cash welfare, child care, child protection, school nutrition, and family nutrition. You are hearing that these programs will be cut, aren't you? Over the next seven years we are going to have an increase in these programs of $356 billion – hardly a cut.

Is it not time for real welfare reform? You know, where I come from it is a sin not to help people who are in need. It is equally a sin to help people who ought to be helping themselves. If you are under the age of 18 and you have babies, you should not get AFDC payments. If you are on welfare and you have more kids, you should not get more benefits. You have to go to work. It is just that simple. We should not be debating this in the Senate. It ought to be done.

Let's talk about Medicaid. We have a Medicaid manual that is 12 inches thick. If you are 19 years old, you can be defined as a *child* under the Medicaid regulations. What we are going to do is give Medicaid funding to the states in block grants and let every state determine how they can best serve their poor population with health care.

Medicaid funding is going to go from $444 billion to $773 billion, an increase of $329 billion. Now, do you think they can make it work with the $329 billion increase? You may shake your head no. But if we can get it back to the states where you are in charge, guess what? I think we have a better chance.

Let us move to Medicare. There are some very wonderful functions the federal government can perform, and one of them is to provide Medicare. But Medicare is a 30-year-old program.

What the bureaucrats tried to do in Washington last year was to take private health care and make it public. What we are suggesting is taking the public health care system and using the innovations in the private sector to keep the system from going bankrupt. Otherwise, the Medicare system will be bankrupt in seven years.

Even under our budget plan that provides a $675 billion increase over the next seven years, when the baby boomer generation retires, we will have a wave of Medicare problems that makes the challenge we have today pale by comparison. We have an obligation as Americans to make a good first start in getting Medicare on a firm financial basis. And Medicare, contrary to what the demagogues all over this country are going to say, is going to increase by $675 billion under our plan.

And let me suggest something to all of you about the demagogues who do not want to address the problems that face Medicare. Maybe they will win this battle. But if they win, it is not a Republican loss. It is not a loss for me. It is not a loss for my committee. It is a loss for America.

While planning this budget, we decided that we did not need 163 separate job training programs. Does anybody want to volunteer to give up your job today so the federal government can retrain you for your next job? Have any volunteers in here? No, I do not see anyone. We decided there should not be 163 job training programs; 23 separate programs to deal with child abuse; 42 programs to educate health professionals; and 300 separate programs for economic development.

Ladies and gentlemen, we need to use common sense in Washington to slow the growth of programs, to clean up the bureaucracy, the duplication and the red tape. This is what I tell my colleagues, "When the lobbyists come to your office and tell you how critical the program is, keep your mind fixed on one thing – the next generation. You have to say no to the special interests to save the future for the next generation. It is not hard to turn them down if you want to put America first."

The President does not have a plan right now, ladies and gentlemen.

This is not good news. He has no plan to balance the budget in 20 years, 15, 10, 5. As scored by the Congressional Budget Office, his plan does not exist.

This fall we are going to take our federal budget plan, under which some of government has been privatized, eliminated, cut, or shifted back to the states and we are going to bundle all of this together. Do you know what it will mean? Less taxes for Americans, less regulation for Americans, and a smaller, more focused federal government. But it is not the final answer. When you go from $9.5 to $12.1 trillion, you have to ask yourself, "Why didn't they do better than that?"

But it is a credible plan to get us to zero, and at the end of the day, it is going to represent the best first step this generation can make to contribute to the future of the next generation. We are going to send that package to the White House, and I hope the President will sign it.

I tell you as one Republican who can get along with Democrats – who has been in coalitions with Democrats probably more than any Republican in the House – we cannot give up on principle. This is about the last best chance we have to right the fiscal wrongs of this country and to have a smaller government. Why? Because you are ready to give. You are ready to sacrifice as long as you are not giving more than your fair share, as long as we have everybody on the table. You are willing to give. We have the leaders in place now in Washington who are willing to make changes, throw out the status quo and initiate growth.

Alan Greenspan, the chairman of the Federal Reserve, says that balancing the budget will unleash a prosperity that nobody can even chart in America. He said that if we can balance the budget, we will finally end the fear that represents America's greatest legacy – the fear that your kids will not be better off than you are. We are going to send that to the President; and if the President says, "No, I want a compromise," I am going to say, "No, no, no, no." There is no compromise with balancing the budget. There is no compromise with that principle.

My dad carried mail on his back, and I rose to become the Budget Committee Chairman in the U.S. House of Representatives – what a great country this is. I want you to understand this: the people do get what they want in America. It takes a very long time for the government to hear them. The American people ended the Vietnam war, not the politicians. It took too long, but the people got what they wanted.

Let me suggest this: We will balance the budget when you stand up and say that you want it balanced. And when the politicians try to stand up and tell you there is a Wizard of Oz behind the curtain in Washington who can fix everything, you will say, "No, there is no wizard. That is just an old man behind the curtain. There is no magic there. I can do it better where I live. Give me a chance."

We will send the budget plan to the President. He will decide whether or not to respond to the mandate of the people in 1994. If he decides not to, you better send him a message. If you do not send him a message, you are going to lose. If you lose, the children in this country will lose. When you go home to your neighborhoods, when you are at the shopping centers, when you are at the family dinners or the church socials – wherever you are – discussion about balancing the budget will come up this fall. They are not just going to be talking about the O. J. Simpson trial. If we get to a crisis where the government may close down, the budget will become the number-one issue. And every American's opinion will count. You need to congratulate yourselves for taking this power and money and influence out of Washington. You need to congratulate yourselves for getting it back to where it belongs and restoring some common sense to the way in which we govern ourselves.

Last night before I came to Dallas, I picked up that great book called *America* by Alexis de Tocqueville. He talked about the beauty of America, the ability of Americans to govern themselves in very basic units at the township level.

Those are the things we ought to be thinking about. This is just the first step. What we have to do as Americans is figure out where we want to go. Why not use tax credits to help people who need assistance? Why not show compassion rather than just create another bureaucracy? We should think about that. Why not let local units of government petition the state government for food stamp money and welfare money? Welfare ought to be run by our neighbors. At the local level, we know if Mrs. Jones has a couple of sick kids and needs more help. We know if Mr. Smith has to be picked up in the morning and put on the road. Compassion is about "one at a time." It is the smallest possible unit.

Do you know what the 21st century ought to be? The 21st century ought to be the beginning of an individual; every individual has to live his or her dream. Incentives, the free enterprise system, rewards for working hard – that is what the 21st century should be. And there is one other being we ought to reinstate in America – God. It is time to invite God back into America.

I firmly believe that to do all of this, we must balance the budget. We must be willing to tighten our belts and know that we do not get bounty from government, but, rather, from limited government. We must be willing to get into the trenches against those liberals who want to defend the status quo. We have to be willing to hold these conservatives accountable who talk one way and vote another. I need your help.

If, in fact, we can right America physically by balancing the budget, reducing the deficit and having a great outpouring of wealth and opportunity in this country – is that enough? Do you know what the answer is? We do not have a more important goal than to make America the strongest country in the 21st century – not only to fix the problems that currently face us, but to help save the world.

God bless each and every one of you. Thank you, Mr. Perot.

Senator
Paul Simon

The Importance of a
Strong, Stable Dollar

ROSS PEROT: Our next speaker is Senator Paul Simon of Illinois. He was born in 1928 in Eugene, Oregon. He attended the University of Oregon and Dana College in Blair, Nebraska.

Senator Simon served in the U.S. Army from 1951 to 1953, in the Counter Intelligence Corps as a special agent along the Iron Curtain in Europe.

At nineteen, he became the nation's youngest newspaper publisher when he bought a defunct newspaper in Troy, Illinois, and named it the Troy Tribune.

He eventually acquired fifteen newspapers in Illinois that he sold in 1966 to devote himself full-time to public service.

Senator Simon was elected to the Illinois House of Representatives in 1954 and to the Illinois Senate in 1962. During his fourteen years in the Illinois Legislature, he won the Independent Voters of Illinois' "Best Legislator" award every session. Senator Simon was elected Lieutenant Governor of Illinois in 1968. He changed the office from one that was largely ceremonial to one of an ombudsman, actively focused on making state government better serve the people.

He was elected to the U.S. House of Representatives in 1974 and served for 10 years before being elected to the U.S. Senate. While serv-

*ing in the House, Senator Simon played a leading role in drafting legis-
lation in the fields of education and disability policy.*

*He was the chief sponsor of the legislation that chartered the
National Center for Missing and Exploited Children. In 1984, he was
elected to the U.S. Senate. In 1987-88, he sought the Democratic nomination for President. Since his election to the Senate, Senator Simon
has held more than 600 town meetings throughout his state – more
than any U.S. Senator in state history.*

*He introduced a balanced budget amendment in 1986 that has been
the cornerstone of the balanced-budget debate since that time. He has
also led the effort to curb violence on television.*

*Senator Simon has announced that he will retire from the Senate
when his current term expires in 1997.*

*For the past 45 years, he has written a newspaper column entitled
"PS/Washington," which has been called "The best on Capitol Hill" and
"Political science at its best" by leading Washington columnists. He is
married to the former Jeanne Hurley of Wilmette. They have two children, Sheila and Martin, and three granddaughters.*

Senator Simon has just completed a very interesting book entitled
We Can Do Better – An Open Letter to the President. *We are fortunate that Senator Simon could be with us today to explain the importance of a strong stable dollar.*

Thank you, Ross. I appreciate and thank everyone who is here
because you are clearly helping to set the agenda for America and
helping to make it great. I applaud you for it. I am pleased to follow
my two colleagues, Senators Sam Nunn and Pete Domenici, for whom
I have great respect.

The subject that Ross Perot asked me to talk about, "What is
Happening to the U.S. Dollar," sounds dull, but let me tell you, it is
extremely important to our future. One of the major economic events
of this past year has been the decline of the dollar against the Japanese
yen and the German mark. Though the slippage has been arrested temporarily, the long-term trend is clear. We know that the drop in the
value of the dollar will affect our future, but we are not sure how. We
know that we should do something about it, but we are not sure what.
In a White House conference on April 18th, a reporter asked President

Clinton about the sinking dollar. The President responded, "In the present climate, the ability of governments to affect the strength of their currency . . . in the short run may be limited."

That is questionable, but the President was right when he followed that by saying, "So what you have to do is work over the long run. The United States does want a strong dollar. We believe in the importance of fundamentals in our economy. We believe in getting the deficit down, getting jobs up and pursuing a responsible course."

The *Washington Post* had an editorial that observed, "Anger and frustration in their voices, Japanese and German officials have been calling on the United States publicly to do something about the [falling] dollar." Then the *Post* stated incorrectly, "There is nothing useful that the United States can do."

There are two basic questions: What does the fall of the dollar mean, and what can we or should we do about it?

Let me address both. What does the fall of the dollar mean? It is significant both for our nation and for the world. Since two-thirds of the world's trade is carried on in dollars, the erosion of the dollar can destabilize economies far from us.

The British publication, *The Economist*, is correct when they have said, "In the long run, the biggest loser from the neglect of the dollar will be America itself."

A *Journal of Commerce* columnist accurately noted that "The weak dollar will decrease U.S. political influence abroad." Peter Passell wrote in the *New York Times*, "No indicator of the American economic decline stands out like the fallen dollar."

Paul Volcker, former chairman of the Federal Reserve Board, is quoted in the *New York Times* as saying, "If you think American leadership is important, then erosion of the dollar is a negative." *Time* magazine quoted the distinguished financial analyst Felix Rohatyn as saying, "We are gradually losing control of our own destiny. The dollar's decline undercuts American economic leadership and prestige." I could quote others.

As if to underscore all of this, the April 12th *Wall Street Journal* had a heading about the fastest-growing economic part of the world, Asia. It read, "Asia's Central Banks Unloading Dollars in Shift Toward Yen as Trade Currency."

Short-term, Americans will see little change. Yes, if we are traveling in other nations, we will be hurt a little by the foreign exchange rates. Our balance of trade with other nations may be helped a little because U.S. products can be secured for less money. Foreign businesses, just like American businesses, rarely drop their prices immediately – both because they want to make some additional profit and because there is a reluctance to adjust prices until the currency market stabilizes.

Our balance of trade is helped because U.S. businesses who buy component parts from overseas producers will suddenly find them more expensive. They will shift to a more cost-effective U.S. manufacturer of the same product, if one is available. That is not always the case. The VCR, for example – invented, developed, and at one time entirely manufactured right here in the United States – does not have a U.S. manufacturing source.

Little-noticed economic consequences will gradually affect us. For example, securing a patent in Japan will now be more expensive for a U.S. firm or individual. Factors like that have a limited, short-term impact, but a much greater long-range impact.

Long-term dollar decline has more serious consequences. First, the increased cost of foreign goods will have a gradual inflationary impact on our economy. That will not only cause the consumer dollar to shrink and discourage savings; it eventually will put pressure on the Federal Reserve Board to raise interest rates to discourage inflationary pressures, and that will hurt our economy.

The financial markets will also push up interest rates. We know, and this is not widely known, that approximately 16 percent of our deficit, or about $700 billion, is held outside the United States. Many nations outlaw holding bonds from another nation. The United States did that at one point. There is additional ownership that is not publicly disclosed; it is hidden by a third party holding the bonds. If the dollar continues its decline, U.S. bonds that are denominated in dollars will become less and less attractive. We will have to raise interest rates to sell this huge chunk of our deficit.

Not as widely known is that 14 percent of our corporate bonds are held by people who live beyond our borders. That money has financed a huge chunk of our industrial expansion and modernization. If the dollar continues to decline, we may either lose the source of capital, or interest rate payments will have to be raised to make these bonds attractive enough to sell.

In addition, there are sizable foreign deposits in savings and checking accounts in our banks and foreign-held certificates of deposit. Indirectly, these help to finance both our governmental sector – because the banks buy Treasury bonds – and the private sector, because the banks are able to make loans to U.S. businesses. If all of this shrinks because of the fall of the dollar, the only way to salvage the situation will be with higher interest rates.

In the long term, higher interest rates discourage industrial investment and reduce productivity. Our economy is hurt, and the phenomenon of a lower dollar is not healthy for our nation. From time to time, interest rates decline, and frequently this is healthy for our economy. But the fairly consistent pattern of the drop in our dollar against the yen and the mark has major long-term consequences that are not good.

I read an exchange that took place between two economists some years ago when the dollar brought 360 yen. One economist predicted that if our policies were not altered, the dollar would eventually slide to 180 yen. The other economist predicted, confidently, this would never happen. A few weeks ago, the dollar fell to 83 yen, and today the dollar is worth 92 yen, thanks to propping up by several central banks.

Recently, the *Washington Post* published a column noting the opinion of an economist and an economic observer who suggest we may have to think about issuing U.S. Treasury bonds in yen rather than dollars to attract buyers and save on interest. The reasoning is very simple. The financial markets want a stable currency for their investments, particularly long-term investments. The yen has shown itself much more stable than the dollar. To continue to sell in dollars will require higher interest rates. Therefore, they argue, we should issue our bonds in yen and pay less for interest. It would be politically unsettling to many Americans for our bonds to be sold in yen, but that is where we are headed.

There are better alternatives. What can we do? It is not difficult to diagnose the problem. But once we diagnose the illness, the patient has to take the medicine, and that is much more difficult when the patient is not accustomed to taking distasteful medicine.

The basic problem is that confidence in the dollar has diminished. Neither cheerleading by U.S. officials nor salvaging efforts by the central banks of Japan, Germany, and other countries will do more than temporarily heal the wound. Confidence-building measures have to be substantial. Those who now hold U.S. dollar–denominated financial certificates, many of whom are uneasy, are not going to be assured by cosmetic actions.

Four steps can strengthen our economy and solidify the dollar. I will spend more time on the first of the four points.

Number one, get rid of our federal government deficit. This is, by far, the most important part of the four actions, and it will help the next three.

It is no accident that the most recent slide of the dollar began the day after the Senate rejected the Balanced Budget Amendment to the Constitution by one vote.

The federal government has been in a deficit situation for 26 years, and for 25 years the dollar has been in a slide against the yen and the mark. It does not take an Einstein to understand there is some kind of relationship there. But it is not a straight line, and other factors are also present. Sometimes when the deficit was high, interest rates were high, increasing the value of the dollar. It is an oversimplification to attribute all the dollar decline to the deficit, but it is the major cause.

And here it is appropriate to repeat what I wrote in a book more than a year ago. "During the 1992 presidential race, Ross Perot spoke more candidly about the deficit and what needed to be done than either Bill Clinton or President Bush."

The *New York Times* reported that "The Germans and the Japanese say the basic problem is America's budget deficit." A month earlier the *Los Angeles Times* quoted Federal Reserve Board Chairman Alan Greenspan telling the House Budget Committee that "Last week's Senate defeat of the Balanced Budget Amendment can be blamed for the sudden plunge in the value of the dollar and the currency will remain under long-term pressure until Washington tackles the deficit."

Business Week commented on the dollar's slide, "What the international markets want is simple: Less debt or higher interest rates." Paul McCracken, economist at the University of Michigan and former chairman of the Council of Economic Advisors under President Nixon, had a guest column in the *Wall Street Journal* titled "Falling Dollar, Blame the Deficit." In the article he notes that the deficits have caused the decline in productive capital investment and that this "... is not trivial. If gains in real income had continued at a pace more in line with our long history, average family income today in real terms would be almost 25 percent higher than our economy is now delivering."

The bipartisan Concord Coalition recently issued a study suggesting that annual family income would be $15,000 higher today, on the average, if we had not had these years of deficit. Trudy Rubin wrote prophetically in the *Journal of Commerce*, "If there were signs that Washington were cutting the deficit, the dollar would probably stabilize."

Lawrence Thimerene, chief economist for the Economic Strategy Institute, wrote in the *New York Times* that to stabilize the dollar, Congress and the President must "demonstrate real seriousness on deficit reduction."

To the credit of President Clinton, he did that: attacked the deficit with his budget of 1993. It cost him politically, but it benefited the nation. To the credit of my colleague Senator Pete Domenici, who chairs the Budget Committee, he proposed that we balance the budget by the year 2002. While I differ with Senator Domenici on how we get there, I applaud his courage in proposing this. We need more bipartisan courage in that direction.

Our task is made more difficult by the one vote we failed to get in the United States Senate for the Balanced Budget Amendment. I hope that the people gathered here and those who are watching on television can influence one of the 34 senators who voted against the Balanced Budget Amendment. What a great contribution all of you could make.

Even the limited action that we have been able to take through the Budget Committee has had an impact. The heading in the *New York Times* story of May 12th was, "The Dollar Surges on New Plan to Cut Deficit." The story, written by Peter Truell, begins, "The dollar staged its biggest one-day rally in nearly four years, rebounding against the German mark and the Japanese yen on speculation that Washington might do more than in the past to cut the federal deficit."

The difficulty with legislation alone is that the financial markets will remain skeptical about whether Congress will follow through. Financial savings from interest that could be applied to things like social programs and Medicare are not going to be fully achieved. On the basis of estimates made by Data Resources and other forecasters, my best guess is that with both the firm goal of balancing the budget and the firm goal of a constitutional amendment, there would be an additional interest savings of at least one percent. Over a seven-year period that would mean $170 billion that we could devote to education or health care or Medicare or things that we need in our nation. The reduction in interest would also encourage home construction, car purchases, and industrial investment.

Washington Post columnist James K. Glassman had a column under the heading "Year of the Balanced Budget." While whoever wrote the headline for the column may not have intended it, there is fear on the part of many that the use of the singular "year" is what will happen. We need "years," plural, of the balanced budget. Our experience with legislative solutions alone – such as Gramm-Rudman-Hollings, an earlier balanced budget try which I voted for – is that they have an impact for a year or two. But when the public squeeze is felt, it is much easier politically to create additional deficits than to make the tough decisions that we ought to make. That is where the constitutional amendment would help.

Unless we confront our fiscal problems, the day will come when we will look back with longing to the time when the yen was 83 to a dollar.

Let me just add here one other point to underscore what Pete Domenici said. The present forecast is that next year the federal government will spend $370 billion on interest. That is 12 times what we will spend on education, 22 times as much as we will spend on foreign aid, and twice as much as we will spend on our poverty programs. We can find better ways to spend our money than endlessly piling up interest payments.

My final three points, briefly. Our trading balances must be addressed. A report from the Congressional Research Service says that studies show 37 percent to 55 percent of our trade deficits are caused by the budget deficit. But there are other causes, varying from our neglect to aggressively market our products overseas to our weakness in trade negotiations. The latter deficiency is caused, in part, by not having a cadre of professionals handling our negotiations, particularly when compared to Japan. Too often it has been long-term professionals against changing teams of U.S. negotiators.

It is worth noting that our firmer stance with Japan on trade matters has come since Japan has been a declining factor in the purchase of our Treasury bonds. It is difficult to get tough with your banker.

The United States also must build products that can accommodate the cultures of other nations. We must learn to sell in their languages, not ours. Tens of thousands of U.S. corporations that do not consider marketing in other nations must change course. We are gradually getting better, but if we can hasten the process, we will reduce the trade deficit that troubles the international currency markets.

Third, our savings rate must be increased. Again, the biggest impediment to our savings rate is the federal government's budget deficit.

But it is more than that, it is our culture. We are not dramatically different from Canada, but we have a savings rate of 4.8 percent compared to Canada's savings rate of 9.1 percent. In addition, Germany saves 10.7 percent and Japan saves 19.7 percent. Because of our lower savings rate, the United States is much more dependent on other countries to buy our debt.

By making some changes in our tax code, we can reward savings rather than debt. Our tax code, for example, rewards businesses that create debt to finance growth rather than financing growth through savings or equity financing through issuing stock. A corporation that buys another corporation by borrowing money can write off the interest payments, even though the debt may create hazards for the purchasing company. If that same corporation more prudently issues stock, the dividends are not deductible. If we change the tax laws to permit 80 percent of interest to be deductible and 50 percent of dividends to be deductible, the net result would be a wash in federal revenue, but many corporations would have a more solid base and our corporate debt base would decline.

Similarly, we should create tax incentives that would not add to our nation's deficit but would add to our productivity by encouraging individual Americans to save, thereby making investment capital more available. Citizens of other nations have incentives to save, whereas Americans do not. This has to change.

Shifts in our culture will not be brought about quickly, but we must work to bring about change.

Finally, we must do more long-term thinking and face our deficiencies frankly. The fiscal deficiency is an example I have already discussed. We have ducked telling people the truth because it is politically more convenient to duck. Too many politicians in both political parties are running by polls rather than the national need. We have to tell people the truth about our finances. We have to face problems squarely.

I was pleased with the applause for someone like Pete Peterson. You may not agree with him, but you are willing to say, "Let us all sacrifice to make this a better country."

We have to face other things. Can we expect to build the kind of nation we should have if we continue to have 24 percent of our children living in poverty? No other Western industrialized nation has anything close to that. Can we expect to build a nation that can lead and compete in the future if we continue to neglect the need for quality education in all the nation?

The national markets look at our deficits and worry about long-term inflationary pressures. When our fiscal policy does not address the deficits, the Federal Reserve Board is forced to look at the long-term implications of inflation. That is why the quality of appointments to the Federal Reserve Board is so significant and important.

If we in Congress and the Clinton Administration address our fiscal policies more directly, and particularly that constitutional amendment, the pressure would be removed from the Federal Reserve Board for action in raising interest rates.

Germany and Japan are far ahead of the United States on non-defense research and probably even farther ahead of us in applying their research to productive purposes. Governmental America tends to live from election to election, and, even worse, from poll to poll. Corporate America too often lives from quarterly report to quarterly report. Unless we do more long-term planning and acting in both the public and private sectors, our future performance as a nation will be less than outstanding.

Others understand this about us. We must understand this about ourselves. If we were to address with courage these four areas that I have mentioned, not only would the dollar continue to rebound, our hopes and spirit would rebound also. The cynicism and negative attitudes that concern many of us are caused not only by the haters and those who see only the worst in our government and public officials. The depth of public concern that results in hostility rather than activity is also caused by good, decent public officials of both political parties who do not have the courage to face our fundamental problems or who see an opportunity for partisan advantage rather than an opportunity to lift the nation.

Yes, we can save the dollar; but much more important, working together we can also save the nation. Thank you.

Meredith Bagby

Our Future, Our Children's Future

ROSS PEROT: Meredith Bagby is the author of The First Annual Report of the United States of America, *the first financial report on federal spending and taxes written for American citizens in the form of a corporate annual report.*

Meredith wrote the annual report as a course project during her junior year at Harvard. She published it in 1994; it was reissued by HarperCollins in 1995.

She was born in Coral Gables, Florida. She is 21 years old. She was the Salutatorian of her class at Palm Beach Lakes Community High School where she was also the President of her debate team. In 1990, she was elected Governor of Girls State, an organization sponsored by the American Legion.

She received a full Harvard-MIT/ROTC Scholarship. At Harvard she won numerous national debating tournaments, and she received the Harvard Grumman Prize for Excellence in Debate. She was also a Coca-Cola National Scholarship winner, and a staff writer for the Harvard Political Review.

Meredith was an analyst for the National Bureau of Economic Research. She was a legal assistant in the state attorney's office in Palm Beach County. Meredith is currently a financial analyst at Morgan

Stanley in New York. She has been admitted to the School of Law at the University of Virginia, where she will study law and business.

She is in the process of preparing the Annual Report of the United States 1996 *that will be published by HarperCollins in 1996.*

I know that you will find this speech and this young lady fascinating. Please welcome Meredith Bagby.

Thank you. Mr. Perot usually never forgets anything, but the one thing that he did forget to add to my list of credentials is that I am not running for President.

Mr. Perot, distinguished speakers, members of United We Stand America, and all those listening at home, I am profoundly honored to be participating in this historic meeting. I do not believe that this many leaders of diverse ideas have come together since 39 of the 55 delegates to the Constitutional Convention signed our Constitution, and look what they created.

Mr. Perot, we thank you for your wisdom in giving America this momentous educational opportunity, and congratulations to everyone in United We Stand America for focusing sharply on ways to prepare Americans to carry our democracy into the new century.

In *Look Homeward, Angel*, Thomas Wolfe captured the interdependence of the past, present and future when he said that every moment is a window on all time.

Please join me at this window of today to see who we are and how we may venture into what may be our tomorrow.

It is May 23, 1995, on the campus of Harvard University where I am a senior. It is a bright Sunday morning. The after-exam relief is suddenly pierced by screaming sirens and the sights of two forever silenced bodies being taken from a dormitory which is near my own. My roommates, my friends, the president of my university, Neil Rudenstine, are all in a state of shock. A young Ethiopian premedical student has murdered her roommate, tried to kill a guest in their room, and then has hanged herself. We hear the media state repeatedly that the killer was not an American. Since many of us are living as hyphenated Americans, it may ease our pain and rage to say that this murder is not part of our particular cultural experience.

Indeed, what do this murder and the other daily tragedies we hear reported by the media have to do with us? It is easier to believe that they have nothing to do with us. But unfortunately, that is not the case. As members of a single community, we are indeed responsible for each other.

For me, for other students and faculty, this event called into question our commitment to be part of a community. We felt that perhaps we had contributed to an uncaring atmosphere where the attitude is often, "I have too much work, too little time, and enough of my own problems, to get involved."

Unfortunately, this tends to be the mentality of modern society. This is what leads to the kind of desperation that can lead to this kind of note, "I have no one," the murderer wrote in her last letter to her friends – "I have no one."

Despite our thousands of social programs, studies of the human psyche and practitioners of psychiatry, many of us simply do not know where to go for help in a complex society that seems fragmented.

In his last book, *America and Americans*, John Steinbeck wrote that Americans have grown cold to one another. Government and business have swallowed up the once more important institutions of church, family, and community. As a result, we produce people without roots, without strong values, and without other people to care for them. As I researched the *First Annual Report* published earlier this year, stark realities fused to enforce this pattern of isolation.

We, as a nation, are acutely set apart by race, language, culture, money, professions, education, and issues of every kind. My generation, born after 1964, is at war with the boomers and the seniors over debt, jobs, and who is to pay for Social Security.

Consider the chart at the top of the next page that shows how the generations are fighting over tax dollars. We must make trade-offs between social programs that care for the elderly such as Social Security – now on the high end of the scale – and social programs for the young. Programs such as education are now receiving less than 3 percent of our tax dollars.

One lobby group is pitted against the next special interest. Diseases are even being polarized, with their proponents fighting for dollars. But perhaps the greatest dividing marker is between the rich and the poor, the educated and the uneducated.

Over the past decades our income distribution has become more

Spending on Selected Government Programs by Year

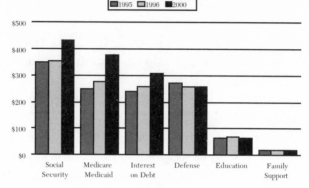

unequal, not less. In 1995, 47 million of us are below the poverty line and an inordinate number of those are women, children, minorities, and the mentally ill. Those in poverty often turn to drugs and crime. They receive inferior educations and thus are less able to pull themselves into higher earning levels.

The chart below shows that children born in lower income areas often score worse than those of high-income families. Clearly we do not have equal opportunities in education.

Average Scores of 12th Graders

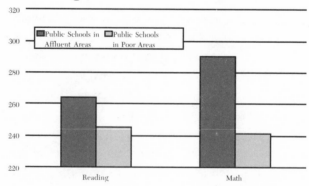

The test was based on a 500 point scale and administered by the National Assessment of Educational Progress

The following chart compares the earnings of a dropout family with the earnings of a degreed family. How can a high school dropout family ever catch up to the advantages of a family degreed in law or medicine that earns almost four times as much?

Comparative Annual Earnings

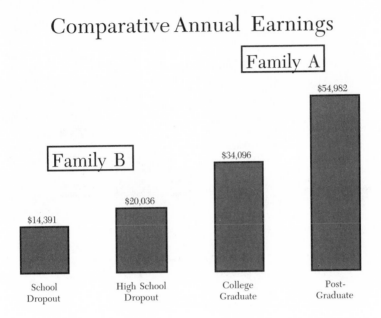

If you want to understand America, do not just look at the best of us, look at the rest of us. Go into any community and try to find a neighborhood where children and Yuppies can learn from our seniors, where English is spoken in every pocket of the population, where we are not walled away or grilled in from one another.

Besides being segmented in our community, we as a nation feel alienated from our government – local, state, and federal – as they spend our tax dollars recklessly and with no accountability. Consider the first chart on the next page which shows that for the past 15 years our debt has skyrocketed with no hope of ever being curtailed, or perhaps the second chart which shows the huge gap between the money the government collects in taxes and the money that they spend every year. Bill Gates' entire $12 billion fortune would be wiped out in less than a month at this rate.

National Debt

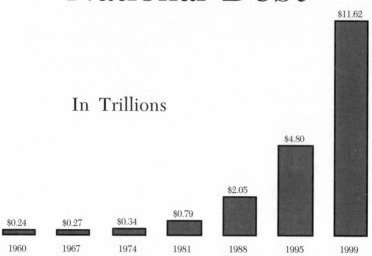

In Trillions

$0.24	$0.27	$0.34	$0.79	$2.05	$4.80	$11.62
1960	1967	1974	1981	1988	1995	1999

Federal Spending & Total Taxes
As a Percent of GDP

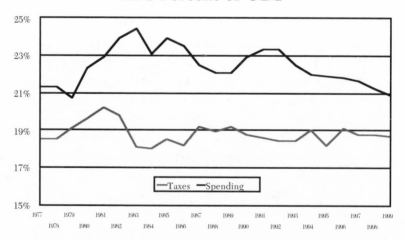

But what is perhaps most startling is the next chart which shows our levels of future financial obligations – $23 trillion – which make our debt look almost small. These are the monies such as Social Security, interest on the debt, and Medicare, that the government has obligated itself to pay in the future.

Financial Obligations of the Federal Government
Year Ending September 30, 1993

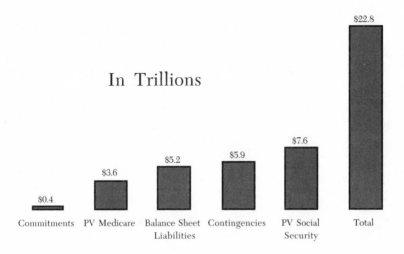

In Trillions

$0.4	$3.6	$5.2	$5.9	$7.6	$22.8
Commitments	PV Medicare	Balance Sheet Liabilities	Contingencies	PV Social Security	Total

Because these future obligations are coupled with our low savings rate shown in the chart below – only 5 percent compared to the other industrialized nations which save 10 percent or higher – we can expect a lower quality of life and an inability to compete with other nations in the future.

Comparative Savings Rates

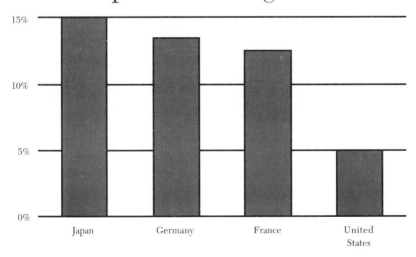

These problems and others seem so huge that many of us give up on making a change. That is why less than 50 percent of us vote in our national elections; 70 percent say they distrust government; and, according to a recent *Newsweek* poll, 40 percent of us do not even believe the United States will exist as one nation 100 years from today.

As a child, as a teenager and as a college student, I was always taught to believe that America was the nation with the most opportunity and the highest economic prosperity for all. And in the global context, America held the world's hope for freedom.

As an adult, I see the status that America once gripped rapidly diminishing. But perhaps more glaring than any of our fiscal problems is the fact that we no longer feel a sense of responsibility for one another.

Senator Trent Lott of Mississippi describes the way America used to be when he tells the story of his youth. He took a baseball from a local game. When he got home, his father knew he had taken the ball because a neighbor had reported the boy's misconduct.

The point is that we used to feel personally responsible for not only our own children but for the well-being of other people's children. My grandfather used to tell me if he saw somebody down on his luck on the street, he would merely pick him up in his truck and help him find work. What happened to this kind of America where it was safe and common to be your brother's keeper?

Perhaps when we complain about the high taxes that go to social programs, we will ask ourselves what we individually do to help those who are less fortunate. It seems more than coincidental that our social programs have grown along with our disregard for one another.

It is we who have created the void where social programs have spread. If we each individually cared for the old in our families, would there be a need for such an extensive Social Security program? If men cared for the children they fathered, would we see so many children and single mothers in poverty? And finally, if men and women would dedicate themselves to each other in marriage and spend time caring for their children, we would see less drug use, less crime, less suicide.

The picture that we view here on this window on all time is not one that anyone wants to see. Yet we must reexamine ourselves if we are to succeed.

America is clearly at a watershed in its history. We can choose to become one nation, one community whose members care for one another, or we can continue down the path to what Arthur Schlesinger calls the "tribalization of America" – fragmenting ourselves by race, culture, education, occupation.

All history cries out to us that to endure, a nation must be of one language, of common goals, of responsive government, of codes of decency and of kept spiritual and moral standards. To succeed, America must unify itself. We must heal the wounds of ethnic tension, of partisanship, of generational and socioeconomic warfare.

Empirically and statistically the enduring power of strong values has been proven by James Collins and Jerry Porras of Stanford University in their book, *Built to Last*. They show in their six-year study that companies that have principles, core ideology, and vision have achieved success more than six times greater than those companies without these qualities. As shown in the chart below, if you had invested $1 in these companies 30 years ago, the dollar would be worth $6,000 today.

Cumulative Stock Returns of $1 Invested

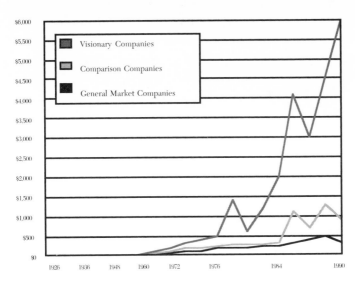

Clearly, principles pay. But the tough question for us is what kind of principles can we design? Indeed, in this year, 1995, what does it mean to be an American and what shared future can we design?

Defining America has always been a difficult problem. Unlike most other nations, we have no common ethnic or cultural background.

Indeed, being an American is more of a state of mind. It is wanting to have a say in your government and being able to create a better way of life for you and your children. More than being a country though, America is an ideal for those searching for liberty around the globe. America represents the desire of men to be free of the shackles of history, of prejudice, and of limits.

As F. Scott Fitzgerald wrote of the settlers who came to this country, "They were face-to-face for the first and last time in history with something commensurate to their capacity for wonder." What does it mean to you to be an American? What about you particularly makes you American? Some, when asked what makes them Americans, think of fictional characters like Mr. Smith who went to Washington, Forrest Gump, or the image of the cowboy or the farmer.

Others mention the great success stories of the self-made men and women who inhabit this country – Jonas Salk, John D. Rockefeller, Oprah Winfrey, Abraham Lincoln, Michael Jordan. When I think of what it means to be an American, I think of people in my life who embody the best of all American values.

There is my grandmother, who is here today, who worked two, sometimes three jobs as a school bus driver, a Coca-Cola bottle inspector, and a dime store lunch counter manager to put my mother through college. Often she has helped me out in college, too, with her Social Security check.

There is a friend of mine at school who, despite coming to the United States less than ten years ago from mainland China, managed to learn English, to be accepted to Harvard, and will now be serving the United States as an officer in the military.

There is another man I know who started a chain of restaurants. In his spare time he runs a boys' camp and manages to be active in South Florida politics. He is a Cuban, and he came to the United States with nothing, in a boat made of Styrofoam and with a sail of plastic raincoats. I mention these heroes because they represent the best qualities of Americans. They are innovative, hard-working, and most of all they have a desire to give back to their community and to future generations.

How do we take this shared and revered quality of Americans and build it into our future? First, let us teach our young more rudiments of life in school, church or temple, to choose truth over lies, honesty over theft, respect over violence, love of self and others, duty to country, pride in parenting and self-control. Let us teach our people to save instead of consume and to prepare for their future and force our government to do the same.

Secondly, let us stress the nobility of all education – college and non-college. Let us emphasize the worth of the trades – carpentry, electrical work, and farming. Those who work with their hands are often forgotten, and college is not the choice of everyone.

If the lights went out in the building today, I doubt our Ph.D.'s here could solve the problem. Millions of jobs are waiting to be created as we build shelter for the world and feed it. We are the best builders and farmers on earth. Let us prepare those who will craft our houses and grow our food as much as we do the graduate students who will write our books.

Let us develop further our enormous strengths as the cradle of higher learning. Our university systems are the best in the world, and therefore we can build loyalties in world citizens as they learn here at our great universities how to fish in their countries. Our foreign aid must be turned into exported education made in the USA.

Third, let us force those we elect to carry our will to city halls, state houses, and Washington. We as citizens can only do this by becoming politically active, just as you in United We Stand America have shown us how to do. Write, call, and hound our elected officials to keep them honest and accountable. And above all, we must vote.

Fourth and finally, let us become one nation. Let us care for our children, our ill, our forgotten. Let us take everyone along with us on this journey for a better tomorrow. Let us be one nation with every type of person and yet a nation unified by a common set of goals and ethics.

If the genes do carry strengths as well as weaknesses, we know that the American gene for courage has always prevailed. We are dominant – not recessive – for success, for innovation, for ultimate triumph. Everything that has tried to destroy us has failed.

As we stand at the threshold of a new century, America is the author of a democracy that is changing the face of the globe. Revolution, civil war, and mass migrations of people are at a high tide. Technology is drastically altering the way we live our lives as we surf the Internet and bring the world home to our personal computers.

Then there is perhaps the greatest force of all – the generations that will come. New generations – my generation – will mold this new world. My generation has been raised on MTV, Kermit the Frog, divorce, Ronald Reagan, fear of death by drugs and AIDS, materialism of the 1980's, and an irreverence for government because it has mortgaged our future. We are loose cannons, latchkey kids. We face a lesser standard of life than our parents. We tend to be despondent, negative. Texans might say of us, "These dogs just won't hunt."

But I urge you to look closer because there is more than just our coarse veneer. There are 25 million of us. More of us are college educated, multilingual, and better traveled than our predecessors. We come closer to wiping out discrimination than those before us. With improvements in technology and transportation, we will be able to explore more, accomplish more, learn more about our bodies and our world. Historically we come of age at a time of peace and plenty. We are the generation without wars, without the tears of assassination, without the hunger of depression, without the threat of atomic destruction. For this reason we begin our journey not fueled by fear or rage or want, but with the precious luxury of peace, the priceless gift of knowledge, the wealth of lessons learned and corrected.

We want to bring more to our table than our predecessors, not less. We want to shed the labels of *Generation X*, *the grungers*, *the baby busters*, and instead be a global generation, a generation of technology, of science, of education, and, above all, a generation that nurtures its children, honors its elders, and carries tolerance and education into a renaissance that knows not a single boundary.

My generation is, of course, not alone in these quests. Older, younger, rich, poor, we are all on this voyage together. And so, as one, we must build our shared vision of the future, to rediscover what it means to be an American and to make America again an estuary for the intellect, the artist, the shopkeeper, the carpenter, the student, the scientist, of any and all backgrounds. We will meet our rendezvous with destiny anew. Refreshed, we bring a shiny magic to a dusty, discouraged world.

If it is true that every moment is a window on all time, then you and I are the reflection of everything past, and we are the promise of everything that is to be. America flows through us. We are the future and we are our children's future.

Thank you.

House Majority Leader Dick Armey

Simplifying the Federal Tax System

ROSS PEROT: *You have heard numerous speakers talk about the need for a new tax plan. Every time they talk, you applaud and react. We have a man who is going to talk specifically about a new tax plan, Congressman Dick Armey from Texas. He is the House Majority Leader.*

Congressman Armey was born in Cando, North Dakota – a great name that epitomizes Congressman Armey's can-do spirit.

He graduated from Jamestown College in North Dakota. He received his master's degree from the University of North Dakota and his doctorate in economics from the University of Oklahoma.

Prior to being elected to Congress, he was Chairman of the Economics Department at the University of North Texas. He lives near Lewisville, Texas, with his wife, Susan, and five children.

To give you some idea of how his constituents feel about him, Congressman Armey is now serving his sixth term in Congress, and he was reelected with 73 percent of the vote. He has served on the Joint Economic Committee, the House Education and Labor Committee, and he is one of the architects of the Republicans' Contract With America.

Before it was popular, he was a leader in the effort to get the budget balanced, cut spending, and reduce taxes.

He is the driving force behind the Flat Tax idea now being discussed in Washington. He believes that simplifying the Internal Revenue Code will restore confidence in our tax system and lead to economic prosperity.

We are delighted to have Congressman Armey with us today to talk about the prospects for tax reform in the United States. Ladies and gentlemen, the Majority Leader of the House of Representatives, Dick Armey from Texas.

Thank you. Thank you, Ross, for that nice introduction, and I want to tell you that the folks in Cando, North Dakota, thank you. We do not get much attention up there, you know. I also want to thank you all for your leadership and your vision. The independent movement that you launched three years ago is a big part of the change that has shaken Washington like nothing I have ever seen.

It took two elections, the unseating of a President, and the toppling of a Congress, but the Beltway establishment is finally getting the message. The American people want a dramatically different kind of government, one that is smaller, more open, and above all, more accountable. That is why, Mr. and Mrs. America, you elected a new majority last November. And, ladies and gentlemen, I am proud to say that in the past 200 days we have made more progress toward creating the kind of government that you want than I have seen in my last ten years in Congress.

Amazingly, we have done this in a bipartisan fashion with a good number of Democrats supporting us on every bill. My view is that this is not a Republican Congress, nor was it previously a Democratic Congress. This is, and always will be, the American people's Congress. We must work together as Americans, not as partisans.

It is inspiring to have Democrats, Republicans and independents gathered in one room here to discuss the nation's pressing problems. I must tell you, this conference stands in sharp contrast to what happened last week when the Speaker of the House, who, as you know, is working very hard to save Medicare from bankruptcy, invited a Democratic congressman and a nonpartisan member of the Medicare board to a meeting to talk about the Medicare reform options. What did that congressman do? He turned down the invitation. Then he showed up at the meeting with a hundred protesters. He disrupted it so that no discussion could take place. That kind of partisanship is not how you conduct an honest policy debate in America.

So, I want to applaud Ross Perot. His new book on saving Medicare is a thoughtful contribution to the debate, one that encourages open, honest and nonpartisan discussion of this urgently important issue.

The Contract With America came about precisely because voters want accountability, not cheap promises and mean-spirited partisanship. That is why our new majority has tried to put our own house in order first. Consider what we did on our first day in office. We cut one in three committee staff members. We applied all laws of the land to Congress. We ordered the first-ever audit of the House's financial records, resulting in $20 million in savings each year to the taxpayers. We adopted honest budget numbers, so that from now on a *cut* is a decrease and an *increase* is an increase. No more phony double-talk. And we imposed term limits on the Speaker and on committee chairmen.

Ladies and gentlemen, we believe no one should be entrusted with too much power for too long. Not even Newt Gingrich or Dick Armey.

More important than that, by putting this government on a seven-year diet plan, we have forced ourselves to make some honest spending decisions, unavoidable decisions. A country that is $5 trillion in the red – a country in which every child born today enters the world saddled with up to $18,000 in debt – is a country that does not have the luxury of more time.

Even as we tackle these huge problems, we know that we must begin looking ahead to the future, to the next stage of this historic transformation. That is why I have come here today to ask your help in taking the next crucial step.

As I said in my new book, *The Freedom Revolution*, I believe the most enduring revolutions bring about the simplest reforms. In my view the simplest and most beneficial reform we could make to spur economic growth and revise stagnant family wages is to scrap today's Internal Revenue Code and start over from scratch.

When I introduced the *Freedom and Fairness Restoration Act* last year, I had no idea how the public would react. The response has been thunderous. Over the past year I have received more than 5,000 intensely enthusiastic letters praising the Flat Tax. In just this past month I have received nearly that many messages over the Internet.

Yes, the Flat Tax has gone third wave with its very own home page on the World Wide Web. The address is:

http://www.house.gov/armey.flattax/welcome.html

Senator Richard Shelby and I have reintroduced the bill, and I must tell you, I am convinced that the Flat Tax is in America's future.

Here is how it works. Rather than tinkering, we scrap the entire tax code, corporate and personal, and replace it with one flat rate that applies to all Americans.

We leave just one exception, a generous family allowance to ensure that every family has the first claim to its own income sufficient to support itself. A typical family of four must earn $33,300 before it owes a cent of federal income tax. For earnings beyond that, everybody pays a flat 17 percent on all the income above the allowance. No deductions. No loopholes. No tax breaks. No tables. No schedules. No nothing.

Each year you calculate your income, fill out a postcard-sized form, make out a check, and drop it in the mail – end of process. Here is the best part. You are done with the IRS until next year. Instead of taking 11 hours to do your taxes, as the average family does today, you could do it in 11 minutes, maybe less. If you have business income, the process is almost identical. Whether you are IBM or a mom-and-pop grocery, you still fill out a postcard-sized form. Just subtract your business expenses from your revenues and pay 17 percent on the remainder.

Imagine the new world that will dawn. Gone will be today's 480 different tax forms and the 280 forms that explain how to fill out the 480 forms. Whole armies of tax attorneys and lobbyists will be out looking for productive work. As for all those IRS agents and auditors, well, instead of harassing you, they will be sitting silently at their desks like the Maytag repairman. They will be feeling bored and I suspect just a little bit lonely.

We have made an important change from last year's bill. Senator Shelby and I have added a new provision that requires a three-fifths super majority to raise the rate, add additional rates, create loopholes or shrink the family allowance. We are absolutely determined that the Flat Tax stay flat.

I talked earlier about all the people that have contacted me about the Flat Tax. Let me share with you some of the reasons why people like the Flat Tax. First, because it is incredibly simple. By one economist's estimate, it would save the American people $232 billion a year in time and paperwork costs. That is more money than the entire federal deficit and a potential savings of $90 for every man, woman and child in this country.

Second, unlike today's code, the Flat Tax is honest. By sweeping away all the special-interest loopholes, it shows us right up front how much government is really costing us. By eliminating the code's social engineering and economic tinkering, it shifts power from politicians to private citizens. The Flat Tax has the decency to respect our ability to make our own financial judgments.

Third, the Flat Tax will be a powerful engine of economic growth. The chief cause of stagnant wages is our anemic savings rate; the chief cause of our low savings rate is the current destructive policy of taxing savings twice, once when a dollar is earned and then again when it produces a return. The Flat Tax wipes out this perverse bias against savings.

As a result, savings will rise, the pool of capital will grow, workers will be better equipped and trained, and their output will expand, leading to bigger paychecks. But a higher savings rate is not enough. We also need greater rewards for work and risk-taking, the true engines of economic growth. Instead of punishing those who would build the proverbial better mousetrap with steeply progressive tax rates, as we do today, the Flat Tax slashes the top rate from 40 percent to 17 percent, enabling America to unleash her would-be Thomas Edisons and Bill Gates to create the inventions and industries and high-paying jobs of tomorrow.

The Flat Tax would make such risks worthwhile, while making America a magnet for foreign investment capital. As a result, the income of the average American family of four would be approximately $4,300 higher in the year 2000 than it would be if we retained the current tax system – higher savings, more risk-taking, higher wages.

Fourth, and perhaps most important, the Flat Tax is fair. When you tax everyone at the same rate, the rich pay a lot more in taxes than the middle class or the poor. It may be a little difficult for some in Washington to grasp, but with three times the income, you pay three times the taxes. With ten times the income, you pay ten times the taxes. And I, for one, want to pay ten times the taxes on ten times the income.

At the same time, by the traditional liberal definition, our Flat Tax plan is also progressive, as progressive as the Code we had under President Kennedy. Thanks to the generous family allowance, even with a flat rate, a family making $33,300 a year would pay no federal income tax. That family making $50,000 a year would pay 6 percent of its income. And a family making $200,000 would pay 14 percent of its income. This means about 20 million lower-income Americans would be dropped from the tax rolls altogether. What is not for a liberal to like about that?

If I might, I would like to take a few minutes to address the four most commonly heard concerns about the Flat Tax plan. The first concern comes from the class-warfare crowd who are alleging that our plan does not tax so-called unearned income. They say we are letting wealthy stockholders off the tax hook. This is completely untrue. Our plan taxes unearned income, as it is called, at exactly the same rate as wages. What we do not do is tax it twice. Under our plan all income is taxed at the same 17 percent rate with no exceptions. To suggest or imply that we do not tax so-called unearned income is a misrepresentation of the plan.

The second concern comes from people who ask, "Will eliminating the home mortgage interest deduction hurt the real estate industry?" The answer is, not as much as lower interest rates will help it. While our plan would end the interest deduction, it also ends tax on interest earnings. As a result, nothing changes. Both borrowers and lenders are held harmless. What the homeowner loses in deductions, he gains in lower interest rates. In fact, he comes out ahead on the deal because the Flat Tax ends the bias against saving, causing the capital pool to swell, and driving interest rates down even further. That is good news for the housing industry.

Frankly, ladies and gentlemen, homeowners are not as wedded to this supposedly sacred cow of the interest deduction as you might think. By a 3-to-1 margin in a recent poll, homeowners said they are willing to forego the mortgage deduction if that loss is offset by a reduction in their tax bill by a similar amount, and that's what this plan does.

I am confident the housing industry will support our approach, knowing that they are not losing a tax break, but gaining a new and better tax code and a bigger economy.

This leads me to an observation, ladies and gentlemen. The American Dream is not just owning your own home, it is getting your kids out of it. What we want is a high-growth, low-inflation economy with opportunities where our children can get out of school, get a good job, raise their family, and be able to afford their own home. The Flat Tax will go a long way to helping them realize that dream.

What about the charitable deduction? Will losing it hurt charities? My guess is they will not even miss it. For one thing, almost half of all charitable contributions today are not even claimed as deductions, so ending the break would have no effect on that giving. But more tellingly, during the 1980s, the so-called decade of greed, charitable giving actually doubled and religious giving tripled, even as the deduction's value as a tax break declined dramatically. We must ask why. Because people had more money in their pockets. Their taxes were lower, and their incomes were higher. The American people responded to greater freedom and prosperity as they have always done, by opening their hearts and their wallets to their neighbors.

Finally, there are those who say the Flat Tax will explode the deficit. This charge, ladies and gentlemen, comes mostly from those who want to preserve the current complicated tax structure. They have even cooked up a scary deficit number, $200 billion a year.

Well – as Ronald Reagan used to say – the trouble with our opponents is not that they are ignorant, it is just that so much of what they know just is not so.

I have been working on this Flat Tax for over a year, and I have devised a bill to close the deficit and make it as deficit neutral as possible. If, for some reason, the official estimators find that it would not raise as much revenue as I predict, then I will gladly adjust the plan to make up the difference. I want the Flat Tax debate on its merits, not on the issue of revenue loss.

What, then, is the Freedom in Fairness Restoration Act? It is a tax plan so simple you could do your taxes on a postcard. But more than that, it is a vision of what America can be again – a land of opportunity, with a rejuvenated economy, liberated entrepreneurial talent, and rising family wages. It is a commonsense plan for returning to a government that is simple, honest, and fair to all our citizens. And who knows, it might just restore the American people's ability to trust their government.

Ladies and gentlemen, as I said earlier, I am here today to ask you for your help. I am asking you to join our crusade. With your vision and your powerful grassroots support, I know the key question inside the Beltway will no longer be whether we have a Flat Tax, but the question will be how quickly can we get the Flat Tax passed for America's future.

Thank you for letting me be here.

Congressman
Bill Archer

Reforming the Federal
Tax System

ROSS PEROT: Our next speaker is the Chairman of the House Ways and Means Committee. He is Congressman Bill Archer from Houston, Texas.

Congressman Archer could not be with us this evening, but he was determined to bring his message to you. He asked me if he could tape it for you. He is such a wise and thoughtful man that I made one exception for this meeting.

Congressman Archer graduated from the University of Texas at Austin, where he received his bachelor's and law degrees with honors. He served in the Air Force, the Texas House of Representatives, and now in the United States Congress.

He is a fiscal conservative. He has never taken PAC contributions and has introduced legislation to get rid of PAC contributions.

Under his legislation 80 percent of the money raised for a campaign would have to come from the candidate's home district. He has never had a campaign fund-raising event in Washington, D.C.

He wants to replace our current income tax system with a new tax system. In the meantime, he does his own tax returns with a pencil and a calculator. He says, "I will either fix it, or I will suffer through it with you."

Congressman Archer's mother attends all of his town meetings in Houston. In 1994, when the election results were coming in, his mother had tears of joy in her eyes when she realized that her son would be the Chairman of the House Ways and Means Committee.

He has cut the staff by one-third and cut costs in that committee by 37 percent.

He is a longtime advocate of the Balanced Budget Amendment. He says, "The Balanced Budget Amendment is the single most important thing that Congress will do in my lifetime."

He and his wife, Sharon, have seven children and eight grandchildren. He clearly understands the implications of the debt and the deficit for his children and grandchildren.

I hope that you will listen very carefully while this highly respected wise man gives his ideas about tax reform to all of America.

Thanks, Ross, for your introduction and for letting me speak to all the active Americans you have assembled in Dallas.

I am grateful also to those of you from Houston who have contacted me with your comments and suggestions. Members of Houston's United We Stand America chapter originally suggested that I talk about tax reform with you today, and Ross seconded that motion in July. That is good, because I cannot think of any subject that is more fundamental to our nation's basic values of freedom and responsibility or more vital to our nation's economic prosperity in the future.

I feel so strongly about what I am about to say to you today that I wish I could be speaking to every American.

Your conference is called *Preparing Our Country for the 21st Century.* I cannot think of a better name. To me, tax reform does not mean what we have done so often over the last 20 years, merely chipping around the edges and resulting in the end with a worse tax code than before.

I want to abolish the income tax and get the IRS completely and totally out of each and every person's individual life.

I have been calling my plans *An Agenda for the Next Century.* We live in an exciting time, on the threshold of the 21st century. What we are talking about is nothing less than the definition of America itself.

What the American people and their representatives do now will forge America's future. Let us put this moment into historical perspective. At the end of the 15th century, the New World was separated from the Old World by an ocean, and so it was destined to be populated by men and women with a pioneering and enterprising spirit.

Americans, from the first, were people of imagination who looked across the surface of the ocean and saw the New World over the horizon. Americans were people who were willing to sacrifice everything to win a better life for their families.

When it came time for Americans to organize themselves into a nation, they were equal to the task. But the odds were even greater. Never before had a nation organized itself around principles. Never before had a nation claimed as its charter the universal laws of liberty and the natural rights and equal dignity of every person, not until 1776, on July 4, in a small room in Philadelphia. Back then the Declaration of Independence was not even taken seriously by the British. They considered it too bold and not feasible. It did not fit with their status quo way of thinking. But that half-page document sparked a new era of concern for individual rights and of unprecedented economic prosperity.

The world has not been the same since. America has charted its course with a careful aim at the horizon, with the same bold vision of what may lie beyond. The world has watched our history unfold as one obstacle after another was overcome by our democratic process.

I was given the chance to address some of the freshmen Representatives who came to Congress this year, and I will tell you what I told them. I feel like a freshman again.

When I started in Congress, I was energetic, full of ideas and felt as if I was going to be able not just to change America, but to change the world. I introduced several bills in those early years, including my first offer of the balanced budget constitutional amendment and the line-item veto, but these ideas languished in Washington.

This year, for the first time, in less than a hundred days, the House of Representatives passed both of them and more. Now I have the satisfaction of seeing many other initiatives I have worked on for years either in place or on their way to becoming law.

The Ways and Means Committee that I chair is doing more with less. I have reduced the majority staff by 40 percent, saving you, the taxpayers, $3 million a year. A balanced budget is on its way, along with capital gains tax relief, incentives to save, and an increase of the earnings limitation for those on Social Security who wish to continue to work.

This month I introduced H.R. 2162, the toughest immigration reform bill in Congress. As a sovereign nation, we must control our borders again. Other Congresses talked about it. We are going to do it. With all of these efforts coming to fruition, I cannot help feeling like a freshman again.

On the threshold of the 21st century, we are all being called to invigorate the American spirit. The only limitations we Americans have are those we put on ourselves. We can reach as far as our imagination and our commitment will take us, and that is very far indeed.

So let us think boldly. Let us put aside our preconceptions about business as usual and forge the best future we can for America.

Today I will discuss tax reform with you from two perspectives. Most of the tax debate has been made on the details of tax policy. That is important, but equally important is the morality of how we tax.

Here is where I stand. My goal is to tear the income tax out by its roots and throw it away so that it will never grow back again. I want to remove the IRS totally and completely from every American's individual life.

Americans are tired of seeing the federal government get first claim on their paychecks. They are tired of seeing the millions of IRS envelopes that show up in American mailboxes each year. They are tired of living under the fear that they will have a confrontation with an IRS agent where they have to provide stacks of records to prove their innocence.

I want to end all taxes on income and provide the essential revenues necessary to pay the government's bills with a tax on the purchase of goods and services.

We are at a unique moment to accomplish these things, but this debate is not a new one. Let me share a little bit of history with you. Thomas Jefferson, our third President, made it one of his career goals to eliminate all taxes from the individual lives of Americans. In his second inaugural address he considered this his most important achievement. He addressed the nation with these electrifying words: "Now it is the pleasure and pride of every American to ask, 'What farmer, what mechanic, what laborer ever sees a tax gatherer of the United States?'" It is my hope that we can soon make that same statement again.

Jefferson saw clearly the moral issue at the root of taxation – where should the government levy the disincentive that comes from taxation? On work effort or on spending?

As the years went on, America saw the same question crop up repeatedly. During the Civil War a temporary income tax was levied on Americans. Many people of the era believed the weight of taxes fell on one man and not on another. What is the income tax levied on? Industry, self-denial, thrift, knowledge, labor and capital. Those are the moral and economic cornerstones of America. What escapes the income tax? Idleness, vice and dishonesty.

One way to think of this concept is a story I tell about two farmers. I call them Farmer Work and Farmer Play. Farmer Work wakes up at dawn each morning, eats his breakfast with his family and then heads to the fields. He works hard until the sun goes down. The Work family lives frugally, saving for retirement, for the children's college and hoping one day to leave the farm to their children.

Across town Farmer Play leads quite a different life. He wakes at 9:30 and by 10:30 he goes to work, but he finishes at 3:00 each day. And on the way home he picks up cigarettes and beer, which he consumes as he watches TV.

The question we must ask is about the morality of taxation. Which of the two farmers' activities should be subject to the tax?

The current income tax is very hard on Farmer Work. Taxes take money from his income, from the capital gains on his savings. When he retires, his Social Security benefits will be taxed severely if his savings earn additional income. When he dies, estate taxes could well mean that his children will not have the opportunity to inherit the family farm.

The question is a moral one. Even a flat income tax would tax Farmer Work more than Farmer Play, for one simple reason – it taxes income. That means it taxes work effort. It taxes ingenuity and bold enterprise. It taxes the very qualities that made America great. The qualities embodied by your host, Ross Perot.

Let us go back for a moment to our history lesson. We all know what happened to the so-called temporary income tax, it became a permanent tax when the Sixteenth Amendment was ratified in 1913.

The first income tax started as a simple tax. The tax law that was created was only 16 pages long, so small I can carry it in my coat pocket. But already there were signs of trouble. A manual published to explain that code was 400 pages long. The rest, as they say, is history. Uncle Sam pulled up a chair at the payroll table, and there he sat and sat and sat.

From the New Deal through the Great Society, that tax code grew increasingly more complicated and more and more onerous. Efforts were made in the 1980s toward reduced rates and simplification, but the roots of the income tax stayed in the ground, and the tree grew back again.

By 1993, President Clinton and the Democrat Congress passed the largest tax increase in American history, even though every single Republican Congressman voted against it.

Remember that original tax law that was 16 pages long, how it looked? A copy of today's tax code is quite a different story. It is 2,823 pages long. Today the IRS tax regulations are more than 80,000 pages.

As the saying goes, the one thing we seem to learn from history is that we never seem to learn from history. I hope we can prove that wrong by removing all federal taxes on income.

We have tried an income tax. It failed. We tried to make it simpler. We failed. On the threshold of the 21st century, we need something better, we must not return to a 19th-century-style tax. Instead, we need to turn to a tax that is uniquely designed to fit the realities of today's America, one that will build the brightest future for our people.

That system, I believe, must have five bottom-line objectives. First, we must get the IRS completely and totally out of our individual lives. This year 40 million Americans will have a confrontation with the IRS. Some will be small, admittedly, but many will be large. And each will cause anxiety and fear.

With the tax on goods and services, there would be no withholding from your paycheck. You would keep your full pay. You would decide when you pay taxes, when you elect to spend your money.

There is an economic argument for this. Complying with the arcane rules of the IRS is a huge drain on our national economy.

I am the first Chairman of the Ways and Means Committee in memory who does his own tax return. It takes several days out of my life each year. I pledge that I will either fix it or I will suffer through it with you.

If it were possible, each member of Congress should be required by law to do his or her own tax return. If that were the case, I can assure you we would have a very different tax law.

The total cost of complying with the current tax code for all sectors of the economy is estimated to be at least $300 billion a year. That is "B" in billion. Some estimates put it at more than twice that much. I have been called a conservative, so I will make my argument using the lower figure.

Imagine if all that time and money were spent in a productive way, adding to the standard of living of working Americans. Some of the brightest minds in this country spend all of their time complying with the arcane tax rules. If this effort and talent were used to produce wealth, instead of merely transferring it, think of the productive jobs that could be created.

Under the current tax system, there are 130 million returns filed each year. With the Flat Tax, you would still have to file a return and be subject to audit. With a consumption tax, you as an individual would never have to fill out a return or deal with the IRS.

Second, the new system must reward people who save, not penalize them. Economists of all philosophies agree on one thing – our nation desperately needs increased savings. But to the IRS, a penny saved is a penny that ought to be taxed, more than once if possible. Taxes have dug a big hole in the nucleus of domestic savings our economy needs to provide jobs and opportunity with businesses owned by Americans. It has forced us to bring foreigners into our country to provide the capital savings to create the jobs. Taxing consumption instead of income puts a zero tax on savings. A flat income tax merely reduces the barriers to savings, but not to zero.

Under a consumption tax, you would receive your full income and have even more money to save. America would become a sponge for savings, and thereby interest rates would decline, reducing the price of homes, the price of automobiles, the price of all items that you buy on credit.

Third, the new tax system must get at the underground economy. Under the current system, honest Americans who play by the rules and pay their taxes are forced to pay 10 to 15 percent more just to make up for those who will not or do not report their income. Under a consumption tax, every time one of those people who lives in the cash economy buys an item in the marketplace, whether it be a car or whether it be a yacht, they would be taxed. Even a drug dealer who buys a very expensive item will have to pay his fair share of our cost of government.

Even a flat income tax would fail to get at the underground economy. Those who do not report their income today will not simply begin reporting it just because the rate is lower. Zero is still better than 17, 20 or 25 percent.

Fourth, the new tax should be border-adjustable. This is very, very important for the future. That means it should be imposed on imports and subject to removal from the price allowed products when they are exported.

A friend of mine in Congress once said, "You know, Bill, I am a fair individual, all I ever want is a fair advantage." And that is all I want for the United States of America, a fair advantage in the global competitive marketplace.

Right now the income tax is a cost of doing business that is passed on to the customer, here and overseas. It is built into the price of every one of our products, and it cannot be taken out. It makes our products more expensive when they compete in the global marketplace.

A consumption tax levied at the point of consumption in the United States would not be included in the price of our products overseas. We would win hands down against foreign products. Domestically no form of income tax, even a flat tax, can be imposed on products that foreign producers sell in America. But under a tax on goods and services, every one of those products would be taxed side by side with American products and would have to pay their share of our cost of government.

It is my hope that in the next century, conflicts between nations can be decided in the marketplace, not on the battlefields. A consumption tax would give us an immense competitive advantage. We cannot afford to lose this battle, or we will witness a decline in the standard of living of the American people.

If we go to a tax on goods and services, America can become the economic juggernaut of the world. What does that mean to you and me? It means more and better-paying jobs for American workers.

Fifth, the tax system must be fair and not create undue burdens on low-income Americans. With a tax on the purchase of goods and services, the more someone has to spend, the more they are taxed.

It also would be fair to home buyers. Because homes represent savings and not consumed items, they would not be taxed.

Equally important, the new tax code must recognize and account for the needs of low-income people who consume every penny of their income to simply make ends meet.

As you can see, taxes strike to the core of what America should be doing to prepare America for the 21st century.

In a cartoon from 1933, a cartoonist saw Congress overly eager to pull America down the wrong path – an income tax. The right road is the consumption tax.

What would that cartoonist say today? Will Congress force America down the wrong road again?

Or will we keep to the bold vision of our forebears and forge a future that will make America the economic superpower of the 21st century?

Let's return to that room in Philadelphia on July 4, 1776, and let us all stand shoulder to shoulder with the founders of our nation. They met to end taxation without representation. They met to be sure that individuals had the freedom to live their lives responsibly, without inter-ference. They met to boldly oppose a system that put the power to tax in a faraway place and to keep that power in the hands of the people.

What form of taxation would they prefer? This one, or one that puts the decision to be taxed or not to be taxed where it belongs, in the hands of each American in their day-to-day lives? Let me assure you that I consider a flat income tax preferable to the current tax system.

My good friend Dick Armey and I often joke about it. He and I are blessed to live in this state, the State of Texas, a state that has never had any form of personal income tax. Texas raises its revenue with a consumption tax. And I like to tell Dick, "Dick, if it's good enough for Texas, it ought to be good enough for the United States of America."

He has some great ideas, and in the end we will be together. But if we are going to reform America's taxes, we ought to do it with the rev-olutionary spirit now afoot in Washington and throw away the income tax completely.

Timid people say to me, "Maybe that's a little too bold, Bill." But I believe that the courage and character of Americans has not really changed and that our nation is ready to meet the challenges of the next century in a bold, new, uniquely American way. I think you are a per-fect example of that. You are a special breed. You have come here from all over the country at your own expense, with personal sacrifice, with only one goal in mind, to stay informed and to make a difference in your country's future.

It is not easy to commit this kind of time and effort, and I congratulate each one of you. I see in your spirit that American spirit that has carried our nation so far. I hope you will have the courage and boldness to walk with me down this ambitious road of liberty and less government.

God bless you, as God has blessed America.

Professor
Laurence Kotlikoff

Generational Accounting: Understanding the Fiscal Disaster We Are Preparing for Our Kids

ROSS PEROT: Dr. Laurence Kotlikoff is Professor of Economics at Boston University, and Research Associate of the National Bureau of Economic Research. He is the author of Generational Accounting – What Determines Savings?

Dr. Kotlikoff earned his bachelor's degree in economics from the University of Pennsylvania in 1973, and his doctorate in economics from Harvard University in 1977. From 1977 through 1983, he served on the faculties at UCLA and Yale.

From 1981 to 1982, Professor Kotlikoff was a Senior Economist with the President's Council of Economic Advisers.

He has served as a consultant to the International Monetary Fund, the World Bank, the Office of Management and Budget, the U.S. Departments of Education and Labor, the Joint Committee on Taxation, and numerous other U.S. and international organizations and corporations.

He has provided expert testimony to committees of Congress including the Senate Finance Committee, the House Ways and Means Committee, and the Joint Economic Committee.

He has co-authored several books and has written extensively for professional journals, newspapers and magazines on various issues, including the tax structure, social security, pensions, the deficit, savings, and insurance.

Dr. Kotlikoff, thank you for coming today to speak about the effects of federal budget decisions on the future generations of Americans.

Thank you, Ross. I am delighted to be here. As Ross told you, I am a college professor, not a politician, and my goal today is to teach you a few things that I am not sure the politicians really want you to learn. Now I want you all to pay very strict attention because there is a test at the end. Anyone who does not pass will be forced to attend my workshop on Sunday.

Today's class has five lessons.

The first lesson is about generational accounting. Generational accounting gets at the heart of why we came to Dallas in the middle of August. It measures directly the amount of the government's bills that we adults will pay and the amount that we are intending to dump on our children and grandchildren.

Lesson number two: U.S. generational accounting shows that our government is preparing a fiscal nightmare for our children.

Lesson number three: Balancing the budget in seven years, as the Republicans propose, or 10 years as the President proposes, is far too little too late to produce generational balance, by which I mean fair treatment of current and future generations.

Lesson number four: U.S. generational policy – our five-decade-long practice of taking from the young and giving to the old – is the primary reason our nation is saving so little, investing so little and growing so slowly.

Lesson five: Congress needs to do generational accounting on a routine basis in setting fiscal policy.

Now, what specifically does generational accounting show? Let's take a look.

The chart on the next page shows the lifetime net tax rate of different generations born in this century based on current policy. Net taxes refer to all the different income, payroll, excise and other taxes we pay to federal, state and local government, less all the Social Security, Medicare, welfare and other transfer payments we receive from these governments.

U.S. Lifetime Net Tax Rates

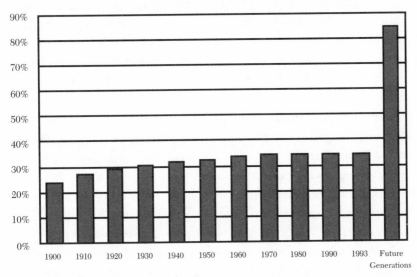

Each generation's net tax rate is calculated by dividing its lifetime net tax payment by its lifetime labor earnings. For you actuaries out there, both of these amounts are calculated as actuarial present values.

Consider the generation born in 1900. This generation paid about 24 percent of every dollar that it earned in net taxes. What about my generation? I'm a baby boomer. I was born in 1951. Well, based on current policy, my generation is projected to pay a third of its lifetime income to government, federal, state and local in net taxes. The same is roughly true for younger generations now alive, again, assuming current policy is maintained.

But can we maintain current policy? Can we continue through time to tax each new generation that comes along at a 33 percent net tax rate and still pay for all the government's spending on goods and services as well as interest on the government's debt?

The answer is no. Assuming those of us now alive don't pay higher net future taxes, future generations will have to cover the difference between what we pay and the government's projected spending. This difference represents not 33 percent of what future generations are projected to earn from working, but a whopping 84 percent!

Now 84 percent is an incredibly large and scary number. And, I'm sure some of you are saying to yourselves, "Things can't be this bad.

This must be based on extremely pessimistic demographic and fiscal projections."

I wish that were true. But the projections used in generational accounting are the intermediate ones, and not the pessimistic ones. They are coming from our government – from the Office of Management and Budget, the U.S. Census, the Social Security Administration, the Health Care Financing Administration, and other government agencies. By the way, the intermediate projections, year after year, have turned out to be too optimistic. Generational accounting uses the same methodology that's being employed by the Social Security trustees in their Annual Trustees Report.

Since we can't tax future generations at an 84 percent rate – for economic, if not for moral reasons – we are going to have to raise taxes or cut spending at some point in order to lower the net tax burden on future generations. The real question is whether we current adults – young, middle-aged and old alike – are going to step up to the plate and pay more and demand less from the government, or whether we will leave today's children as well as tomorrow's children to face sky-high taxes.

Now the Republicans are telling us not to worry, they will fix things. And the Democrats are telling us not to worry, God will fix things. Well, we really should worry.

The chart below shows you what happens if we adopt the Republicans' budget proposal, which involves balancing the budget seven long years from now.

U.S. Lifetime Net Tax Rates
Under Alternative Policies

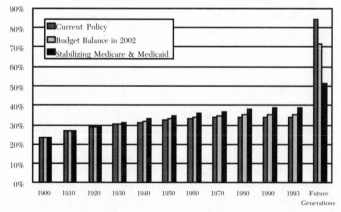

In cutting some government spending and some of the projected growth in Medicare and Medicaid, the Republican plan ends up raising our net taxes and lowering those facing future generations. That's the good news. The bad news is that the net tax rate facing future generations falls only from 84 percent to 72 percent under the Republican plan, which is still astronomically high.

Should we be surprised that the Republican budget proposal, for all of its good intentions, doesn't really come close to achieving generational balance? We should not be surprised the plan does not reduce government debt. Instead, it lets government debt grow by hundreds of billions of dollars for seven more years and provides no guarantee that it won't grow at record rates after seven years. The plan doesn't stabilize the growth of Medicare and Medicaid benefits. These benefits continue to grow, under the Republican plan, year after year at roughly twice the rate of the economy. And the plan doesn't change our demographic dilemma – the fact that the enormous cohort of baby boomers start collecting Social Security benefits in 13 years and Medicare benefits in 16 years.

The Republican plan is both shortsighted and mistargeted. The plan looks ahead for only seven years. Now seven years may be a long time for a politician, but it's a pretty short time for my five-year-old. And the plan's target is budget balance, not generational balance. But budget balance doesn't necessarily imply generational balance. We could triple Social Security taxes tomorrow and use the extra revenue not only to balance the budget but also to double Social Security benefits. This would produce budget balance but would move us farther away from generational balance because it would greatly benefit today's elderly at a huge cost to young and future Americans.

So this weekend, when you hear the politicians tell you about their plans to someday soon achieve budget balance, tell them you've heard it before. Tell them that you heard it in 1982 when they passed the Tax Equity and Fiscal Responsibility Act. Tell them you heard it in 1984 when they passed the Deficit Reduction Act. Tell them you heard it in 1985 when they passed the Gramm-Rudman-Hollings Act. Tell them you heard it again in 1987 when they passed Gramm-Rudman-Hollings II. And then tell them you heard it in 1990, and again in 1993, when they passed the 1990 and 1993 Omnibus Budget Reconciliation Acts.

Finally, tell them that the real issue is not budget balance in ten years or in seven years, or even this year. Tell them that the real issue is generational balance – whether our country's long-term fiscal policies will protect our children and grandchildren from exorbitant rates of net taxation. And tell them when they come up with a credible policy to achieve generational balance, you will be, as Ross Perot would say, all ears.

One suggestion you might give them, which apparently hasn't crossed their minds, is to put an immediate stop to excessive growth in Medicare and Medicaid. These programs are so large and are growing so fast that simply limiting their growth to that of the economy is enough to lower the net tax rate facing future generations from 84 percent down to 52 percent. To further lower the lifetime net tax rates facing future generations, we could adopt the non-Medicare and non-Medicaid elements of either the Republican budget plan or that of the President. The point is that achieving generational balance is still feasible, but the hour is extremely late.

Incidentally, the way most economists advocate reforming Medicare and Medicaid is not to limit payments for particular medical procedures, nor to try to bribe the elderly into enrolling in HMOs, nor to waste time setting up another commission of politicians to study the problem. The economists' way is to divide the country into small geographical regions, provide a fixed budget for each region, and use that budget to purchase health insurance coverage for the region's Medicare and Medicaid populations. Each region's budget would grow through time at roughly the same rate as the economy – no faster and no slower. Competition by insurance companies would lead to the best quality of care that can be purchased given the available budget.

But I'm digressing. Let me get back on track by recapping our first three lessons. First, generational accounting measures who will pay. Second, U.S. generational accounting reveals that a fiscal freight train is bearing down on our children. And third, our politicians are responding to this imminent train wreck by selling tickets.

Lesson four concerns the economic impact of our government's ever-growing redistribution from young and future Americans to older ones. To begin, let's look at what has happened to rates of U.S. saving and investment since 1950.

The following chart shows U.S. saving and U.S. investment rates in the 1990s and the previous four decades. To an economist, this is not a pretty picture. It shows that the U.S. savings rate has averaged only 2.7 percent since 1990, compared with 9.1 percent in the 1950s and 1960s. Less saving means less investment. And, since 1990, our investment rate has been running at less than half the rate that we observed in the 1950s and 1960s.

The Postwar Decline in U.S. Saving and Investment

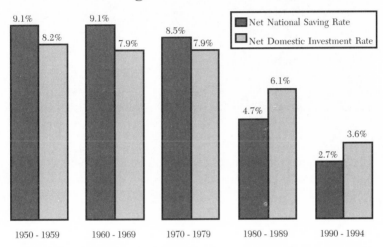

So, investment refers to the addition of new plant and equipment to our economy. Hence, the more that we invest, the more capital goods of different kinds our workers get to use in producing goods and services, and, consequently, the more productive they are. More productive workers earn higher wages, so there is a direct line of causality running from low rates of saving, to low rates of investment, to low rates of labor productivity growth, to low rates of real wage growth.

Has our lower rate of national saving led to slower growth in labor productivity and real wages? It certainly has.

The chart on the next page shows that labor productivity and real wages are pretty closely related and that both are growing at much slower rates now than was the case in the 1950s and 1960s.

Okay, if low U.S. saving helps explain low U.S. real wage growth, what explains low U.S. saving? Well, the flip side of having a low national saving rate is having a high consumption rate. So, let's consider who is consuming at such high rates these days.

Labor Productivity and Real Wage Growth

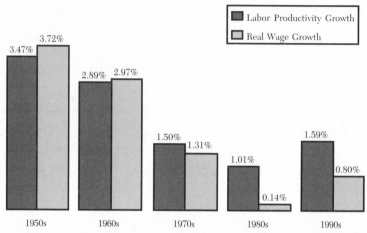

The answer is the household sector. It's not the government. As the chart below shows, household consumption is a larger share of our national output now than it was in the past, whereas government consumption is a smaller share.

Postwar Household and Government Consumption Rates
As a Percent of Net National Product

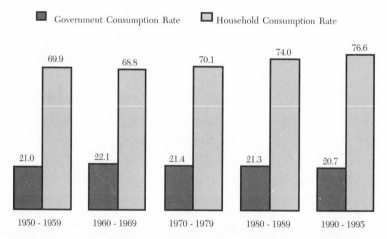

Okay, if our household sector's rate of consumption is to blame, who within the household sector is consuming so much more? The answer, you may be surprised or not surprised to learn, is not the supposedly spendthrift baby boomer generation or the members of the X generation. Instead, it's the elderly whose consumption, measured on the per capita basis, has risen enormously compared to that of the young and middle-aged. Let's look at the example below.

Resources and Consumption of 70-Year-Olds Relative to 30-Year-Olds

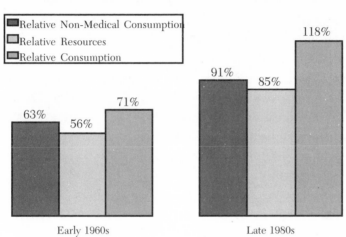

The above chart considers two periods – the early 1960s and the late 1980s. It shows how the average consumption and economic resources of 70-year-olds has grown relative to those of 30-year-olds. In the early 1960s, 70-year-olds consumed only 71 percent of the amount consumed by 30-year-olds. By the late 1980s, 70-year-olds were consuming 118 percent of the amount consumed by 30-year-olds. Some of this dramatic increase in the relative consumption of the elderly reflects increased consumption of medical goods and services. But nonmedical consumption of the elderly has also risen drastically compared to the young. In the early 1960s, the nonmedical consumption of 70-year-olds was 63 percent of the nonmedical consumption of 30-year-olds. In the late 1980s it was 91 percent.

This chart also shows that the average economic resources of 70-year-olds has risen from 56 percent of the resources of 30-year-olds to over 85 percent. The measure of economic resources being used here includes all forms of income, including government transfer payments received by individuals.

What we saw in the preceding chart is really not surprising. The dramatic growth in the relative consumption of the elderly has coincided with the dramatic growth in their relative incomes. The principal reason that the income of the elderly has grown so much faster than that of the young is the fantastic growth in Social Security, Medicare and Medicaid.

I'm telling you this: I'm certainly not trying to bash the elderly. Some of my closest relatives are older and some are even members of the AARP. But we need to face the facts. In transferring ever larger sums from young savers to old spenders, the government is destroying U.S. saving. It's destroying not only U.S. saving, it's destroying U.S. investment and real wage growth and hitting our kids with a double whammy. It's handing them a very large and growing tax bill in an economy in which their pretax wages are growing very slowly. In the process, the government is transforming the American Dream that Ross spoke about earlier today – the belief that each generation would enjoy a higher, indeed, a significantly higher, living standard – into something it has never been, just a dream.

Our final lesson is the urgent need to get the Congressional Budget Office to start doing generational accounting and to get Congress to start using generational accounting to achieve generational balance. Generational accounting has been around for a number of years, but relatively few members of Congress seem to be aware of it. The Congressional Budget Office is Congress' number one number cruncher. If the Congressional Budget Office starts using generational accounting to evaluate every major fiscal proposal, Congress will have to pay attention.

In my view, much of our fiscal mess reflects the abysmal way we've been keeping our books. Had we been using generational accounting starting in the 1950s to evaluate fiscal policy, we would truly be in much better shape. The reason is that the successive expansions of pay-as-you-go entitlement programs during the Eisenhower, Kennedy, Johnson, Nixon, Carter, Reagan, Bush, and now Clinton presidencies would have been exposed for what, in large part, they were and still are – a way for current generations, both rich and poor alike, to rip off future generations.

But here we are in 1995. Generational accounting is now being done by foreign governments around the world, from New Zealand to Norway. It's being used by the International Monetary Fund, the World

Bank, and the Organization for Economic Cooperation and Development. We have marvelous computers, reasonable data, and a very clear body of economic growth theory, indicating that generational accounting is the way and, indeed, the only correct way, to do long-term fiscal planning. We've also got a demographic/fiscal Armageddon around the corner. But, despite all these facts, the Congressional Budget Office is doing no systematic, long-term fiscal planning, which means that Congress is doing no long-term fiscal planning.

Instead, the Congressional Budget Office remains fixated on doing short-term deficit accounting. But this is worse than doing nothing because in focusing on the deficit, the Congressional Budget Office is giving the mistaken impression that the deficit is the right number to be looking at in evaluating our fiscal policies, including our generational policy. Nothing could be further from the truth. The deficit, to be quite blunt, is not a well-defined economic concept, because unlike generational accounting, it doesn't provide the answers to well-posed, well-defined economic questions. Because it's not well defined, the definition of the deficit is entirely up for grabs. This is why every politician has a different definition of the deficit. This politician wants to include Social Security; this one wants to adjust inflation; this one wants to factor in economic growth; that one wants to include unfunded Social Security liabilities; this one wants to add the S&L bailout; and on and on it goes. Since the Congressional Budget Office appears, for good reason, to have no idea what the deficit is supposed to measure, it routinely puts out a range of different, but equally worthless, measures of the deficit in order to keep all their customers happy. It's time for the Congressional Budget Office to stop manufacturing economically meaningless measures of our fiscal vocabulary, and to start providing answers to fundamental economic policy questions, the most important of which is the rate of net taxation facing our children.

Of course, the Congressional Budget Office is not the only fiscal agency in Washington. Until this year, generational accounting was being included by the Office of Management and Budget as a routine part of the President's Budget, even though its findings were undercutting many of the administration's policy proposals. Apparently, it was getting more public attention than the White House wanted. So this year, two days before the budget was published, the White House overruled Alice Rivlin, the director of the Office of Management and

Budget, and completely deleted the generational accounting section, notwithstanding the fact that the Office of Management and Budget had spent several months carefully preparing the material with my help and that of my co-developers of generational accounting, Professor Alan Auerbach of the University of California at Berkeley and Dr. Jagadeesh Gokhale of the Federal Reserve Bank of Cleveland.

The fact that our administration wasn't willing to devote five pages out of a 2,000-page budget to examining the fiscal consequences of its policies for our children speaks volumes about their real priorities. It also reminds us that we won't get our politicians to do long-term fiscal planning until we make it clear that their election depends on it.

Let me turn to the last point, which is that we have a test, which you all have to take. The question that I'm posing to you – and I want you to answer yes or no, and if your answer is yes, I want you to raise your hand – is this: will you petition Congress to do generational accounting and produce generational balance?

You all passed! It has been a great pleasure speaking with you.

Thank you.

The Issues

Jobs

The Reverend Jesse Jackson

The Ladder of Opportunity

ROSS PEROT: Next, we have a speaker who needs no introduction, Reverend Jesse Jackson. Reverend Jackson is the Founder and President of the National Rainbow Coalition, the national social justice organization devoted to empowerment, education and mobilization. Born in Greenville, South Carolina, he attended the University of Illinois, North Carolina A&T, and the Chicago Theological Seminary. He was an assistant to Dr. Martin Luther King. He went on to direct Operation Breadbasket and he founded Operation Push. He was a Democratic Presidential candidate in 1984 and 1988. Reverend Jackson is known for his commitment to our youth. He has visited thousands of elementary schools, high schools, and universities encouraging excellence in school work and urging young people to stay away from drugs.

He is also a major force in the American labor movement. He has worked with unions to organize workers, and he has successfully mediated labor disputes. Reverend Jackson is an author, activist, orator, politician and spiritual leader.

He and his wife, Jacqueline, live in Washington, D.C. They have five children.

It is my privilege to introduce Reverend Jesse Jackson.

Thank you, Ross. I want to express thanks to Ross Perot for having the courage and good judgment to convene much of the nation's political family. There has been the need to convene, but there was a gap. Labor could have filled it, Democrats could have filled it, Republicans could have filled it. It was not done, so Ross stepped in and filled this gap.

I want to talk about the challenge of direction, priorities, and values. God has enabled and empowered us as a people. As citizens of a great nation in the cherished tradition of democracy, we must call our leaders in to account. We must participate in the formation of our nation's priorities. The history of America is a history of citizens moving outside of parties and traditions, reaching for our better and our truer self. The great movements were always led by outsiders – the abolition of slavery, women's suffrage, the civil rights movement, the peace movement, the nuclear disarmament movement, the environmental movement, and the labor movement were all driven by men and women of conscience and conviction.

We have always moved outside to expand the nation's views and visions. In our lifetime, great movements have transformed this country, always against the powerful bipartisan consensus that marked our common sense and shared values. The highest form of patriotism is that of risk-taking, life-risking citizens who are willing to be transforming agents for change and for justice, willing to put their bodies on the line as living sacrifices. These are people who will measure *character* by how we treat the least of these, especially at this time when one party with two names, or two with one assumption, become hip-locked and say they are "gridlocked."

The people have to open up the process as an act of patriotism and survival. The parties face expansion or extinction. The new powers on Capitol Hill assume that the rich are too poor and the poor are too rich, and that corporations are undertaxed, and that the military is weak. They assume that hope for the locked-out is an illusion, and cynicism is acceptable.

Now citizens are moving again, and for good reason. The country is headed in the wrong direction, with Washington out of touch and so often getting in the way. You are part of that movement. The Rainbow Coalition is a part of that movement. People across the country are looking for new options. Massive deficits symbolize that irresponsibility.

Under the Reagan years we doubled the military budget in peacetime, cut taxes on the affluent, and stuck the next generation with the bill. Those who could not afford to go to the party, who were never invited as a matter of fact, are now told they must pay for the party. We tripled the national debt in four years. Perot, the Rainbow Coalition, and United We Stand America say we cannot go down that path again. We must go another way.

Rising anxiety and fear of the extremes of wealth and poverty must be in the nation's debate. The top 1 percent of the people own 10 percent of the wealth. The top 20 percent own 80 percent of all the wealth.

Last week's merger of Westinghouse with CBS, and ABC with Mickey Mouse, will have several predictable outcomes. A few people will become billionaires and will instantly be called *geniuses*. A few friends of theirs will become millionaires, and they will be called *smart*. Many will lose their jobs, and they will be called *untrained*, *unlucky*, and *unblessed*. We must go another way.

But that is not all. Look around society. Crime rates are rising, not among blacks, where it is already too high, but among young white men and women. Wages are falling, and families are breaking up. Drugs, sex, and violence are peddled each night on our television and sold every day on our streets. More and more affluent people retreat behind high walls and private police forces, like Latin American oligarchs divorced from democratic space. The crisis is economic downsizing. The crisis that has us anxious today is economic downsizing and economic domination.

Military bases are closing without conversion. Offshore we are investing $45 billion a year defending South Korea from North Korea, 40 years after the war. The NAFTA-GATT trade agreements are undercutting good labor, replacing it with cheap labor, not better labor.

The American worker *can* compete with the Mexican worker or the Chinese worker. The American worker cannot compete with slave labor and should not have to. Let us raise their standards and not lower our own.

They are allowing billionaires to move offshore to legalize tax evasion, while we are making less and feeling less secure. This avoidance leaves all of us with a crisis of anxiety. Instead, the debate shifts to the diversion of affirmative action and race-baiting. They call opening the doors of opportunity "reversing the door of opportunity." They call goals and timetables to end quotas a "quota of reverse pain." They think lower ceilings for women, and deeper holes for blacks and browns, and closed doors will go away with time rather than a plan of inclusion.

Equal opportunity has turned tax consumers into taxpayers. It enables two workers in one family to maintain a household. It has made our economy stronger and more diverse, trained more workers, produced more affluent consumers, and resulted in the best military force in the world.

Now radical conservatives set the agenda in Washington, and claim a moral tone. They say they are undertaking your work, but let us take a closer look. We need a movement to set America on course for the next century, and make her strong from the inside out and from the bottom up.

The President and the conservatives come here looking for your support because of their mythical commitments to balance the budget in seven to nine or ten years. But you and I know that those plans depend on a range of assumptions that are virtually wrong by definition. We are in a hole. If we are in a hole, the first thing we must do is stop digging that hole. Then the next generation must figure out a way to climb out. If you were going down a road at night and it was dark, and the longer you drove the darker it got, it would not take a rocket scientist to figure out what to do. Put on your brakes and back out the same way you went in.

Do we really need an independent voice in politics? A citizens' movement on the move is vital, but "money politics" still dominates Washington. Political reform has been buried by Republicans, as it was by the Democratic majority before them. Now, spectacled corporate lobbyists are invited in to explain the bills they have drafted to the legislators assigned to argue for them. Never has there been so much money flowing in Washington – never so much legal graft going on. The privileged few with power want every kind of reform for the poor, including the reform of schools, but not campaign finance reform. Let Gingrich explain why he will not reveal the sources that invest in him.

Their *mush, hush, slush* funds and sources are untouchable. They get their votes from the common people and their oaths from their investors. In a democracy, votes must have more power than oaths. Let the power rest with the people.

Money politics are reflected in choices that are being made. The Pentagon, the biggest bureaucracy of them all, has two-thirds of all federal paychecks. But the Pentagon is the largest source of waste, fraud and abuse in the federal government. For example, $35 billion in Pentagon funds were paid out without proper records. Basic book-keeping was so bad that it could not pass an outside audit. We have another $35 billion invested in excess military inventory. The Russians are not after us. Their military cannot beat the Chechnyans at a hospital. They are virtually out of the business, but we are still spending about the same amount as the rest of the world put together on the military.

Where is the money coming from to reinvest in America, when we are spending $40 billion a year defending South Korea from North Korea 40 years after the war? Why are we spending $1.5 trillion in the military budget defending Europe and Japan from Russia, while Europe and Japan are now subsidizing Russia? Let Europe and Japan share more of the burden of their own defense. In the first place, they have strong, stable economies now. We are not abandoning them. Second, there is no foreseeable military threat coming from a Russia that is essentially out of business. Third, they can afford it. And fourth, we need the money to reinvest in our own country to put America back to work.

Even Newt Gingrich admits we do not need to spend this much to defend the United States. Yet, as astonishing as it may seem, the Congress will vote next month to give the Pentagon $9 billion more than it asked for. Much of it is pure pork. For example, construction projects that the Pentagon does not want will be built in districts that do the appropriating. And weapons that the Pentagon does not need will help to support military-industrial jobs. That's $9 billion! – and all this is happening while $1 billion is being cut from the poorest school districts, rural and urban; $3,000 per classroom is being cut from the poorest urban schools; $500 million will be cut by ending summer jobs programs for teenagers, leaving 650,000 teens on the streets next summer with little hope of work; and $1 billion will be taken out by ending home heating for the elderly, leaving the World War II retirees literally in the cold. This is immoral. This neither makes good sense nor shows good judgment.

This is not about balancing the budget; it is about how we spend the money we plan to spend. These decisions offend common sense and basic decency. Somewhere I learned that we will be judged by how we treat the least of these. These choices offend basic values and basic hope for our country.

Both parties promise to balance the budget eventually. But you must not stop there. You had better take a good look at the choices they are making with the money that they will spend, and you will find what we all know to be true.

Let us focus on welfare, and in particular, Aid to Families with Dependent Children. Of the 14 million people in that program, 9 million are children. So let us stop Aid to Families with Dependent Children – which helps 14 million people of which 9 million are children – because it costs us $17 billion a year. But what about the other AFDC – Aid for Dependent Corporations – the $230 billion that is spent on them? It is easy to pick on vulnerable women and children, but what about the giant corporations who invest in our politicians? Corporate welfare exceeds the support given to poor mothers many times over, because poor mothers do not make campaign contributions, cannot hire lobbyists and do not even vote much because their spirits are broken.

They are talking about raising taxes on the working poor, even as they offer the richest 1 percent of Americans a $22,000-a-year break. But then, working poor people do not make campaign contributions, cannot hire lobbyists to write legislation, and they do not even vote much because their spirits are broken. They are throwing money at the biggest bureaucracy of them all while cutting money that aids working people – that gives poor children some small badge of hope against the great odds that they face.

Money politics explains why we cannot do what every other industrial country has done, and that is to provide every American with comprehensive health care, even as we get health care costs under control. You cannot get the budget in balance without getting health care costs under control. One more time – You cannot get the budget under balance without getting health care costs under control. And you cannot get health care costs under control simply by whacking away at Medicare and Medicaid – putting the costs on the poor and the elderly. In fact, those costs will be spread by hospitals and doctors to private insurers.

Many of you bought the Republican line last year when they said there was no crisis. Now they are here this year to say that Medicare and Medicaid must be cut, not to pay for their tax breaks, but to meet a crisis too severe to ignore.

Our parents and grandparents, veterans of World War II and the Korean War, were on a basic health care plan, the same kind that the Congress has today. They were provided comprehensive medical care for as long as they needed it. A government of, for and by the governed must accept that moral responsibility.

Understand this – after we waste more years and more hundreds of billions of dollars, the only way to balance the budget, bring health care costs under control, and provide Americans with the best health care possible is through comprehensive universal health care reform. The longer we wait and let the special interests and the ideologues and schemers put that off, the more we are going to pay.

Money politics explains why we sustain a trade policy that serves Wall Street, not Main Street; that exports jobs and not goods; and that allows other countries to employ lobbyists from both parties to control access to their home markets while Uncle Sugar opens up our markets.

Leaders of both parties – Bush, Clinton, Gingrich, Gramm, Dole – pushed this NAFTA treaty through. Brother Perot and I were called the Odd Couple for opposing it. But everything we said turned out to be true. Wages plummeted in Mexico. Mexicans are poorer. Jobs have been lost here. When the crunch came, the $30 billion bailout did not bail out the American workers who lost their jobs, nor did it bail out Mexican workers. It bailed out the speculators and the investors. We must have a fair international trade agreement that lifts up the private working people.

Now they want to go farther down that road next year with GATT and NAFTA – bringing Chile into NAFTA – and tell us it will be a major foreign policy victory. We cannot afford too many more victories like that.

We must insist on a trade policy that serves working people, not Wall Street speculators – one that lifts wages and conditions abroad and does not lower them here. But to do that we must take our government back. We must end the reign of money politics that makes a mockery of our democracy.

Now, my brothers and sisters, as we look about this audience, there is an America that is not represented here. The cities are behind high walls. There is an absence of jobs, of a tax base, of good schools and adequate housing. Hospitals are closing. Families are disintegrating. To that we have a quick answer, "Three strikes and you're out," rather than "Four balls and you're on." If the crime is vicious enough, if the person is sick enough, one strike is enough. For Susan Smith, one strike is enough. For those who bombed the building in Oklahoma, that is enough. For those who bombed the building in New York, one strike is enough. Judges already have that power.

But the vision for the cities of this country really must be "Four balls and you're on." It must not just be about lockup, but lift-up. Prenatal care and Head Start, ball one. An adequately funded public education, ball two. Marketable skill and access to college, ball three. And a job, ball four. Let us put America back to work and lift our children up, not just lock them up.

Those who appeal to our fears instead of our hopes have a vision of America that, by the year 2000, would have more parolees than graduates. Presently 650,000 African-Americans are in jail, slightly over half the nation's prison population. Only 520,000 are in college, and the gap is growing. Is this the way we want America to go?

The highest single contributor in Governor Wilson's race in California was the California Corrections Union. They gave $425,000. The national prison budget in 1980 was $4 billion. But in 1992 that budget was $31 billion, an increase of 329 percent. Do you feel any more secure?

Here is another alarming fact. Among the people taking private ownership in jails are American Express, Smith Barney, Merrill Lynch and Prudential – all "investing in the future of our cities." The number one growth industry in urban America is jails. Half of all public housing built in the last ten years has been jails. America has the largest prison population in the world – 1.4 million people. Is this where we really want to go?

In Florida and California, they have as much money for prisons as colleges. In 1972, 169,000 people worked for the penal system. In 1992 the number was 523,000. Over a ten-year period, California went from 19,000 people in jail to 124,000. That is 12,000 people a year. In 1948, the prison population in America was 155,000. In Texas alone in 1995, it was 155,000.

We have been privatizing this growth industry. In 1993, some 43,000 prison beds were built by private companies, an average of one every 12 minutes. Why does the big money want to invest in jails?

If you are caught with five grams of crack cocaine – that's five Sweet'n Low sugar bags, a five-dollar high – a first-time nonviolent offense, with no previous arrest record, you will be given a mandatory five year sentence in federal prison. That is a $40,000-a-year federal penitentiary scholarship. First-time, non-violent offense, no gun involved, no previous arrest records – five years, five grams. If you are caught with 500 grams of powder cocaine, you can get probation.

Ninety-one percent of all those caught with a five-dollar high are young black males who were not previously on a prison scholarship. They will be our parolee graduates by the year 2000. Fifty-four percent of those who use crack are white. The U.S. Sentencing Commissioner said this is unfair, it's disparate, it's racist, it's beneath the dignity of our country, it costs too much, and it does not solve the problem. By comparison, to get five years for marijuana possession, you have to have $42,000 worth of marijuana. For powder cocaine, for five years, you have to have $3,000 worth. For crack, you have to have $29 worth for five years. There is no study to prove crack is deadlier than powder. What is the difference? You take powder from the big guys on the outside, the young kids put a match to it and the powder becomes crack.

Small towns are now offering prison officials memberships in country clubs and other perks, because they now want to get a jail in their district. If you get a jail in that district where you have lost a farm, lost a job, lost a plant to Mexico or China, then new jobs are created. You can have construction, you can have maintenance, and once you privatize the jail, you can rent out the uniforms. The inmates make five telephone calls a day collect, and somebody makes money from that. The uniforms have to be cleaned, and somebody makes money from that. There is a $30,000-a-day food contract. Somebody makes money from that. It seems that the idea of a "jail-industrial complex" making our schools secondary is not really the great hope and promise of America. There must be a vision to save these children, redeem them, revive them, reclaim them. These are Americans, these are God's chosen. Somebody must speak out. I declare I am going to do it today.

Our American cities have become the catch basin for the poor. Seoul, Korea, is flourishing. Tokyo is flourishing. But the American cities have become the catch basin for the poor, the abandoned, and the broken. Contrary to media stereotypes, most poor people are not on welfare. They work every day. Contrary to stereotypes, most poor people are not black. They are white, female, and young. There are 40 million Americans in poverty, and 29 million of them are white. They are mostly children, but whether they are white, black or brown, hunger hurts them all alike. These are our children. These are American citizens, often trapped in poverty, not by plan, but by a predicament that is the human predicament. They work the hardest and they work the longest on the nastiest of jobs. They cut up our chicken. They develop carpal tunnel syndrome. They sweep our streets. No, they are not that lazy. You do not see them every day – because they catch the early bus.

They really are not lazy; they raise other people's children. They are not lazy; they cut the grass in the parks. They really are not lazy; they work in the hospitals, they mop the floors, and they change the beds when we get sick. They wash our faces when we are full of fever, and they empty our bedpans, our slop jars, because no job is beneath them. And yet when they get sick, they cannot afford to lie in the bed they make up every day. We are a better nation than that!

Why are they in this trap? Their wages have been falling every year for over 20 years. Their conditions grow worse every day. Their neighborhoods are terrorized by crime. Their children go to schools that are a little bit dangerous to their health. Their young cannot find work. Their brightest students cannot afford to go to college. Those who escape face extra obstacles to find loans to launch a business or to buy a home.

And now, my friends, Washington has abandoned them. You must not. This Congress is not making "hard" choices to cut the deficit. It is not cutting weak programs, but programs for the weakest workers, displaced from their jobs through no fault of their own. And those workers lose those jobs when ABC meets Mickey Mouse. Those workers have simply been caught in the crossfire. Children born to poverty through the hand of fate are born with three strikes against them – a mother who is sick, a father who is absent and without a job. We need a new proposition for them. We must accept new responsibilities.

The Rainbow Coalition has a program that I want all of you to join as a family. We have mobilized a hundred ministers in 50 cities to meet with juvenile court judges in that city, and to reclaim 20 youth each as alternatives to unnecessary jailing. These are our children. Some children just need parenting, and tutoring, and they need caring adults. If judges and ministers will reclaim 2,000 youth each in 50 cities, that is 100,000 youth we can reclaim. Better that we have 100,000 youth in churches with 25,000 coaches nurturing them than 100,000 police chasing them. After all, these are our children. We can reclaim them. It costs too much to disclaim them.

But let us go a step beyond that. In those same 50 cities, we want to get 20,000 parents to do five things – take your child to school, meet your child's teachers, exchange home numbers, turn off the TV three hours a night, and pick up a report card every nine weeks. Teachers teach children differently when they know the parents, and children behave differently when parents and teachers know each other. I believe that if a million parents joint venture with teachers, and ministers joint venture with judges, we can break the cycle of crime and self-destructive behavior and save our children. We can use that money to build schools and not jails. We can make America safer and more secure. That is our challenge. It is also our possibility.

It is our challenge and our possibility. On this, I appeal to you. We talk so much about values these days in the political dialogue. One big debate is whether we could stop people from breaking out into character collapses – crime, dishonor, abuse – if we would just have a minute of prayer in school. That would solve it. Well, Moses was not that ambitious. When he looked at a recently freed people whose lives had become loose in their options and styles, a people who no longer honored their God or their parents, a people who had lost a sense of trust and confidence, he knew a minute of prayer with a pistol in your pocket was not enough.

Here was Moses' plan – he went to the mountain and he did the praying. The leader prayed, and when he came back to the valley, God gave him a comprehensive plan. He gave them a land for economic opportunity, the right to political self-determination, adequate food, and ten ethical commandments by which to live. This same idea will work here. We need to tell those who think a minute of prayer is the answer to the problem, "Let us have a *life* of prayer and service and care and feeding. And let us have an urban policy plan that consists of economic development, a little self-determination, and an abiding loyalty to ten ethical commandments."

Watch out when someone tells you a political solution to our education problems is to offer a few choice schools for a few choice children. That was Nebuchadnezzar's plan in the first book of Daniel. The Bible says that when he took over Jerusalem, he sent his chief eunuch out to the people who were in despair, who did not have jobs, who had been taken over. He was instructed to find certain kinds of youth, to choose children in whom there was no character blemish, the kids who had no jail records and were cunning in science, knowledge and wisdom. So the eunuch picked the most blessed and talented ones, and took them away to train them.

In so doing he changed their names, their language, their diets, and eventually got them good jobs and removed them from their base of people. But when they refused to turn their back on their people and their spirituality, Nebuchadnezzar attempted to destroy them by water and by fire. But God spared them for their loyalty.

Jesus comes at that from another angle. He did not start with the most talented, the most blessed and the most gifted, but rather, the least of these – Simon the leper who was otherwise quarantined, the woman at the well who faced execution. He came at the bottom to those who were homeless and hungry. He said, "I shall measure character by how you treat the least of these." And while we often focus on saying, "I would not mind having Michael Jordan as my next-door neighbor or maybe Colin Powell," we must ask ourselves, "But what about the *unchosen* people, everyday people like you and me? What about the ones who drive buses and trucks, those who are janitors and maids, those who are teachers, those who are retirees, those who are veterans of foreign wars, those who could never make the major leagues, those who could never sing or dance or run? What about the unchosen? What about those who are not perfect, or are kind of fat, or short, or do not have perfect rhythm or cannot sing? What about the rest of them?"

That is what makes America different, that we care about everyday people. It is a measure of the American character how we treat the least of these. That is why I do not want to be color-blind; I want to be color-caring. I want to be caring. I want to see people for who they are and what they are, and embrace them in a high enough fullness of their humanity. That is why I say to you today that the issues we face are about priorities, direction and character.

Several years ago there was a big struggle of sorts in Los Angeles known as the Rodney King crisis. Four white police who were apparently driven by racism tried to beat a man to death. They probably would have lied and got away except that it was on camera. But it would be wrong to assume that all whites are racist on that basis. In truth, had it not been for George Halliday, a white photographer who filmed the incident and took it public, the outcome might have been quite different. But strangely enough, no university has given George Halliday an honorary degree or special award because it seems there is no value on character. The police are writing books about what they did and did not do, and Rodney King got money, but the man of character who learns something about fairness has been ignored.

Beyond color, beyond culture, there is something called *character*. He knew Rodney King was black. He knew the police were white. He also knew it was wrong. Character.

And then four young blacks beat Reginald Denny, a white truck driver. They beat him nearly to death. One broke a block over his head. They tried to kill him, it seems. But it would be wrong to assume all young blacks are racist on that basis. In truth, four other young blacks saw the incident as they were home watching television. They left their individual homes, and they stepped forward and saved Denny from his attackers. They took him to the hospital where one of those black Affirmative Action doctors performed surgery and saved his life.

Somewhere beyond color, beyond culture, is something called character. We are all American citizens. We are all God's children and deserve to be included. We must have a place as Americans and reorder America's priorities. God bless you. Let us live under one big tent, and keep hope alive!

Congresswoman Marcy Kaptur

Creating Jobs in the U.S.A.

ROSS PEROT: Our next speaker is Congresswoman Marcy Kaptur, a lifelong resident of Toledo, Ohio.

Her parents ran a small family-owned grocery store. After her father had a heart attack, they had to sell the store, and her dad worked in a local automobile factory. Her mother also worked in a factory in the Toledo area.

Congresswoman Kaptur started working at thirteen to earn money for college. Her mother cleaned doctors' offices and worked in a beauty salon to help pay her college tuition.

Congresswoman Kaptur summed it up when she said:

> *My Polish grandparents came to America in steward class in the bottom of a ship in 1912, through Ellis Island, seeking a better way of life. Someone told them the streets in America were paved with gold. Little did they know that they would be the ones who would lay the roads and work in the big factories to bake the bricks.*

She graduated from St. Ursula Academy in Toledo. She earned her bachelor's degree in history from the University of Wisconsin, and her master's degree in urban planning from the University of Michigan.

Congresswoman Kaptur worked as an urban planner for fifteen years, and was a doctoral candidate at Massachusetts Institute of

Technology. She served as Urban Advisor to President Jimmy Carter from 1977 to 1979.

Congresswoman Kaptur is now in her seventh term in Congress. Since 1986 she has received more than 70 percent of the votes in her district in each election. She serves as a member of the House Appropriations Committee. The Appropriations Committee is responsible for spending cuts and setting budget priorities for the federal government.

Congresswoman Kaptur, as a matter of principle, refuses to accept congressional pay raises.

She works night and day to create jobs in the USA, and she is an outspoken proponent of keeping our good-paying manufacturing jobs in the United States. She is an outspoken proponent of the need to keep a strong manufacturing base here in the USA. It is an honor and a privilege to introduce Congresswoman Marcy Kaptur.

Good morning, my friends. Thank you for that simply beautiful welcome. And to the independent-minded, irrepressible, indefatigable Ross Perot, thank you.

Today this daughter of a blue-collar family from Toledo, Ohio, the Jeep capital and the Cherrios capital of the world, is indeed privileged to address a national gathering dedicated to America's future in the 21st century. Let me first say to Ross Perot: thank you. In 1992 you helped usher in an earthquake in our political system that is still being felt. The national media pilloried you. But you had the audacity to refuse to go away. Glowingly, you danced with your wife! You kept your sense of humor and sense of purpose.

And Ross, you made the special interests in Washington and Wall Street uneasy with all of your pointed questions – about NAFTA, about balancing the budget, about who benefits from insider trade deals, about which hired guns were meddling in our politics. Ross, we appreciate your perseverance and your patriotism.

A speaker yesterday said he hoped the next century for America would be known as the century of "the individual." Let me say my hope for the 21st century is that we as Americans regain our sense of nationhood and advance the cause of freedom globally. That speaker also said it was timely to invite God back into America. Well, let me respectfully quote my pastor from church last Sunday, "You may be the only face of God your neighbor ever sees." Let us today recommit to a higher purpose than individual gain and make our cause not *I the person*, but *We the people of the United States*.

I am especially pleased to be here with this warm and enthusiastic assembly of citizens who in 1992 began a movement to transform our political system. Last night Ross Perot talked about a second Contract With America – beginning with real campaign finance reform – to be delivered to the American people by Christmas of this year. I will be the first member of Congress to sign on to that contract.

Those here today, and millions of others who are watching and listening to these proceedings on television and radio, employed the sacred right to vote as a powerful weapon for change last November. Their vote for change was not a vote for an ideology, not even for a party. They want a nation that preserves their freedom, defends their interests, and protects their future. Our people have had their fill of political doublespeak and the corrosive impact of special-interest money on the governance of our nation. Wouldn't it be historic to usher in the 21st century by reforming campaigns in America through tight spending limits? Wouldn't it be historic to require, as a condition of any license to broadcast in America, free and equal time from the media for all candidates?

Yesterday we also heard a lot about what is wrong with the government. I remember the old cartoon with Pogo saying, "We have met the enemy, and he is us." As a member of Congress who voted for three balanced budget amendments, let me say that there is no doubt that the government is important and needs reform. But the government constitutes 20 percent – or one-fifth – of our gross domestic product. What happens in the other 80 percent, the private sector, is where we all must focus our attention. That is what I want to talk about today. When the government and the private sector work together in the national interest, all things are possible. We want our nation made whole again before the 21st century begins.

What happened to Linda LaChance of Biddeford, Maine, describes part of our quandary. In 1979, Linda earned $10 an hour making shoes in NIKE's last shoe plant in America. In 1985, six years later, NIKE moved her job and thousands of others overseas. Since then, Linda has been unemployed three times. Today she is making $5.50 an hour. As

Linda says, "NIKE's motto is, 'Just do it.' Well, they did it to me."

NIKE now manufactures 100 percent of its shoes overseas using 30,000 contract laborers in China and Asia, paying them 30 cents an hour. It costs NIKE eight dollars to make a pair of shoes, which they then ship back to the United States and charge us $69.99 to $150.00 a pair. Then, NIKE paid Michael Jordan $20 million for advertising campaigns to make us "feel good" about NIKE, while NIKE pocketed $3.8 billion in revenues in 1994 and paid Phillip Knight, its chief executive officer who smiled all the way to the bank, three-quarters of a million dollars in salary plus $718,000 in bonuses and stock options. Is that what we want for America?

As far as I am concerned, if any company with a charter to conduct business in the United States moves our jobs to another country to get low-wage labor, and then U-turns their wares back here for sale, I say we charge them a "Pledge of Allegiance" market entry fee to get inside the marketplace of the United States. Further, any foreign firm that wishes to advantage itself in our marketplace should have to demonstrate that the workers who produced those goods earned living wages under decent conditions. Otherwise, all we are doing is cashing out our jobs, our standard of living, our liberty, to the lowest wage environments where workers are locked in the dark ages of serfdom.

When I think about Linda, I am reminded of a conversation I had with the chief executive officer of Boeing Corporation, the airplane giant that for decades has advantaged itself as a major U.S. defense contractor. Last year while Congress was debating why China should be granted favored trade status to send its goods into our market, I happened to sit across the table from this gentleman in Washington. Recall, Boeing is laying off another 7,000 workers this year in our country – skilled workers America cannot afford to lose. Our national defense and industrial might rest on their shoulders.

He said to me, "Congresswoman Kaptur, why are you questioning Most Favored Nation trade privileges for China?" I replied, "I am against MFN for China because their people do not have basic political rights. And I do not think you can have true free enterprise if you do not have political freedom first."

He said to me, "You really don't get it. I had dinner with the Premier of China a few weeks ago. I want to tell you something, Congresswoman. He plays the violin. Any man with music in his heart cannot be all bad." I replied, "Adolph Hitler loved Wagner. What did you think of him?"

If Boeing makes a deal to outsource airframe production to China, who benefits? Does the productive wealth of America increase? Do jobs here at home increase? Does our defense grow stronger? Or do a handful of executives and unaccountable shareholders merely pocket millions for themselves?

There is a difference between "money for a few" and the "wealth of a nation." Further, does the edge of freedom advance from that transaction – or do Chinese men and women workers, denied basic freedoms, work for "hunger wages" in a society that does not value liberty nor their inalienable rights as human beings?

For 20 years America's middle-class families have not had an increase in their real wages. You know that. Our checks do not buy as much. Today a high school graduate with five years' work experience makes 27 percent less in real wages than his counterpart did in 1979. In the 1950s, one working person in this country could provide for a family of four. In the 1990s, it takes two family members working full-time, sometimes at two and three jobs, just to keep the family afloat. Isn't there something wrong when worker productivity in America has steadily risen, but workers' wages and benefits continue to decline?

Our international trade agreements have been a net destroyer of millions of jobs in our country for over two decades. Wouldn't you think someone in Washington would notice? Since 1980, the United States has accumulated a net loss of wealth of over $1.5 trillion in traded goods. One result is that we have lost more than two million well-paying manufacturing jobs in this country: 300,000 jobs have been lost in textiles, 287,000 jobs in steel, 128,000 jobs in construction equipment, and 60,000 jobs in high-tech computers and office equipment. The list goes on.

This past year alone, in spite of the gentle recovery, permanent lay-offs in just the textile, apparel, and chemical industries together amounted to over 103,000 more lost jobs. America has never had a recovery where we have lost so many manufacturing jobs!

Why doesn't our media cover these casualties? Could it be even our media has become beholden to the corporate advertisers that fill their coffers? It is, after all, corporate advertising that pays for the rubbish we are subjected to over the public airwaves.

Our mass media is becoming increasingly owned by a few corporate giants. For example, General Electric, which has terminated thousands of workers in our country, owns NBC; billionaire Lawrence Tisch owned CBS until he agreed to sell it to Westinghouse; and Capital Cities, which owned ABC, is being swallowed by Disney.

Behind these financial empires lies an even more tangled web of interownership. Wells Fargo International Trust, for instance, is the biggest shareholder in General Electric. It is also the fifth largest shareholder in Capital Cities, the seventh largest shareholder in CBS, and the fourth largest shareholder in Time Warner. And, just to round out the circle, Wells Fargo is also the third largest shareholder in Disney.

Wells Fargo is not unique. Other major institutional investors such as Bankers Trust, Capital Research & Management, and Fidelity Management & Research all own substantial holdings in each of these giants. Sound familiar? These are the same barbarians at the gate we met back in the 1980s as merger mania hollowed out the productive wealth of this country. Is it not a fact that the one who pays the piper generally calls the tune?

Now, a bill just swept through Congress that actually sanctions even bigger media monopoly control in our country. In your town, a single multinational company will soon be allowed to own your newspaper, two television stations, all the radio stations, and your cable company. This brings me to Westinghouse, a company that terminated about 15,000 workers over the last year, laid off over 25,000 workers in Pittsburgh over the past decade and is now buying CBS.

Do you think that under Westinghouse's ownership CBS news shows will ever tell the truth about our economy, about unemployed Westinghouse workers, or about the kind of price-fixing problems the company has experienced? Or, will America be subjected to brainwashing? Will NBC's broadcasts be free of General Electric's influence? Will ABC's Sunday morning news shows be insulated from its sponsors' dictates? And will Rupert Murdoch's Fox Channel reveal his political sidewinding in our nation's Capital, as his network subjects our children to the lowest common denominator trash like *Melrose Place* and *Models, Inc.*?

I say let the President veto the telecommunications bill. Then start from scratch. Take the money out of politics by getting free time donated by the media for candidates across our land before any bill granting broadcasters the privilege to use our airwaves moves through the Congress again.

Now, think about this. Not a single U.S.-owned television manufacturer exists within our shores. In 1965, every color television set produced in our country was made by an American-owned domestic plant. In that year, the people of our country purchased 2.6 million television sets manufactured by companies like Sylvania, Motorola, Admiral, Philco, Sunbeam, RCA, Quasar, Magnavox, Wizard.

By 1991, sales of televisions to U.S. consumers skyrocketed to 21 million sets. But, by 1995, there were no U.S. producers left, as Zenith bit the dust. Our country has sustained a loss of hundreds of thousands of jobs, income, and productive wealth in just this one sector.

Some say these trade policies provide bargains for consumers. But please tell me where prices have gone down – in shoes, in cereals, in cars, in homes, in anything! While the purchasing power of American households has fallen, prices keep going up at a steady pace.

Look on the shelves – shoes from China, canned fruit from Thailand, VCRs from Japan, fuel from the Mideast, and televisions from Mexico. Every year the deluge of imports gets larger. When a retail clerk at Wal-Mart, who works part-time for minimum wage with no benefits, rings up a $100 pair of tennis shoes made in China, does she analyze who benefits from that transaction? Not the U.S. workers who lost their jobs. Not the communities and small businesses that once thrived from strong employers and well-paid workers. Not our nation's productive wealth. And certainly not she.

Who benefited? The importer and globe-trotting manufacturer who kept prices high, drove wages and benefits down, and siphoned off exorbitant profits by paying Chinese workers a pitiful 30 cents an hour. We should remember what Henry Ford knew – consumers must have decent jobs before they can buy a company's goods, or, ultimately, the nation gets "cashed out."

Fortune 500 companies have not increased their manufacturing workforce in the U.S. for a decade. Virtually all their investment in production has been overseas. We are seeing unilateral disinvestment of huge segments of our economy. America's workers are being asked to compete against three forces: (1) capital that can move anywhere; (2) foreign cartels in nations like Japan that block entry of U.S. products into their market; (3) millions of low-wage workers of the world who live under undemocratic regimes. Is it any wonder that the downward pull on U.S. wages and benefits never abates? Is it any wonder that the workers of America are restless? They know that their future economic security rests on companies with no allegiance to America's freedoms, just their own.

Our national political leaders have also become a party to an insidious shift in our perception of how to achieve national prosperity. They have shifted our national emphasis from selling to customers at home to selling to customers abroad, while ceding our home markets to imports. And they have painted a false picture of the difficulty in selling to customers abroad – whether that be in cartel-controlled markets like Japan, or in developing nations like Mexico. Which, of course, brings us to NAFTA. Let's measure the promises made to pass NAFTA against the promises already broken.

NAFTA to date has been an emergency room case. NAFTA has ushered in an era of *Alice in Wonderland* trade policy where failure is called success, truth is turned upside down, and billions are spent to prove that those who were wrong were actually right.

Since NAFTA went into effect, more than one company a day has left our country for Mexico. Nearly 390 more companies are projected to build on the Mexican side of the border in the next five years. If it is not a giant sucking sound, it sure is a loud swoosh.

A Congressional Joint Economic Committee report found that in the first nine months of NAFTA, Mexican imports to our country cost the United States 137,000 more jobs. Major economic analysts now predict NAFTA-related job losses in the U.S. at 350,000 over two years, growing to over half a million by the year 2000. Who speaks for these Americans who are rendered voiceless in our political system?

NAFTA also promised to help Mexico's workers. They said their wages would increase and provide a market for our goods. In fact, their workers' pitiful wages have been cut in half. Mexico needs its own misery index. My friends, there is a new Mason-Dixon plantation line inscribed on our continent, and it is called the U.S./Mexico border.

Before NAFTA our country held trade surpluses with Mexico. NAFTA proponents predicted a rising U.S. trade surplus with Mexico, reaching $12 billion by the end of the decade. But, this year we will run the highest trade deficit with Mexico in the history of our commercial relations, estimated at $20 billion. And our deficit with Canada has more than doubled for a 1995 trade deficit of $17 billion. Remember, for every billion dollars of deficit we sustain with each of those countries, 20,000 more jobs in this country are at risk.

We were promised that NAFTA would reduce illegal immigration and drug trafficking across our Mexican border. In reality, the Border Patrol reports a 30 percent increase in detained illegals, and the *New York Times* reports that Mexico is replacing Colombia as the drug capital of the Western Hemisphere.

Increased heroin shipments are spreading death across our land. FBI official James Moody reports that many companies privatized by former Mexican President Salinas were bought by drug lords. Frankly, the only nations with which the United States should sign free trade agreements are those which block the flow of illegal narcotics to our country.

Then there is the Mexican peso bailout. We were told by our Treasury Department that NAFTA would strengthen the peso when they knew all along that Mexico was leaking reserves like a sieve.

Now, 20 billion of our tax dollars are out the window without a vote of Congress. Shouldn't those who bet their hot money in Mexico and earned 66 percent returns be expected to eat their own losses? The speculators got the profits; we taxpayers got the losses. That hardly seems fair.

Of course, there were some winners from NAFTA. Remember former Canadian Prime Minister Brian Mulrooney, one of the three signatories of NAFTA? Well, before the ink was even dry on the agreement, he was appointed to the board of one of NAFTA's biggest beneficiaries, Archer-Daniels-Midland & Company. He is being compensated at the rate of $100,000 a year just for that board seat. You might recall, that is the multinational company that is being investigated by the U.S. Justice Department for international price-fixing in agriculture.

And then, of course, we have former Mexican President Carlos Salinas, another signatory of NAFTA. He was appointed to a lucrative board seat of Dow-Jones, which owns the *Wall Street Journal*. Prior to NAFTA's passage, do you think paid corporate advertisers had anything to do with the fact that the stories in the *Journal* were slanted ten to one against NAFTA's critics?

Now, there is a proposal on a fast track in Washington to expand NAFTA to include other Latin American countries, starting with Chile. I ask: Why not fix NAFTA instead of expand it? Let's renegotiate trade agreements in the interest of our nation that are fair to all sides concerned. I will shortly be introducing a bill to that effect.

NAFTA is not the only instance where political manipulation has been used to absolve Congress from a real debate about America's economic future. Last November, a lame-duck Congress – people who would not be coming back – voted to pass GATT. A 22,000 page bill that took seven years to negotiate. It weighed ten pounds. It cost our Treasury $40 billion in lost tariff revenue. And it fails to address the nontariff barriers to free trade that are at the heart of the gigantic trade imbalances in the world. Yet, it got only a few hours of debate time with no amendments allowed. Under GATT, the United States cedes power to a supranational organization located in Geneva, Switzerland, dominated by nations which vote against us 80 percent of the time in the United Nations, and we have no veto power. Is anyone in Washington paying attention?

From the misguided policy of Most Favored Nation trade status for dictatorships, to the promotion of sweatshop zones in the Caribbean, to GATT, to NAFTA, and to the failed U.S.-Japan auto talks, our nation's trade policies over the last two decades have diminished the livelihoods of millions of our citizens. Just with Japan, our trade failures have cost America over one million jobs.

Further, America's long-term interests with the majority of the world's people in the developing nations have been jeopardized by our failure to translate internationally our highest ideals of liberty, justice, and the rule of law. Hence, our policies pretend ignorance of slave labor in Asia. We turn a cold shoulder to teenage girls in the Caribbean and Latin America who labor for us 80 hours a week for 56 cents an hour.

Meanwhile, our highest elected officials cozy up to regimes that have a standing policy of entrenching powerful economic oligarchies at the expense of their own people. During the Cold War, America stood for the concept of freedom over repression. Today, America is aligning itself with the most unsavory of regimes for a goal no loftier than a few business deals. Shouldn't America's foreign policy champion political liberty first?

In closing, let me ask, "Where do we wish America to be ten years from now – fifty years from now?" The answer is clear.

We want a free and economically secure nation here at home, with a stronger middle class whose standard of living rises with rising productivity. We want to protect and spread the spirit of liberty among our people, as well as the forgotten millions across this globe. We want the best educated people, the most sustainable agriculture, the most sophisticated defense, and the finest health care. We want the hearts of our cities and towns to again bloom with high-wage jobs through investment in both human and physical capital. Let's close tax loopholes – including capital gains tax loopholes – that encourage footloose companies to ship our jobs overseas. Let's reform our tax system to encourage saving and reward work rather than speculative investments. And then, let's fully fund our private and public retirement systems, reinvesting their assets to yield the highest return for beneficiaries.

Stand united with us for an America that exports more than she imports. Let's create real wealth here at home, not just money for a few, and use the power of our marketplace to pry open the closed markets of the world.

Concurrently, America should only sign free trade agreements with free people. Let's use our economic power to jump-start democracy and rising living standards elsewhere.

And, how about balancing America's budgets with no foreign borrowing? Let's reinvigorate the quality of self-reliance and reduce our debt level so it does not outstrip our ability to pay it back. Why can't our U.S. Treasury embark upon a "Save the USA" campaign in which our U.S. Treasury bonds are offered for sale at post offices, denominated at prices affordable to everyone, so America is again owned by Americans?

And while we are at it, let's wean America from our dangerous dependence on foreign sources of energy and move to an energy self-sufficient nation with new fuels and sources of power to sustain life in the 21st century.

Our generation must advance the edge of freedom and representative democracy to the world's people given expression by our Statue of Liberty. For our earth, which will grow by 85 million people a year, we aspire to cleaner water, purer air, sustainable forests, the restoration of our oceans, and an end to nuclear proliferation.

So let's infuse the spirit of America with the renewed optimism Carl Sandberg captured when he eloquently penned, "I see America, not in the setting sun of a black night . . . I see America in the crimson light of a rising sun, fresh from the burning, creative hand of God. I see great days ahead."

The Issues

Social Issues

Pete Peterson

The Silent Crisis in Social Security:
Fixing the System for the 21st Century

ROSS PEROT: Our next speaker is Pete Peterson. Mr. Peterson is Chairman of The Blackstone Group, a private investment banking firm founded in 1985. He is currently on the Board of Directors of Rockefeller Center Properties, Transtar Corporation, and Sony Corporation.

He is the founding President of The Concord Coalition, a bipartisan citizens group he organized in 1992, which is dedicated to building a constituency for fiscal responsibility. He is also the Chairman of the Council on Foreign Relations and the Institute for International Economics.

Mr. Peterson received a bachelor of science degree with highest honors from Northwestern University in 1947. He received his masters of business administration degree with honors in 1951 from the University of Chicago.

Mr. Peterson's business career began in 1948 with Market Facts, where he became executive vice president in 1952.

That same year, he joined the McCann-Erickson advertising agency and became vice president at age 27. He later served as general manager and director. In 1958, Mr. Peterson joined Bell & Howell as execu-

tive vice president and director. In 1963, he became the CEO and held that position until 1971.

Mr. Peterson joined President Nixon's White House staff in 1971 as the Assistant to the President for International Economic Affairs. He was named Secretary of Commerce by President Nixon in 1972 and also assumed the Chairmanship of the National Commission on Productivity.

Mr. Peterson was the Chairman & CEO of Lehman Brothers from 1973 to 1977, and after the merger with Kuhn, Loeb, he became the Chairman & CEO of Lehman Brothers, Kuhn, Loeb from 1977 to 1984.

Last year, President Clinton named Mr. Peterson as a member of the Bipartisan Commission on Entitlement and Tax Reform, co-chaired by Senators Kerrey and Danforth.

Mr. Peterson has received numerous awards throughout the United States and has authored several books, including Facing Up: How to Rescue the Economy from Crushing Debt and Restore the American Dream *and* On Borrowed Time: How the Growth in Entitlement Spending Threatens America's Future.

Mr. Peterson is married to Joan Ganz Cooney, Founder and Chairwoman of the executive committee of Children's Television Workshop. He is the father of five children.

Mr. Peterson is living proof of the American Dream. His parents came from Greece with little education. They worked hard and saved enough money to open a Greek restaurant in Kearney, Nebraska. For over 25 years the restaurant stayed open 24 hours a day, 365 days a year.

From this humble beginning, their son became the first Greek cabinet member in the United States Government.

Mr. Peterson, thank you for agreeing to speak with us today about the problems facing our Social Security system.

[Note: Mr. Peterson was preceded at the podium by the Reverend Jesse Jackson.]

Ross, I deeply appreciate your putting me after Reverend Jackson. The last time I followed Jesse Jackson on a speaking platform, it was at the U.S. Conference of Mayors. He was so eloquent that when he finished most of the mayors jumped up and followed him out of the room. Ross, it made "a giant sucking sound."

I can't help but be afraid that everyone here is going to follow Jesse out of the room, except the candidates for the Republican nomination for President. But come to think of it, that would still leave a pretty substantial crowd.

Before I go any further, I want to salute Ross Perot and United We Stand America. Just a few years ago the wisest names in Washington were saying that megadeficits were a political fact of life. Now, in no small part due to your efforts to raise this nation's fiscal IQ, we have galvanized public sentiment behind a need for a leakproof constitutional amendment that will make balancing the budget not a distant goal, not just rhetorical advice for politicians, but the fundamental law of the United States of America.

I also want to thank Ross Perot for inviting me here to speak about Social Security. I say that so you will know who to blame when I'm done.

Sometime ago, Ted Sorenson, John Kennedy's aide, told me of a dream he had. In the dream, he and I were flying together to the Middle East. Shortly before landing, a terrorist leaped up, brandished a gun, and announced that he would shoot both of us former White House aides – on a bipartisan basis. But first, the terrorist said, he would give each of us one last wish.

The terrorist looked at me and I said, "I do have one last wish. I'd like to make one final speech about the relationship between entitlement and Social Security and the deficit."

The terrorist then turned to Ted and said, "Mr. Sorenson, what is your last wish?" And Sorenson says, "I've heard Peterson give a speech and my last wish is that you shoot me first."

What I, at least, find so gripping – and terrorizing – about entitlements is, of course, not the numbers themselves. It's what they mean for America. Where the Social Security numbers are taking us – and what we can do about it – is my subject today.

Now, Ross, if you don't mind, I brought along a chart or two, something you just might want to try yourself sometime. Actually, Ross is delighted I'm using them. I understand that every time a speaker uses a chart, Ross gets a royalty.

Before we dim the lights, let me tell you what I'm going to tell you.

I'm going to tell you that most of what we think we know about Social Security is wrong. I'm going to tell you that Social Security is simply too big and growing too fast to either be left under the budget table or off the budget table. That does not mean I am singling out Social Security for the budget axe.

To the contrary, I believe everything must be on the table. Welfare and defense to be sure, but everything else as well – from federal pensions to farm payments, from Medicare to veterans benefits. What I am insisting is that trying to balance the budget without touching Social Security is like trying to clean out your garage without moving the Winnebago. You might be able to make a start – but you'll never be able to finish the job.

Finally, I'm going to tell you where we will end up if we do nothing and what reforms we can make to avert a crisis. Along the way, you will see that reforming Social Security is not just another fiscal challenge. The heart of our challenge is how to adapt our economy, our culture and, indeed, our values to the demands of a rapidly aging society. It's one of the paramount challenges confronting America in the 21st century, and it will involve – in a very fundamental way – the soul of our society.

This will be a short presentation, and then for anyone interested, I'm making the charts available that I'm going to be racing through today.

And I just want to add that I'm not here to suggest that the right choice on Social Security is painless. But the fact is – contrary to what you might have heard – America can solve its Social Security problem fairly and humanely, provided that we act soon.

Now, to the myths – starting with the biggest one of all. Turn on a talk show or ask a friend and what do we hear?

Myth One: WHAT'S EXPLOITING THE FEDERAL BUDGET IS "THEM."

- The underclass – and all of their welfare cash.
- The third world – and all of their foreign aid.
- The military – and all their gold-plated bombers.

The first disturbing fact I'm going to offer is the cost of "them," meaning these three items, is falling – from half of the budget 30 years ago to only one-fifth of the budget today.

The second fact is the cost of "US" – meaning the major middle-class entitlement, Social Security, Medicare, federal pensions – is rising fast. "US" took up only 17 percent of the budget 30 years ago but has grown to 38 percent today, and will grow even faster once the massive baby boom generation starts retiring. You all know this, but too many citizens do not.

Meanwhile, the deficits we have been running to pay for "US" are gnawing at posterity. Let me just cite one number. Back in 1965, interest on the national debt only amounted to one-sixth of all our defense spending. By the end of the 1990s, we will spend more on the interest on the national debt than on national defense.

The point here is that we are not going to solve this problem by searching for scapegoats. Who's to blame? Not just the pandering politicians, but so many of us also are to blame – including all of us in the broad middle and upper classes who damn the government for gobbling up our taxes and then stand by as government borrows trillions to give us more benefits. To mask our failure, we engage in denial. We endlessly rehearse the mythical middle-class mantra: "I'm not part of the problem, and I should not be part of the solution." And to support our denial, we invent myths. And none is so powerful as those surrounding the biggest of all government benefit programs, Social Security.

So let's proceed to Myth Two: HOW CAN THERE BE A PROBLEM? THE SOCIAL SECURITY TRUST FUND, WE ARE TOLD, IS REALLY A BIG SURPLUS AND WILL BE SOLVENT FAR INTO THE NEXT CENTURY.

One part of this myth is true – the program has a small surplus right now – but it will start running deep annual cash deficits beginning around 2015, as shown in the chart on the next page.

Social Security Will Be Deficit Spending by 2015
(in billions of dollars)

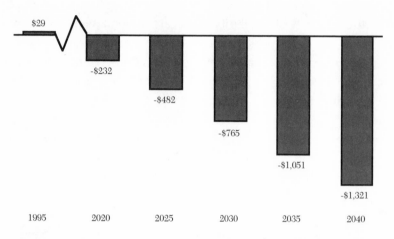

After 2015, too many retirees and too few active workers make the Social Security balance fall like a bungee jumper who forgot to buckle his cord. There will be a Social Security deficit of a half trillion dollars a year by 2025 and deficits of trillions of dollars thereafter. Add in Medicare and the deficit plunge is more than twice as rapid, as indicated by the chart below.

Medicare is Already Running a Cash Deficit
(in billions of dollars)

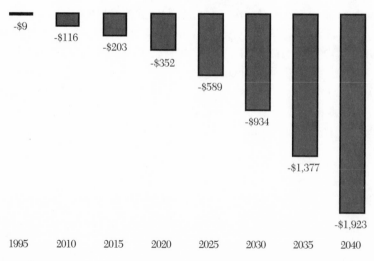

Everyone knows that Medicare is rapidly going bankrupt, but that's not my assigned subject today. As for Social Security, however, some officials still claim that despite these stunning deficits, its "trust fund" will remain "solvent" until 2029.

The very name "trust fund" conjures up a vault somewhere where Social Security taxes are stacked up, to be paid out years later. But this image is totally false.

Better to call it the Social Security "Dis-trust Fund." Social Security is strictly pay-as-you-go – obligations are paid out each year from the revenue taken in each year. Future obligations are backed by nothing more than so many promissory notes – that is, by the government's "promise" to compel future workers to pony up more taxes. Calling it the "Social Security Trust Fund" is the ultimate oxymoron – right up there with the phrase "Congressional Intelligence Committee."

Myth three: SOCIAL SECURITY IS A SACRED "CONTRACT" BETWEEN GENERATIONS.

Sounds great, but if it's a contract, I'd wager that the signatures of the younger people of the country have been forged.

As you can see below, the terms of the contract keep changing – and always to the disadvantage of younger taxpayers.

Social Security as a Percent of Worker Payroll

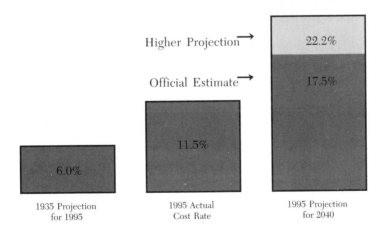

What's more, it's a "contract" that results in the federal government spending 12 times as much on each elder than it spends on each child.

And – most devastating of all – it's a "contract" in which young people have so little confidence that more believe in UFOs than think they
will ever receive Social Security.

There is an old adage about robbing Peter to pay Paul. In the Social
Security shell game, we're robbing Peter Junior to pay Peter Senior –
even when Peter Senior in question – me, for instance – doesn't need
the benefit.

And Peter Junior is already forking over. In 1993 a retired couple on
Social Security with $30,000 a year in income paid, on average, $850 in
federal taxes. Meanwhile, their young son and daughter-in-law, struggling to raise a family on the same income, paid a total federal tax of
$7,100. No other country tilts the tax code toward the elderly as much
as we do. And very few gouge the young as we do.

Myth Four: BASICALLY, SOCIAL SECURITY WORKS LIKE
ANY FUNDED COMPANY PENSION.

The fact is that Social Security is not a funded pension in any sense
of the word. Instead of retirement savings, it's accumulating unfunded
benefit promises. Try a financing scheme like that for a private pension, and you would be sent to jail. It's more like trusting your retirement to the proceeds of a chain letter.

The chart below illustrates the size of these unfunded promises.

Unfunded Benefit Liabilities
in Billions of Present Value Dollars

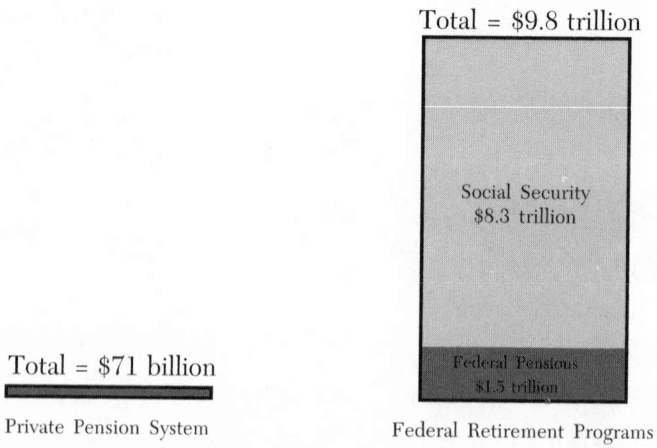

Total = $9.8 trillion

Social Security
$8.3 trillion

Total = $71 billion

Federal Pensions
$1.5 trillion

Private Pension System

Federal Retirement Programs

For Social Security alone, the unfunded promises amount to $8.3 trillion. Combined with unfunded federal pensions, the burden comes to $9.8 trillion – about 140 times greater than the unfunded liabilities of every private pension system in America. It's also more than twice the size of our official national debt.

Let's put it another way. As the chart below indicates, if federal law required us to fund Social Security the way private pensions must be funded by law, it would instantly add $670 billion a year to the federal deficit or about $800 billion if we add in the unfunded federal pensions.

Restating the Deficit to Reflect Unfunded Benefit Liabilities

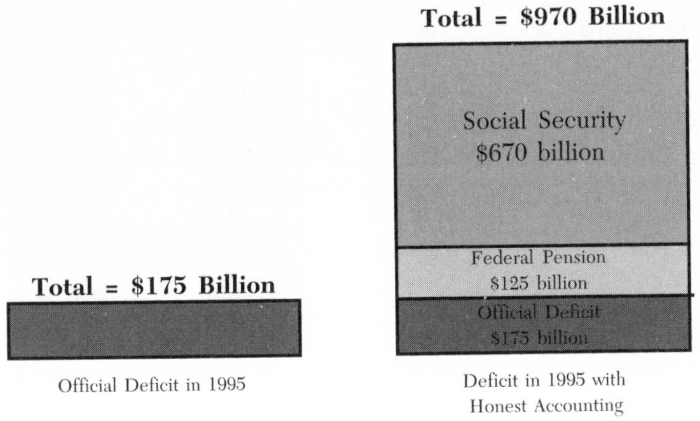

Total = $970 Billion

Social Security
$670 billion

Federal Pension
$125 billion

Official Deficit
$175 billion

Total = $175 Billion

Official Deficit in 1995

Deficit in 1995 with
Honest Accounting

In Washington, they worry about what the policy wonks called unfunded mandates – in other words, promises the government has no plans to pay for. But comparing welfare or any regulatory mandate to Social Security is a little like mistaking Woody Allen for Arnold Schwarzenegger. Social Security is the mother of all unfunded mandates.

Now for Myth Five: MOST OF THE ELDERLY ARE POOR AND THEREFORE REALLY NEED ALL THEIR BENEFITS.

This is simply wrong. It is a lie. In fact, poverty in America is today three times more likely to afflict the very young than the very old.

I'm going to repeat that because it is so important. Poverty in America is three times more likely to afflict the very young than the very old.

And in recent years, while the average incomes of young families have fallen off a cliff, the incomes of the elderly have continued to rise at a steady clip. Yes, about two out of every five Social Security recipients make $20,000 or less – and for these households Social Security is a lifeline. Everyone agrees these people must be protected.

But, in fact, about 40 percent of total benefits go to households with incomes above the U.S. median average – the same Americans who are far more likely to be getting private pension checks and investment income. And, as you can see, they get the bigger Social Security checks.

Average Social Security Benefit in 1990 by Total Household Income

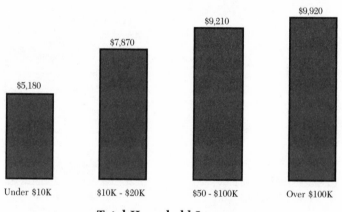

Total Household Income

But maybe need isn't the issue – which leads us to Myth Six: NEEDY OR NOT, I PAID INTO THE SYSTEM AND IT'S ONLY FAIR THAT I GET BACK WHAT I PAID IN.

The graph on the next page indicates that people retiring today do far better than that. Even including interest, an average one-earner couple retiring in 1995 gets back far more than was paid in. That average married worker will get about $127,000 more out of the program than he and his employers ever put into it, plus interest. Calculate just the personal taxes, and interest, and the windfall comes to $182,000. With Medicare thrown in, it rises to nearly $350,000, much of it tax-free. And it must be obvious that our children and grandchildren will never enjoy these windfalls.

Payback in Excess of Contributions
For One-Earner Couple in 1995

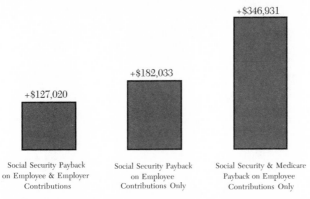

+$127,020	+$182,033	+$346,931
Social Security Payback on Employee & Employer Contributions	Social Security Payback on Employee Contributions Only	Social Security & Medicare Payback on Employee Contributions Only

Let's turn finally to Myth Seven and that ticking time bomb – the greying of the baby boom generation.

Myth Seven: WHY BE CONCERNED? THE BOOMER GENER-ATION IS JUST A PASSING DEMOGRAPHIC EPISODE.

The truth is that the generation of 76 million Americans is unprecedented in size. Once this tidal wave of aging Americans starts washing over our economy beginning around 2010, their impact will be transformational, not temporary. There is a tradition in this country of retiring to Florida.

The chart below indicates that sometime around the year 2025, the share of elderly all over America will be the same as in Florida today. We will become, in effect, a nation of Floridas and then keep aging.

Percent of Total U.S. Population
Age 65 & Older

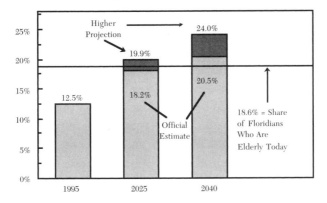

Over the next 50 years, while the number of people under 65 will grow slowly, the number of people over age 65 is destined to double or more. This many golden oldies will be like adding the equivalent of a new California plus all of the New England states – populated entirely by people over 65.

Percent Growth in the Population by Age Group
From 1995 to 2040

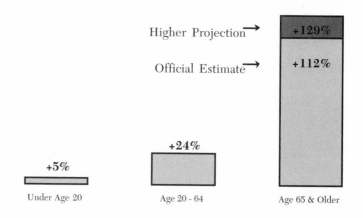

Rapidly rising life spans are, of course, good news for all of us – retirees in the 21st century can look forward to living seven to eight years longer after age 65 than when the Social Security was founded.

But the curmudgeon in me requires me to point out the bad news in the graph on the next page – the extra tax bill for our kids. More people in the wagon and fewer people pulling it. Back in 1955, there were nearly nine taxpayers to support every Social Security beneficiary. Today there are between three and four. But by the time today's newborns reach the peak of their income-earning years, there will be two or less – each married working couple, in effect, will be supporting the Social Security costs of an anonymous retired household in addition to whatever the couple can do for their own retired parents.

Number of Workers per Social Security Beneficiary

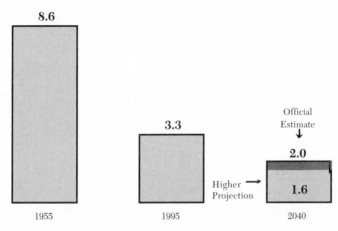

Sound incredible to you? Well, here's another stunner on the changing demographics of 21st-century America. As recently as 1970 there were 12 preschool kids under the age of five for every senior over the age of 85; today there are five. By the year 2040 there may be no more than one. Imagine adding a whole New York metropolitan area full of additional old-oldies – those over 85 – who consume two and-a-half times the health benefits that the very "spry" 65-year-olds do.

In short, the founders of Social Security 60 years ago could never in their wildest dreams have imagined the shape of America that is destined to unfold over the next several decades.

The system is simply not sustainable.

When do we hit the wall? In about 15 years. Think about it, it was only 15 years ago that Ronald Reagan was elected president.

We all know that wasn't very long ago.

So what are our options?

Option one: Do nothing – and watch the Social Security shortfall become a full-scale economic emergency as the program's insolvency drives interest rates into the stratosphere. The economist – and sometime humorist – Herb Stein once said, "If something is unsustainable, it tends to stop." Or as the old adage has it, "If your horse dies, we suggest you dismount." Just as we can't sustain the unsustainable, we can't finance the unfinanceable – these shortfalls are unfinanceable.

There's option two – we raise taxes – and I mean really raise taxes as Professor Kotlikoff has made clear today. By 2040 the cost of Social Security as a share of worker payroll is projected to rise from today's 11 percent to between 17 and 22 percent. Add in Medicare and we're talking about 35 to 55 percent of every employee's paycheck. Obviously, this would kill the economy, but more important, kill these taxpayers.

Obviously, then, these kinds of tax increases are unthinkable – both politically, economically, and morally.

Then there's alternative three: Wait until the ballooning deficits have left our economy in a condition of unrecoverable weakness and then slash Social Security benefits at the last minute. We would deprive tens of millions of Americans at all income levels of the chance to do any sort of advance planning. We would plunge the lower-income beneficiaries – the ones who really depend upon these checks to stay afloat – into a panic so severe we might call it a "demographic depression."

Let's also brace ourselves for the political consequences. Those consequences that could be seismic, even revolutionary – and I'm not using that word to be rhetorical.

I want to pause for a moment – long enough to let those three visions of our future sink in. Because if we do nothing, one, and perhaps all three, will happen.

Which leads me to the final alternative – three reforms – which if we can muster the intelligence and the courage to make them now – can avert the coming crisis in Social Security. These reforms would keep Social Security truly solvent for our children and our grandchildren. They would defuse a crisis that could turn our economy upside down.

Reform number one: Raise the eligibility age for full Security benefits starting next year, by three months per year, until it moves from 65 to age 70 by the year 2014. That's the way we've got to approach this – don't change the rules with two minutes left to go in the game. Give the boomers who will be retiring in 2014 plenty of time to plan now. And consider this – by the year 2014, because of rising life expectancy, the average retiring 70-year-old will still receive Social Security for two years longer than the average 65-year-old retiree in 1940 – the year Social Security paid its first benefit.

Reform number two: Apply an affluence test to Social Security. Right now, about 40 percent of all Social Security benefits go to seniors with incomes above the U.S. median average. We should reduce by 10 percent the benefits going to households with total retirement incomes above $40,000. We should add an additional ten percent cut for every extra $10,000 income. These income thresholds should be indexed for inflation and phased in by the year 2000. Now, how would this work?

Let's say this year that a household receives $10,000 Social Security benefits. If its total income is under $40,000, nothing is withheld. At $50,000, $1,000 in benefits are withheld, at $60,000, $2,000 are withheld – and so on until an income level of $125,000 is reached, at which point $8,500 in benefits are withheld. And that's the maximum. The affluence test would be applied each year so that if someone's income should suddenly plunge, seniors will be guaranteed their full level of Social Security protection.

Reform number three: Make 85 percent of all Social Security benefits subject to tax. I say 85 percent because this would ensure that no one gets taxed twice on their own contributions, and it would make the taxation of Social Security the same as the taxation of private pensions. Beyond this, I don't believe it's fair that retired persons should be exempted from the same universal affluence test – the progressive income tax code – that all working people must submit to. This code, of course, would not require anything from the low-income retirees.

The result of these three reforms? Take a look.

Result of Three Proposed Social Security Reforms

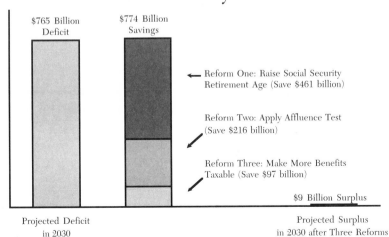

$765 Billion Deficit

$774 Billion Savings

Reform One: Raise Social Security Retirement Age (Save $461 billion)

Reform Two: Apply Affluence Test (Save $216 billion)

Reform Three: Make More Benefits Taxable (Save $97 billion)

$9 Billion Surplus

Projected Deficit in 2030

Projected Surplus in 2030 after Three Reforms

We would wipe away trillions of dollars of red ink – and may actually leave Social Security with a small surplus in the year 2030. In fact, Social Security would remain above or near balance far into the 21st century. In other words, a sustainable balance as shown below.

Result of Three Proposed Reforms

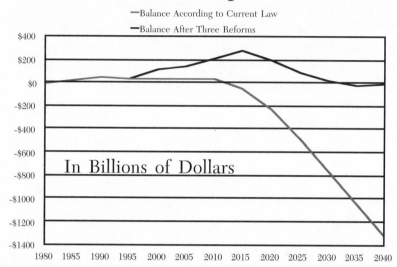

In Billions of Dollars

Now, Ross has asked me to stick to Social Security – and for me one speech is one too many. Still, I'm tempted to launch into my case for a total transformation of our Social Security and tax system. I would create a universal and portable and personally owned thrift plan, where each worker could invest and manage his own funds. With a few other modest reforms in our entitlement system, we could start funding these private-sector accounts – as Senators Bob Kerrey, Jack Danforth and Alan Simpson have proposed – by diverting toward them some one and one half percent of payroll that now goes to Social Security. To encourage additional contributions, I'd also like to see the shift toward the progressive consumption tax – a tax on what we spend rather than on what we save.

Now I realize that these suggestions go beyond Social Security – but so do our problems. A final word. I have been talking for years about America's "entitlement ethic" – the idea that all of us have grown far too fixated on what we have the right to spend and consume and borrow today, and far too passive about what we have the duty to save and invest for tomorrow. You may have seen the new book by Craig Karpel called *The Retirement Myth*. He turns this entitlement ethic into a frightening vision of an entire generation – the baby boomers – entering elderhood without any financial planning. Back in the 1980s, we knew them as Yuppies – Young Upwardly Mobile Professionals. By the 2020s, unless America relearns the thrift ethic, we may meet them again as "Dumpies" – Destitute, Unprepared Mature People. By then, the only way they will be able to keep themselves above water will be to pull under their own children.

One hundred fifty years ago, Alexis de Tocqueville predicted, "The American public will endure until the politicians find they can bribe people with their own money." Today it's worse than that. It is our children's money that we are spending. And that brings me to where I began. After seven myths and facts, three alternatives and three reforms, I know it all starts to swim together and sound like the Chicago Seven or the Secaucus Seven. It reminds me of Henry Kissinger's answer when asked what he thought about the Indianapolis 500. He said, "I think we should free them."

But the real issue here goes beyond numbers. Straightening out Social Security and balancing the budget is not just an economic imperative. It is a moral imperative – a litmus test of what kind of citizens we are.

A wise man said, "The ultimate test of a moral society is the kind of world that it leaves to its children." So today, let me suggest what all of us can do – as parents, as grandparents, and as citizens. In a world rife with lobbying groups and special pleaders, what we can do is take a "special interest" in the general good. United We Stand America has led the way. And to get the facts out to the American people, an unprecedented coalition – the Coalition for Change – is coming together. Along with the Business Roundtable, it includes United We Stand America, my own Concord Coalition, headed by my colleagues Warren Rudman and Paul Tsongas, a youth organization called Third Millennium, as well as the Seniors Coalition, and I think it's great to have young and old working together in common cause.

Bringing our youth into this crusade is key. Keeping the future taxpayers in the dark only makes the problem worse. It reminds me of the old joke about the philosophy professor who asks his class, "Which is worse, ignorance or apathy?" From the back of the class comes, "I don't know, and I don't care." Well, when our children learn about where Social Security is heading, ignorance and apathy will turn to anger. I'd rather harness their energy and fix the system now.

Those of us who are older might reflect on what my friend Paul Tsongas likes to say, "It's not enough for our children to love us. We should want them to respect us." So what will our answer be when our children ask us – and they will – "Where were you when you knew this crisis was coming at us?" I would hope our answer will be, "We were there and we fought for you."

Now, people tell me, "Pete, you're right. But the politics are impossible." They say, "You can't ask politicians to go head-to-head with the American Association of Retired Persons – the AARP – and other special interest groups." And the politicians go on to say you can't ask them to take on Social Security either, without signing their own death warrant. They say Social Security is really the "third rail" of American politics – one touch and you're toast.

So what does that mean for all of us? It's the role of citizens to make it safer for the politicians to do the right thing. And I believe America's senior citizens are ready to play that role. I have talked to many groups of American seniors about this problem – and I don't believe for one moment they're ready to shrug their shoulders and send their grandchildren the bill. It's not in their character – not in keeping with the spirit of sacrifice that has summoned their generation to greatness so many times in this century.

This is the generation that survived the Depression, stormed the beaches at Normandy, scrambled up the summit of Mount Suribachi, under fire – to paint a flag. And when the war was won, this is the generation that built this nation into the freest, the strongest, and the most prosperous society this world has ever known. Against these monumental accomplishments, the modest action it would take to solve our Social Security crisis does not compare.

So, I don't accept for one moment that this generation has forgotten the meaning of sacrifice – that this generation has surrendered its citizenship.

I think there is one last challenge left for this generation. A challenge that takes its bearing not simply from our rights – but our responsibilities.

I'm not here to put down the "greedy geezers" – I'm a geezer myself. But I am here to tell you that I hope we remember that our first loyalty is not to the AARP, but to our country and to our children.

This is our last battle, and we're not fighting for an island this time.

We're not trying to liberate Europe this time.

We're trying to save our country for our children.

Trying to give them the chances we had.

That's a fight worth waging.

And I think we've got one more big fight in us.

That's what I'm here to say – let the battle begin.

Thank you, Ross, for this unique opportunity.

Bernadine
Healy, M.D.

An American Prescription
for Health Care

ROSS PEROT: *Our next speaker is one of the leading authorities on medical matters in the United States.*

Dr. Bernadine Healy is currently the Director of Health and Science Policy at the Page Center of the Cleveland Clinic. She is also Professor of Health Service Management at the Ohio State University. She is a native of New York City. She graduated from Hunter College High School. She earned her bachelor's degree with honors from Vassar. She earned her medical degree with honors from Harvard Medical School in 1970. She completed her postgraduate training in internal medicine and cardiology at Johns Hopkins School of Medicine.

From 1976 to 1984, Dr. Healy was on the faculty of the Johns Hopkins University School of Medicine. In February of 1984, President Reagan appointed Dr. Healy as Deputy Director of the Office of Science and Technology Policy at the White House. In January of 1991 President Bush appointed her Director of the National Institutes of Health. Prior to her appointment at the National Institutes of Health, she was Chairman of the Research Institute of the Cleveland Clinic.

As Director of the National Institutes of Health, she led a federal agency that employs 19,000 people, with an annual budget of over $10 billion. Under her leadership the National Institutes of Health formulated its first strategic plan to guide its research efforts into the 21st century.

In recognition of her numerous accomplishments, Dr. Healy has received many awards. Her latest book, A New Prescription for Women's Health, *will be released this fall. Also, this fall, she will become Dean of the Ohio State University College of Medicine.*

We are very fortunate that Dr. Healy would interrupt her busy schedule to talk with us about health care reform in the United States. Let us welcome Dr. Bernadine Healy.

Thank you so very much. You know, throughout this meeting Ross Perot keeps telling us to buy books. We need to read. We should have our brains being challenged. He actually is giving you some of the best medical advice you are ever going to receive. Getting educated and keeping educated results in healthier lives. You live longer, you get less heart disease, you are less apt to get Alzheimer's, and you will contribute to health care reform.

One thing we all stand united on is our interest in our own health and the health of those we love. Health is the greatest of all riches, and you often don't know it until you lose it. As a doctor, I can tell you it is difficult to evaluate any health system unless it's through the eyes of someone who is sick.

Imagine if at this very moment in Dallas, you were suddenly stricken with severe crushing chest pain, like an elephant sitting on your chest; you are sick to your stomach, sweating, feeling dizzy and having trouble catching your breath. These frightening symptoms would erase all other things from your mind: your success; your job; your plans for tonight; how much money you made last year. Illness has a way of forcing itself to the top of your priorities.

And in this city and almost anywhere throughout this country, you would probably find in a matter of minutes a team of paramedics, ambulance or helicopter personnel, emergency room doctors, nurses, and other health care workers ready and waiting to help you – just because you are one soul in distress. And that's the case whoever you are – rich or poor, old or young, with or without insurance, Texan or not, Republican or Democrat. This is also the only time you might be happier to have me here with you than Newt Gingrich or Bill Clinton – or even Colin Powell.

Now if it is a heart attack, I assure you that you will have the best chance for survival and healthy recovery than you would find anywhere else in the world. Doctors who have trained for up to 20 years and are likely to have been in the upper 10 percent of their college classes; skilled nurses and technical support; computers and other telecommunications monitors; the latest drugs and biotechnology wonders to dissolve clots and save heart muscle; coronary care units, catheterization labs and operating suites are on standby 24 hours a day. All this to give you close to a 95 percent chance of surviving that heart attack and resuming a normal life.

Today's American system of health care is here, ready and waiting for every one of you for one central reason: because of our American political system.

I know this may seem counterintuitive at a time when the public's faith in politics is at an all-time low – some 80 percent mistrust the government some or most of the time. But even when Americans lose faith in their politicians, they never lose faith in the republic for which we stand – that is the energy of United We Stand America. And as for health care, it has blossomed magnificently because of our American political framework with its robust free-market economy and pluralistic democratic society that values the individual. Any plans for health reform must never lose sight of that.

Let me explain this tight link between a political system and health care – not just here but throughout the world.

One news story made it crystal clear to me. Shortly after the breakup of the Soviet Union, I saw a report on CNN about a mental hospital for children and adolescents in Moscow. Under glasnost, cameras were able to film docile kids lining up, their mouths open like birds in the nest, to get their regular doses of psychiatric drugs. The head of the hospital acknowledged that most of these children were there for relatively minor behavioral infractions, what we might call *being a teenager* – running away from home, not going to school, or sniffing glue. Very few had medically defined psychiatric illness.

The reporter asked the head of the hospital how this mass institutionalization could have been tolerated. He replied, "You must understand that in our communist system of government, we do not value the individual – only the group. Our practices do not harm the group." In the United States, we take for granted the fact that we place as much value on the rights and well-being of the individual as of the group.

Sadly, it will take a long time for Russia's health care system to recover from this mind-set. The *New York Times* just last week reported that life expectancy is dismal in Russia, and getting worse. For the Russian male, it has fallen to 57 years of age – unlike the insistent rise in life expectancy in this country and most of the free world. Heart disease, cancer and accidents are big killers. The country has a miserable infrastructure for medicine and public health. One out of 10 babies is born with a genetic defect caused in part by a horribly low rate of vaccination against diseases like rubella that cause birth defects, and by grotesque environmental pollution.

The Soviet Union, a superpower that could put men in space stations, offered its people third-world medical care. The value of an individual human being and a people's sense of the proper role of its government are reflected in a nation's health care system.

This picture is dramatically different from what developed under our political system. American health care is unique on this planet. It is deeply rooted in a largely autonomous private system of care, based on our sense of the individual, but it is one that has also been empowered by some strategic contributions by our government.

The steel pillars of our health care system go back to World War II, deeply rooted in four events, and we must understand them.

First, that war brought us private health insurance paid by employers. To get out from under the yoke of wartime price and wage controls, employers gave workers so-called free health benefits instead (Americans always find a way to get out from under price controls.) Called benefits, not wages, they were income tax free. Fifty years later, we have a large private insurance system for health care – but unfairly, it is tax-free only if your employer pays for it.

Second, President Roosevelt declared that after the war our nation would direct the power of science and technology – so successful in winning the war – towards civilian goals. Medicine was at the top of his list for bringing maximal benefit to the lives of all Americans. Our next war would be on human disease; the ramparts America watched became medical, not just military.

The government's commitment came mainly in the form of that great institution, the National Institutes of Health. The NIH made grants to research institutions and universities throughout the country, and grants to medical schools to train doctors and scientists. "Get the money out of Washington, where it will be wasted," was the cry. Sound familiar?

So today our private sector is the home of a highly talented and innovative medical brain trust. Our medical training and research is now the envy of the world. And every one of us here has benefited, whether we realize it or not.

A third pillar built in this postwar period was our diverse private medical infrastructure. During President Truman's administration, the Hill-Burton Act was passed, which gave federal grants to communities all over the country to build hospitals, provided the community would raise matching funds. As with medical research, the law specifically commanded that the federal government not meddle in hospital care or policies. Today, as a result, there are very few towns or cities anywhere that don't have good, private, not-for-profit hospitals.

Finally, while the government strategically supported private sector–based expansion of hospitals, research and medical education, the American public resoundingly rejected Truman's postwar plans to use taxes to become the provider of universal insurance or of universal health services. Truman was trounced when he tried to nationalize medicine. But he was not the only President to be resisted on this – so were others like Johnson, Carter, and Nixon. Even when Medicare and Medicaid were passed to help the poor and the elderly, they initially came with few strings attached and tapped into the existing private system.

President Clinton thought times had changed, and he declared the push for a national health plan to be the cornerstone of his presidency. He offered soothing promises of health security for all – health care that is always there.

It may be human to want a nanny, particularly when you are sick. But when the American people figured out that it would be the federal government choosing their doctor; either directly or indirectly, telling them what care they could or could not get and where; invading their privacy by putting their medical records on a government computer bigger than the one the IRS has; and taxing them mightily for it all; the public decided that that same government would only be the nanny from hell.

Where has our steadfast American prescription for health care gotten us? What was medicine like when we embarked on the distinctively American crusade to expand our health care the American way – and what's it like now?

Just after the war, our medical care was a lot like that of Russia today. Our life expectancy was dismal. We were in the midst of an epidemic we didn't understand – an epidemic of heart attacks and sudden death among middle-aged men. If you had a heart attack and made it to a hospital, you faced a 35 percent chance of never making it home. Worse, more than half of those stricken with a heart attack died before even getting to a hospital.

Cancer was an unspeakable, incurable disease. Those with severe mental illness were seen as hopelessly insane. We actually had institutions called the Hospital for the Incurably Ill.

Much was incurable then. There was no heart surgery, no artificial hips or knees, no kidney dialysis or organ transplantation. We had few antibiotics, little help for high blood pressure and, except for surgery, no treatment for cancer. Frontal lobotomy was the breakthrough treatment for severe depression, since we had virtually no medications.

I vividly remember summer fears of polio. Some of you probably do, too. I recall the health officials closing the public swimming pool in our neighborhood because of the risk of polio. I saw the fear on the faces of many moms when their children came down with a summer fever or sore throat. And there was the little boy who lived next door to me. He got polio – he survived but was left paralyzed.

With these few remembrances, you know in your heart, not just your head, how far we have come these past few decades. Medical innovation, dominated by America's science, has revolutionized our lives. Polio is no longer a summer dirge of our inner cities. The iron lung has gone the way of the Iron Curtain. We can now treat virtually all cancers. We have dramatically decreased death and destruction from heart attacks and stroke. We've replaced lobotomy with all sorts of brain medicines (we even found Prozac).

Given such advances – the American way – is it illogical or wrong to preserve our uniquely American system as we make needed reforms? In the health care debate of last year, you were rarely reminded of these wonders. The deafening cry was that things were miserable here. Our system was in crisis. We were unfavorably compared to other countries in the free world which long ago chose government-run systems. But they are they – and we are we.

They are used to nannies. They have strong socialist traditions, reflected in their health care and other areas, such as transportation. Their hospitals and clinics, medical schools and research labs grew up as mostly government owned and run. The government imposes vastly higher taxes to pay for everyone's health, whether they want the government's choices or not.

The socialized health care tradition is reflected in their people's expectations about their health care. Their citizens are willing to wait in long lines and accept tight rationing imposed by global budgets that themselves are getting tighter. The elderly are the first to suffer. I saw firsthand how sick people in Finland tolerate up to a two-year waiting list for heart surgery – many dying while on that very list – and those over 65 are not eligible at all. In England, it's mighty hard to get hemodialysis if you are over 55.

Quality-of-life needs are often the first to be rationed out. In Canada, getting scheduled for back surgery can take years. Women in that country may not be able to get an epidural anesthetic during childbirth. In some countries, a higher quality of private medicine is available for a very few – but it is prohibitively expensive for most families and, even then, sometimes they have to leave the country to get it.

A recurrent example used by those who attack our American health care system is our infant mortality rates. My response is, "Yes, look at our infant mortality." Did you know those statistical comparisons are tallied by each country differently? Some countries neglect to count babies who die within 24 hours of birth, and many don't even record in their statistics the very low-weight preemies who die. We are just about the only country in the world where 500-gram babies are even counted and actually have a chance to survive.

In fact, you will find among the lowest infant mortality rates in the world right here – for example, in Maine, Utah, Vermont. What's different about these states? Not medical care, but rather that they have fewer teen pregnancies and crack babies, less drug addition and poverty – all of these are issues that must be addressed urgently, but not used as an excuse to nationalize everybody's health care.

In truth, medicine's successes in infant health are a marker of our compassion and ingenuity and of the value we place on every human life – old or young.

But so much of health care is not even reflected in mortality statistics.

Medicine is also about improving quality of life, not just quantity of life. It's about treating osteoporosis, depression, stroke, diabetes; it's about relieving someone's pain and being able to offer rehabilitation after a paralyzing injury. It's about better wheelchairs for the handicapped and computer aids for the blind. It's about making everyone count.

And that is why we lead the world in health care, but also why that care is so expensive. As one critic put it, "In most countries of the world, death is inevitable; in America, it's an option."

Medical care has been holding at about 14 percent of our GDP for the past three or four years, right up there with food, housing, and transportation. This number on its own is not a problem in that health care is a highly productive sector of our economy. It employs over ten million Americans in generally higher-paying jobs. Our health care industries are among the most competitive in the global market, with a very favorable trade balance, a steady stream of life-saving products, and a hefty investment in research and development.

But high costs have caused problems for the individual patient, problems we cannot ignore. Too many people don't have health plans, and others fear they could lose their insurance if they lose their jobs or get a major illness. In fact, in poll after poll, year after year, Americans say that the biggest problem with our health care system is the fear of financial ruin due to a serious catastrophic illness in their family. We all share that fear.

At any given time, almost 40 million Americans don't have insurance. That number is increasing, in part because of the growing number of jobs being formed by smaller businesses, which can't buy insurance as cheaply as big companies can.

The current payment systems insulate most consumers who have insurance from cost. That drives up consumption but also drives up the cost of health care for those who don't have insurance.

A vicious cycle of cost-shifting occurs: The uninsured who are working actually pay for other people's health care through their income and payroll taxes – often thousands of dollars; and then they, when unable to pay their own medical bills, get uncompensated care. Their uncompensated care is paid for by dollars shifted from those paying patients, driving up the costs for everyone. On top of that is cost-shifting from government health programs to private paying patients.

Many aspects of our financing system are simply not logical. They must be changed and they can be changed – through both public and private action.

To find solutions to these problems of cost and coverage, we have to tease them out one by one, make a diagnosis, and embark on a plan of treatment. Our actions should be guided by a few principles.

First, we must test each solution before casting it in stone. All too often – as Ronald Reagan used to say – when the government enacts a program, it takes on eternal life.

Whatever we do to improve the financing structures of our health care system, we must test some of the changes, gather information, look for intended and unintended consequences, and modify the program if it doesn't work – just as the private sector does.

Second, we must accept that the private sector will take the lead in bringing down costs through price competition and the development of a robust consumer market that demands both quality and value. Governmental attempts to control costs – namely, price controls – are a proven failure. They invariably have the opposite effect, driving up costs. The government still must play a critical role by providing tax incentives, removing barriers to cost control, allowing waivers to test different models, and encouraging individual responsibility.

A third vital principle must be honored. Listen to the patient – in this case, the American public. That was one of the critical failings of the Clinton health plan. The attitude last year, as expressed by one senator, was that they would "push through" Clinton's health reform "regardless of the views of the American people." We saw what happened. The views of the American people are never to be pushed aside. They have spoken time and time again: Americans don't want nationalized health care, and they don't want more taxes.

That doesn't mean the government should take no action. On the contrary, we need to make a few changes now.

First is tax reform. A compelling idea would be the radical simplification of the whole tax system, either with the flat tax proposed by Congressman Armey or the consumption tax proposed by Senators Domenici and Nunn. But until then, we must do a better job of helping families within the existing tax system. The government has always tried to encourage responsible behavior through the tax code – for example, IRAs and the tax deduction for charitable contributions. There is nothing more responsible than setting aside tax-free dollars for needed health care. But the present tax deduction for health insurance is grotesquely unfair. We need to remedy this immediately, in three ways.

We should allow a full tax deduction for those who don't get their health program paid for by their employer. The cost of this could be paid by putting a cap on the size of the health policy tax deduction for everyone.

We should allow a medical savings account option. If you want to purchase only a catastrophic care policy and set money aside each year in an IRA-type savings account that can build up over the years for routine health expenses, you get the same annual deduction. This approach will lower health care costs by making consumers more cost conscious and would encourage personal savings.

We should also think about a tax deduction for long-term care insurance. After all, *family values* sometimes means taking care of our parents when they cannot care for themselves. We must encourage people to insure themselves or their parents against the costs of long-term medical care. For too long that vital family responsibility has been passed off to the government even by those families who could at least partially afford it. Long-term care now consumes over half of the Medicaid budget. Our elderly population is exploding, so we had better start this now.

Along with tax reform, the government must enact basic insurance reforms. This addresses the obvious concerns about policy *cherry picking*: Insurance plans should not be able to turn you away because of a medical condition, exclude covering your preexisting health condition, or cancel your coverage if you get sick. One way or another, health plans must be portable.

Insurance reforms should also facilitate the formation of large purchasing groups of individual and small businesses to pool risks so that they can then get the same rates for health plans as big employers do.

Third, the government has to focus on its primary responsibility – the financial mess it has created with Medicare and Medicaid. These mega-programs purchase about one-half billion dollars worth of health care in the private sector. When they cough, the entire system gets sick. Incidentally, Ross Perot's prescription recommends *Intensive Care*; his and Debbie Steelman's advice should be heeded – let our elders have a say in what to buy with their money, and they might just do it more efficiently. Right now, costs in Medicare are rising three times as fast as in the private sector. We can't afford *not* to give freedom of choice a chance.

As for Medicaid, we all believe in a medical safety net. Although the American public spends some $140 billion for that net, complex and often perverse eligibility requirements make coverage spotty. There is little help for an intact, working-poor family, and the elderly who need long-term care must spend themselves into poverty to get help. A safety net should not be all-or-nothing; people should pay what they can, even if it is a lesser amount, also making it easier for others to move from welfare to work without suddenly losing all health coverage.

Fourth, it has been estimated that as many as 10 to 15 million people in this country who do not have any kind of health plan can afford it, but choose not to buy it, sometimes even turning down contributory plans offered by their employers. This is irresponsible. Everyone who expects to use the health care system must pay for it for themselves and their children if they can afford it. Shelter and food and health care may be seen as a right, but that doesn't mean you don't have to pay for it. If tax incentives, insurance reforms, and Medicare and Medicaid reform don't work to expand access, we might need to consider an individual requirement to buy at least a catastrophic health plan.

Finally, in addition to these, the government must reevaluate how well it performs some of its other roles. The medical malpractice system plays a key role in protecting patients, but the system is too arbitrary because of limitless damages awards for some and little recompense for others. We must have a just system, driven by science and common sense, not a high-stakes lottery.

In the regulatory arena, both federal and state governments must get rid of outmoded mandates that increase the cost of health care. This includes state insurance mandates that force all insurance policies to cover services that some people could never use or would never even want – ranging from acupuncture, to *in vitro* fertilization, to hair pieces, to marriage and parent counseling. One size does not fit all; and one person should not be forced by the state or federal governments to buy shoes that don't fit.

You can see the government has a lot on its hands without adding any new roles and responsibilities. In the American spirit, as history has proven, the private sector and an informed public must do the rest.

The private sector is actually doing a great deal already. The private sector kicked into action with extraordinary innovation and lightning speed. As proof that the markets do respond, the cost of employee health benefits actually declined last year by 1.1 percent, for the first time in almost a decade. Employers achieved this by shifting to more economical forms of health coverage: managed care networks, HMOs, PPOs, and at least first-generation medical savings accounts. About 63 percent of employees are now enrolled in some form of managed care program.

Our private sector health care system is for the first time competing on both cost and quality, and those systems that win on both counts will prevail. Providers have responded by rapidly forming alliances to offer employers the same quality care, more efficiently rendered and at lower cost. Not everyone is comfortable with these market-driven changes.

Doctors have figured out that they will be less independent as they become part of larger groups; hospitals are having to compete for services and close if they fail; large, integrated health plans – in which "providers" including some combination of primary care and specialty doctors, hospitals, outpatient clinics, long-term care centers, or other critical medical services are aligned to offer an *integrated* service directly to a patient for a fixed price – are taking on financial risk with capitation, sometimes entirely eliminating insurance companies as middlemen; and big employers are becoming self-insured, giving them a bigger stake in employee wellness.

Individual consumers, too, are asserting their will in the midst of all this change. HMOs originally were *closed networks* and patients complained that they lost their choice of doctor. Now closed HMOs are facing stiff competition from open networks that offer a so-called *point-of-service* option, so that you can go to a doctor or hospital outside the network, but you will have to pay more.

And the pressure is on hospitals and doctors to become more consumer oriented. This means giving consumers – giving individuals – understandable information about the prices of various services, about outcomes, and about overall quality.

And that is as it should be. In health care, more than anywhere else, the consumer – the patient – must be at the center. After all, disease and death don't happen to a nation or to a group; they happen to individuals, one by one. One cannot tamper with the choices, privacy, and rights of the individual when it comes to their one real possession, their mind and body. We hear a lot about rationing; but when it is done by the patient – with love from the family and good counsel from a doctor – it can actually be compassionate. Look at the decisions that Jackie Kennedy Onassis and Richard Nixon made just prior to their deaths, with no coercion – a choice to forgo expensive medical treatment that would have been futile and to die with dignity.

In all of these efforts to improve the health care system, we cannot lose sight of our American traditions – who we are. But also we must never forget that health care does not exist in a vacuum. It is intimately connected to other goals of our nation, particularly a thriving economy and educated people. A country is not healthy if its people are not working or have a poor education. Better education runs in parallel with better health and better jobs. Conversely, a nation that cannot care for its sick will never succeed in these other endeavors.

A good economy, good education, and good medical care – these three combined – are the golden triangle of a successful nation and a healthy one. On this, too, United We Stand.

Thank you. Thank you, Ross Perot, and thank you, all of you.

Deborah Steelman

The Truth About Medicare

ROSS PEROT: *Our next speaker is Deborah Steelman. She is an authority on Medicare, Medicaid and other federal health programs.*

She was born in Salem, Missouri. She earned her undergraduate degree and her law degree from the University of Missouri.

Ms. Steelman has worked in the Medicare arena since 1981 as a staff member of the Aging Committee that was chaired by the late Senator John Heinz. She served as Associate Director of the Office of Management and Budget during the Reagan Administration, and was responsible for monitoring the Medicare and Medicaid programs.

In 1991, President Bush appointed Mrs. Steelman to chair a bipartisan commission – the Advisory Council on Social Security and Medicare. The council conducted a two-and-a-half-year survey of Medicare's financing and benefit structure. They reported in 1991 that Medicare must be completely restructured.

Ms. Steelman is now an attorney in private practice and she is still working to create a sound and sensible Medicare program.

We are pleased to have her with us today to talk about the need for action to save Medicare from bankruptcy.

Ross, thank you. Everyone agrees that Medicare is one of our most important federal programs. It is the cornerstone of a secure retirement plan. It brings peace of mind to young and old alike. It is one of the many blessings of living in this great country. And we must work hard to make sure it always will be.

This is why we have to talk turkey. We have to face up to the facts. We all owe Ross Perot a colossal thank you for his book, *Intensive Care*. I don't know how many of you have had a chance to buy this book, but you must do it because it spells the issue out in black and white.

Medicare has three problems. You have heard a lot about the first of them. Medicare Trust Fund, Part A – the part that pays for hospital bills – is going broke.

Medicare's second problem is the Supplemental Medical Trust Fund, Part B – which is the part that pays for doctor bills and some other services outside the hospital – and it is going through money faster than a teenager spends his allowance.

Problem number three is that the Medicare benefit package fails to cover basic health care needs. With all we spend for this program, the benefit package still fails to keep up with the times.

It is important to keep all three of these problems in mind as we tackle the job of keeping Medicare alive and well for today's beneficiaries, your children, and your grandchildren. If we only solve one of these problems, but not the other two, we have not done our job.

It is also important to understand that we pay for Medicare in different ways. The part of Medicare that pays for hospital bills, Part A, is funded a little bit like Social Security. You and your employer – if you are self-employed you pay both parts – pay a payroll tax. But unlike Social Security, there is no cap on your wages subject to that tax. There is no tax freedom day for Medicare. You pay for Medicare in every single paycheck all year long. And Part A is only a little over half of the Medicare program. It is about 60 percent.

The other 40 percent of Medicare that pays for doctors and other services – Part B – we pay for in two different ways. Right now income taxes pay about three-quarters of the bill and Medicare beneficiaries pay the rest through monthly premiums deducted from your Social Security checks. Right now that deduction is $46.10 per month. Now, Medicare did not start out this way. In the beginning, taxpayers and beneficiaries split the cost 50/50. But as the costs of the program have cascaded beyond the wildest dreams of those who passed the legislation, more and more of the bill has been shifted to the general taxpayer.

Now, you would think that with all this money going into the program, the government could deliver a benefit package that has kept up with the times, a benefit package that is as good as any benefit package in the private sector. Think again. Medicare's benefit package easily ranks among the lowest packages offered by employers today to their work forces.

It is important to understand the three ways we pay for Medicare: payroll taxes, income taxes, and monthly premiums. And it is important to understand that the benefit package has not kept up with today's medical miracles. Every one of us has a stake in this program and every one of us must be responsible for getting Medicare out of the trouble it is in today.

Let's take a look at all three of Medicare's problems at one time.

Problem Number 1: The Hospital Trust Fund – Part A – is going broke. You may have heard a great deal about Medicare's bankruptcy this summer. Medicare's trustee board issued its annual report in April. Since then, many in Congress have sounded the alarms.

Medicare's Trustees issue this report every year. All of President Clinton's appointees and the Trustees appointed by President Bush came together and issued a unanimous report. They said that the Hospital Trust Fund – I will read from the report – "is severely out of financial balance and the Trustees believe that the Congress must take timely action to establish long-term financial stability for the program."

The trustees recommend that Congress do one of two things – either increase payroll taxes by 44 percent immediately, or immediately cut Medicare spending by 30 percent. These are terrible, drastic measures. I am sure the Trustees gave these options just to bring home how much trouble the program is in.

Let me assure you, nobody in Washington supports actually cutting Medicare spending. No one. No matter how much trouble the program is in, too many people rely on Medicare to cut spending arbitrarily.

Some people do think raising payroll taxes is a great idea to help Medicare's problems. We have done this before. I believe we cannot continue to raise taxes. Raising payroll taxes to keep up with a program whose costs are growing over ten percent a year cannot be the answer. As shown in the chart below, payroll taxes would have to triple just to keep up with the spending demands of Part A alone. No, this time we have to face up to the fact that the costs of Medicare must become reasonable. Costs will still go up – we have to face that fact, too. But costs must escalate at a slower pace.

Medicare Part A Payroll Tax Rate

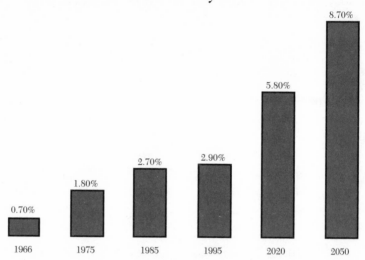

You will also hear that we should not worry, because technically the trust fund won't be bankrupt until 2002. That is seven long years from now. This is the classic brinkmanship approach: "Don't worry; Medicare is always on the verge of bankruptcy. We'll take care of it after the next election."

In other words, why do something today that can be put off until tomorrow? Even though you already know the answer to this, let me give you another reason: Next year Medicare will start paying out more than it collects in revenue, and every year we wait, the problem will be 20 percent more difficult to solve. The graph on the next page indicates the negative cash flow of the Medicare program beginning in 1996.

We can hardly solve the easy problems – what sense does it make to wait to solve this problem when it will be harder?

So I say forget the next election. I say it is time to roll up our sleeves and get to work. I have to say that is why it is such an honor for me to

Negative Cash Flow of Medicare
(in billions of dollars)

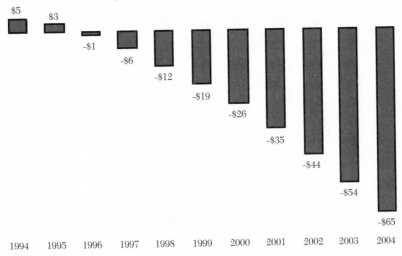

$5 $3   -$1   -$6   -$12   -$19   -$26   -$35   -$44   -$54   -$65

1994   1995   1996   1997   1998   1999   2000   2001   2002   2003   2004

be here, because I think that is the way all of you feel.

Medicare Part B, the program that pays for doctor bills and other services outside the hospital, has averaged 15 percent annual growth over the last 20 years. The program will double in size roughly every seven years.

Remember that Part B is partly paid for by income taxes and partly by premiums. The Part B premium is tied to the increases in the cost of the program. Throughout its history, these premiums have risen as the costs of the program have risen.

Today, the Part B premium costs $552 per year; by 2000, beneficiaries will pay over $700 per year for Part B coverage. Current premium costs equal a little over 6 percent of an average beneficiary's Social Security check. It we do nothing to check program costs, the Part B premium could cost more that 13 percent of the average beneficiary's Social Security check by the year I turn 65, the year 2020.

To keep this from happening, we could always ask the taxpayer to foot more of the bill. We could say, "These premiums are getting too high for beneficiaries to pay. Let's have the taxpayer give more of their income taxes to Medicare." Guess what? We have already done that.

Let's take a look at these two parts of the program together and let's really get a picture of how much this is costing. How much do we cur-

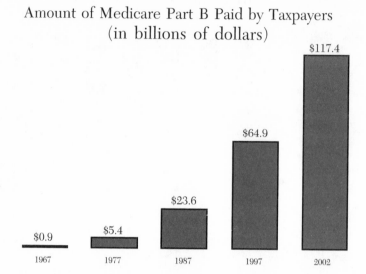

Amount of Medicare Part B Paid by Taxpayers (in billions of dollars)

Year	Amount
1967	$0.9
1977	$5.4
1987	$23.6
1997	$64.9
2002	$117.4

rently pay for these programs? If you earn about $25,000 today, you are paying about $1,150 a year for the Medicare. In the year 2002, you will pay $1,800, about $650 more. Every year that will go up. If you make $75,000 today, you pay about $3,450 for these two programs a year. In seven years, you will pay over $5,300, almost $1,900 more per year.

Cost of Medicare by Income Categories

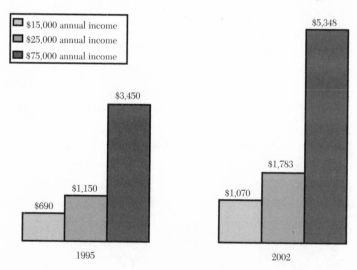

- $15,000 annual income
- $25,000 annual income
- $75,000 annual income

	1995	2002
$15,000 annual income	$690	$1,070
$25,000 annual income	$1,150	$1,783
$75,000 annual income	$3,450	$5,348

Now these are rough estimates, but they show the costs are going up
and up and up. Taxes, whether they are income taxes or payroll taxes,
cannot keep up with this burden. What has to happen? We have to
slow the rate of growth in the Medicare program. The high rate of
growth in the Medicare program produces a Ponzi scheme that simply
is not sustainable. Today – this is the truth, and like Pete Peterson says,
I know you don't want to hear it – today all beneficiaries are getting
more in benefits than they paid into the program, including all the payroll taxes, all the income taxes and compounded interest.

The average – no, I understand there is no average beneficiary – but
the average one-earner couple enrolled in Medicare this year will use
an average of $126,700 more in Medicare benefits than they paid in
payroll taxes, income taxes, premiums, and interest.

The average two-earner couple will use $117,200 more. The single
female will use $65,000 more. The single male, $40,000 more. Those
differences are primarily due to life expectancy. That work was done
by Gene Steuerle of the Urban Institute and he has made a tremendous contribution to date, because it brings home the question, "How
can we keep doing this?" We can't. You cannot keep paying more out
in benefits than you collect in taxes.

Medicare Costs More Per Beneficiary than a Beneficiary Pays in Taxes and Premiums

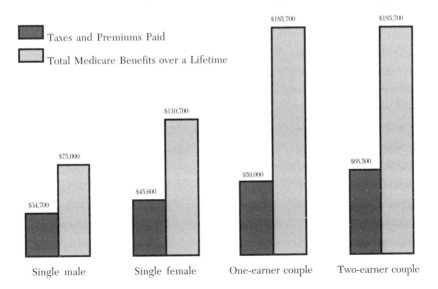

Again, you might ask, how can this be? It is not because the government does not invest your payroll taxes, and it is not because the government did not credit every speck of that interest to the trust fund. It would be easier, I admit, to think that somebody just stole all the money – the payroll taxes, all the income taxes – and spent it all on foreign trade or some other item, but that is not the truth. The truth is that Medicare grows faster than the funding sources can keep up with.

You can see it for yourself in the trustees' report. You can see it for yourself in Ross' book, *Intensive Care*. I have to say it is not the beneficiaries' fault, either, that you get this windfall. It is not. It is because Medicare is a 30-year-old government program, and beneficiaries are having to live with the confusion, the perverse incentives, the screwball rules, and the waste. It is a program that has to be redesigned.

Medicare spending simply grows so fast that the funding cannot keep up with it, and the beneficiaries in today's program are virtually powerless to do anything about it. So the question is, "How much longer can Medicare continue to pay so much more than it collects?" The money has to come from somewhere. Americans are getting older. Medicare enrolls more new beneficiaries every day. Where will the money come from? Higher premiums? More taxes? More borrowing?

I think we know what the answer is. It is what the government has done for a long time, and we cannot allow that to happen this time. We cannot allow more borrowing. We can also no longer ask the beneficiary or the taxpayer to keep footing the bills for a program that is so out of control. This is not rocket science – we must reduce the rate of growth in Medicare.

For decades the trustees have called for lower Medicare growth. In fact, there already have been many bitter battles in Congress over how to reduce Medicare's extraordinary inflation rate. For about the last 15 years you have heard time and time again about Draconian cuts, about slashing Medicare, about all these battles in the Congress. What good has it done? Not much, according to the chart at the top of the next page.

To make a long story short, we have seen that just cutting fees to doctors and hospitals does not do the job. We have cut doctors' fees. We have cut hospital fees. We have tinkered around the edges. We

Medicare Costs Are Still Rising
(in billions of dollars)

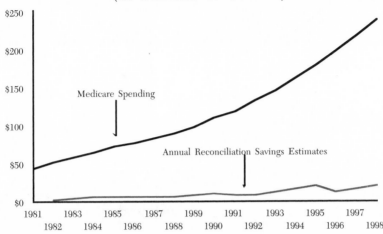

have screwed down all the screws. We have done all of that and it may have helped some. Goodness knows where the program would be if we had not done that. But just cutting fees does not reduce the rate of growth in the program because it does not do anything to affect the underlying causes of Medicare's growth. It does not do anything to get at the incentives that have fueled this inherently inflationary program.

Now, maybe we have cut some of the fat, but the bad providers figure out how to gain on the system immediately and make even more money out of it. And the good providers are maybe near the edge. The good providers have felt these cuts over the last 15 years. And the bottom line on all of this is that Medicare's costs are still growing too fast. We still have the problem ahead of us.

In fact, Medicare is the only major government program for which we continue to spend more and more as a percent of our Gross Domestic Product. Our economy is the source of all the benefits of this society, and we have continued to spend on Medicare more and more as a percent of GDP. We have reversed that trend in agriculture. We have reversed that trend in the government. We have reversed that trend in welfare. Medicare, a few other health programs, and interest payments are the only things for which we continue to spend more and more as a percent of our GDP.

Projected Change in Federal Outlays
From 1995 to 2000 as Percentage of GDP

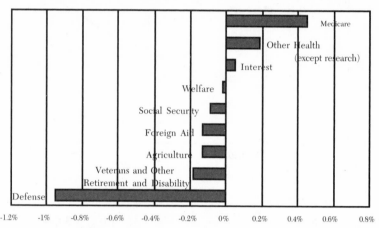

We have to slow the rate of growth in Medicare – the trustees know this, leaders in both parties know it, our representatives in Congress know it, and our President knows it.

Those are problems one and two. Two parts of the program – both skyrocketing costs, both at the end of their rope – that must be changed.

Problem Number 3: Medicare's benefit package fails to cover basic health care needs. As bad as Medicare's financial problems are, the state of its benefit package, in my opinion, is worse. Medicare's benefit package, and the way it is administered, is absolutely irrational. To be charitable, Medicare was designed for the way medicine was practiced in 1965, but this is 1995. Medicare has changed – we have changed. Medicaid, the program for low-income individuals, has changed. Medicaid has a benefit package that has been improved many times, but Medicare does not. Medicare is the package that lags behind.

For example, in Medicare you have a $700 deductible that is indexed to the rate of inflation. It goes up every year. You do not know how much it is going to be next year. Medicare has no stop loss. Private plans all have stop-loss protection so when you really have a catastrophe you are not turned loose. That is when Medicare does it to you. Medicare does not cover many health products and services. Most astonishingly, it does not cover most pharmaceuticals at a time when we routinely fix ulcers with pills instead of surgery, when we are going to be able to address Alzheimer's and osteoporosis and all sorts of other terrible diseases with drugs in the next few years. Medicare does not cover most pharmaceuticals. So you buy a Medigap policy. That is another $1,300 a year, give or take.

Let's add this up. You have Part A and Part B. You have Part A deductible, Part B deductible. You have half a dozen different co-pays in Parts A and B. You have limitations on days here and days there. You have maybe a couple of thousand dollars of coverage regulations and quirks. You buy Medigap, and then you have Medigap's co-pays and limits.

Now, is any of this making sense yet? And I have not even discussed the fraud and abuse and the waste – the bills paid twice, the errors in doctors' offices, the hospital billing centers, the bills five feet long that you cannot read so you do not know if you even got what you needed. You see this every day. You call the department, what do they do? Usually nothing.

So that is problem number one: Part A is going bankrupt. Problem number two: Part B we cannot afford any more. Problem number three: we have got a benefit package problem. What do we do? How, if this program is so unaffordable, can we even begin to think about fixing problem number three?

There is only one thing to do, and one of your native sons here said it – Gene Kranz, the Apollo XIII flight leader, said it. He said, "Let's work the problem, people. Let's get together and work the problem."

Unless Congress passes legislation, the beneficiary has practically no ability to change Medicare's pattern of escalating expenses and inadequate coverage. Unless the President signs it, you have the same problem. If Congress does not pass a bill this year to keep Medicare from going bankrupt, you know who to hold accountable. If the President does not sign the bill, you know who to hold accountable. We must have a law to fix Medicare.

We have talked about lots of problems. I am sure you are about ready to throw me off the stage. It is time for a break. This woman is full of bad news, get her out of here. But guess what? There is some good news when you start to talk about the solutions in Medicare. There is some very good news.

Number one, we can solve Medicare's problems without cutting Medicare spending. Just like Pete Domenici said on the budget, we can solve this problem without cutting, all we have to do is slow the rate of growth.

The best way to think about Medicare might be the way you think about buying a health care plan when you are working, when you are younger. Let's say your health care today costs $2,500. Now, you do not want the cost of that plan to double or triple in the year 2002, but you realize it is going to cost more. We have technology, we have inflation, we have more people – it is going to cost more.

Well, Medicare spends more per person than a health plan covering young people, obviously. Seniors have greater health needs, so it is more expensive. So Medicare spends approximately $4,800 per person today. You can think of the $4,800 Medicare now spends on average for each beneficiary as what Medicare would pay on your behalf if it were buying you a health plan.

Now, by the year 2002 Medicare should spend more than that, but it should not spend double or triple that amount.

Medicare Spending Per Beneficiary

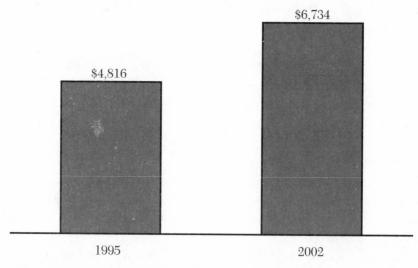

Some people believe that Medicare spending should go up to $6,700 per person by the year 2002. If we do that, we have solved problems one and two. We have solved problems one and two if we go up to only $6,700 by the year 2002. So the question is, can we also solve problem number three? Can we get the benefits we want? Solving all three of these problems has to be our goal for the Medicare problem for the 21st century.

Now, at this point you might expect to hear me say that in order to achieve this idea for Medicare we have to do something radical, we have to do something dramatic. You would expect to see me pound the table and say we have to overhaul the program. But this would be non-sense. It would not be fair to the beneficiaries in the program. It would not be fair to the people who have paid taxes all their lives to not get in the program when they retire. Thanks to our founding fathers and our own common sense over the last 200 years, it is not the way our democracy works. No, we have got to do some very simple things to Medicare. If we do these very simple things, we can solve all three of the problems.

What are those simple things? Letting the beneficiaries change Medicare one by one on your own timetable. Don't you think you could find a better way to buy a health plan than Medicare has? I do. And the reason I think this is because I have seen what the people have done in the private sector to turn around health care costs. When health care costs have gone through the roof in the private sector, people stood up and changed the way we buy health care and reduced the rate of growth. The private sector has turned to managed care and lots of other innovative ideas, like medical savings accounts and flexible spending accounts. All of these ideas reduced cost.

In my opinion, we need to enact the you-choose rule. You choose. If you want to keep your Medicare coverage just as it is today, you should be able to do that. But you should also be able to choose traditional fee-for-service and not be restricted to the doctors who take assignments in Medicare. You should be able to choose all the different kinds of managed care, if you want to – health maintenance organizations (HMOs), point-of-service and preferred provider networks. And you should be able to choose medical savings accounts.

I know the alphabet soup in Medicare is tough to digest, but so were automated bank tellers when we first got them. I did not use one for ten years because I thought they were so impersonal. Then I realized how much quicker they were and how much cheaper they were. Medicare beneficiaries are no different.

Beneficiaries want the best health care at a better price. I think this is the way we can get it. In fact, one of the plans is available in Medicare today. It is an HMO. It is only one option, but one option is better than no option. An HMO is a health plan that provides comprehensive benefits for a fixed prepaid premium. It is virtually the only option the government offers to beneficiaries. But like I say, one is better than none.

What have we learned? Generally these beneficiaries get a better benefit plan than plain vanilla Medicare, and they do not pay plain vanilla Medicare co-pays and deductibles. The main reason more of these plans are not available now, needless to say, is the government's stranglehold that they have on putting more of these plans in place. That is the law we need. We need a law that says if you want plain vanilla care, choose it. Then you are staying in a system you know is more expensive than it should be. You should pick up some of those extra costs. You should take a greater role in policing the system. You should review every single bill. You should mark it up and send it back to Medicare and say, "Do not pay this, I didn't get it. " You should make sure you have a government agency that will crack down on this kind of fraud or waste – innocent waste or incompetence – when you call.

If you want a less expensive plan, say a catastrophic plan, choose it and you may pick up more of the routine costs yourself, either on your own or through a medical savings account. If you want a comprehensive plan that covers everything from A to Z – a hearing aid, eyeglasses, pharmaceuticals – one plan, no deductibles – choose that one. A plan like this may cost more than plain vanilla Medicare, if it is fee-for-service, or it may cost the same as plain vanilla Medicare if it is an HMO. But it is your choice – you choose.

I can hear you thinking right now that this sounds too good, too easy. I came here ready to hear this drastic solution and this sounds too easy. How can this be? Two answers. First, plans that do not have to jump through Medicare's hoops offer better benefits at a better price. We have seen that already.

Second, Medicare and its three revenue streams – payroll taxes, income taxes, premiums – will still pay for your plan. They will fund Medicare's payment to the plan of your choice. Now, this payment will vary, obviously, depending on the beneficiary, because a sick beneficiary costs more than a healthy one. But they would average approximately the $4,800 per year that Medicare now spends on you. Then, over time, that payment to each of the plans would rise, maybe to $6,700 a year.

Some worry that this kind of payment would not be enough to cover the cost of a good plan. I do not worry about this. Number one, $6,700 is a lot of money. We ought to be able to get a good health plan for that amount. Number two, we already have seen a plan operating outside of Medicare that delivers better benefits for a better price. Number three, Medicare's guarantee is what this debate is all about, Medicare's guarantee that this will cover a good benefit package. If we are not talking about a Medicare guarantee, we are not talking about anything. I am talking about a way to make sure Medicare's guarantee is there without breaking the bank, without breaking the future generations. I am talking about a way to make sure Medicare can adapt to modern technology and has a modern benefit package. I think we can get that.

No matter what plan you choose, if your neighbor chooses the same plan, it would cost you the same. If your neighbor chose a different plan, a more expensive one, it might cost him a little more. If your neighbor chose a cheaper plan, it might cost him a little less. But Medicare would make the same contribution to you. If you chose the same plan, it would be the same deal for both of you. That is a guarantee I think all of us would be happy and proud and thankful to stand behind.

Let me just close by saying it is that simple. Write to your Representative; write to your Senators; write to the President – and tell them the road to a better Medicare program is clear and the changes are not very dramatic. They will make those changes.

We do have leaders in Washington who want to do this. You need to listen to them and you need to make sure they listen to you. But we also have leaders in Washington who want to scare the living daylights out of anybody who says we have to change Medicare, and you should give those so-called leaders what they deserve. It is all up to you. Let's work the problem, people.

Thank you.

Governor
Tommy Thompson

Welfare and Medicaid
Reform

ROSS PEROT: Our next speaker is Governor Tommy Thompson of Wisconsin.

In 1994, Governor Thompson became the first Governor in the history of Wisconsin to be elected to a third four-year term.

He is the Chairman of the National Governors Association. He worked in his dad's grocery store and graduated from Elroy High School. He earned his bachelor's degree and his law degree in 1966, both from the University of Wisconsin. He is a former Army captain and a member of the Army Reserve.

His public service began in 1966 when he was elected to the Wisconsin State Assembly at the age of 24. He became Assembly Assistant Minority Leader in 1973 and was elected Minority Leader in 1981.

He was elected Governor of Wisconsin in 1986. He has a firm commitment to revitalize the economy of Wisconsin and to run state government like a successful business.

Since taking office, more than 450,000 new jobs have been created in his state.

Wisconsin's unemployment rates have remained below the national average for the last six years. It is the only state in the nation to reduce personal income tax rates, balance its budget every year, and not raise any major taxes.

As a result of Governor Thompson's welfare reform programs, Wisconsin has experienced the largest decrease in welfare cases in the nation. He established the first parental school choice program in the nation. Governor Thompson and his wife, Sue Ann, have three children.

Today, Governor Thompson will tell us about some of the remarkable strides that the state of Wisconsin has made in the areas of welfare reform and Medicare reform. Let's welcome Governor Thompson.

Thank you very much for that wonderful introduction, Ross. I am very happy to be here to speak to all of you, the individuals who lit a fire under the American political system a couple of years ago. One of my main heroes is Vince Lombardi. He used to say there are three things that should matter to you: your family, your religion, and the Green Bay Packers. All of you, just by being here today, show that you care deeply about three things: your families, your faith in ordinary Americans, and the future of this great country.

There has been a lot of talk and speculation lately about what exactly all of you mean to the political landscape of this country. I am here to tell you what I think you mean. Because all of your ideas – ideas which have only been talked about for years – are finally beginning to be acted upon. They may not seem radical to you, they may seem a little slow in coming, but believe me, things are happening. The little wake-up call you delivered in 1992 led to a political shake-up that sent a clear message, "We do not care if you are a Republican or a Democrat, we expect you to do your job." The election on November 8 was a revolution.

I cannot tell you how great it is for me as a governor to be able to go to Washington and see the change of attitude. The arrogance is gone, blown out of the bag. In fact, I go up on Capitol Hill now and it is nice. People come out and say, "Tommy, how are you? Got any good ideas on school choice or welfare?" They are nice and happy to see you, and that is only the Democrats.

There is a big difference between common sense and what I call "government sense." For decades now we have seen the federal government gathering more and more power into its grasp. For 50 years we have seen a federal government who thought it could do a better job when it came to running our states, to running our schools, to run-

ning our businesses, and to running our personal lives. What has happened in those 50 years? We have seen crime go up, respect for
authority go down, more families breaking up, and a government that
does not pay its bills. It's a good thing they have been telling us what to
do, right? Perhaps the one good thing to come out of this experiment
will be the conviction that it is time to start moving away from government sense and back to common sense.

I come from Elroy, Wisconsin, a very small community in the middle of Wisconsin. Elroy is so small that 2nd Street is on the outskirts of
town. You can call somebody up, get the wrong number and you still
talk for half an hour.

My father ran a grocery store in town. He used to tell me, "Tommy,
you have two ears and one mouth. Use them in that proportion and
you will do just fine." That is common sense.

In 1785, Thomas Jefferson wrote, "Every government degenerates
when trusted to the rulers of the people alone. The people themselves
are its only safe depositories."

So that is the challenge facing you and me, to move away from the
Washington mindset, to move away from government sense and move
back to the people, back to common sense. The welfare system is a
perfect example of what I refer to as government sense. When you pay
people not to work, not to get married, and to have children out of
wedlock, guess what happens? People do not work, they do not get
married, and they have more children out of wedlock.

We have spent more money on welfare today than we spent on
World War II, and poverty rates are higher today than when we
started. That is government sense. Common sense tells you that you do
not simply hand money out and ask for nothing in return. In fact, I
believe that handing out a welfare check and expecting nothing in
return is not public assistance, it is public apathy – "Here is your
check, see you next month."

So while Washington stood around and talked about how welfare
needed to be changed, we in the states – I started back in 1986 – started
doing something about it. We started offering hope and opportunity
along with the welfare check and expecting certain responsibilities in
return. Common sense. We put common sense reforms in place. We
required young men and women between the ages of 10 and 19 to go to
school; and in the case of chronic truants, we took away that portion of

the welfare check attributable to that young man or that young woman.

Some of the young opponents of mine said, "You cannot do that, Governor. What happens if Johnny and Susie do not want to go to school?" And I said, "Tough."

Can you imagine when you were growing up and you were walking down to the kitchen table at 7:30 or 8:00 in the morning, saying to your dad or mother, or both, "I have just decided this semester I'm going to drop out of school and not go to school." My mother or father would have said, "Don't let the door hit you," as I was flying through it. It's common sense.

After starting this program, I received a letter from a young lady that said, "Governor Tommy, I thought you were the worst person in the world. My grandmother was on welfare, and my mother was on welfare with me. I had my first child when I was 13 and my second child when I was 14. I was on AFDC, and that was supposed to be my lot in life. That is what I was expected to do. You started working on welfare reform and you made me go back to school so I could get a welfare check. I went back to school and thought you were the worst person in the world. But since I have been back in school, I am getting A's and I am going to graduate from high school with honors. Then I am going on to college and I am going to graduate from college. I am going on to law school and I am going to become a lawyer."

Now, you may criticize that young lady for her choice of profession, but you have to give her a great deal of respect for what she has been able to accomplish. Her whole life has changed for the better.

I do things a little bit differently. I bring people on welfare into the Governor's mansion for dinner and give my ideas on how to change welfare to the people who are actually on it. At one of these gatherings we got one young mother started who was needing some help.

She wrote me a letter last week. She said, "Since that luncheon at the executive mansion, I want to tell you, Governor, you helped me. I got a job, and I got promoted and my two children and I are doing well. In fact, I got promoted again, and now I got transferred out of Wisconsin – which I'm not happy about – but they gave me a promotion to run the office in Phoenix, Arizona. I want you to know, Governor, that the next time you are in Phoenix, I want to take you out for lunch, and I can afford to pay for it." Isn't that what is supposed to be happening, ladies and gentlemen? That is common sense.

I also started a program called Children First. I have no time for people who bring children into this world and do not take care of them by walking away from their responsibilities. In the program Children First, the individuals who do not pay their child support are brought in front of the judge and given two choices: Either go to jail, or go to work and start paying your child support.

The guy usually raises his hand and says, "Oh, Judge, I will take choice number two, but I can't find a job." The Judge says, "Okay, we will give you 16 weeks of nonpay status to go down and clean out the brush out of the ditches or sweep the streets or be a crossing guard." You know what happens in about 10 days? Like manna from heaven, they get a job and they start paying their child support. It's nothing but common sense.

It is amazing how quickly jobs materialize. In the counties where we started the program, child support payments have increased by 150 percent. And you say, "How do all these reforms work?" In Wisconsin we have reduced our welfare caseload by 27 percent. We have taken more people off of welfare than the rest of the country combined.

When I first started, we were sending out checks totaling $47 million each and every month to AFDC recipients. This past month it dropped down below $30 million. We are saving the federal and state taxpayers – you – $17 million each and every month. We are giving people hope and opportunity and a chance to have a job and a part of the American way. That is what it is all about. That is common sense, ladies and gentlemen, that is not government sense. That is what needs to be done in this country.

Now I am undertaking the most radical program I have ever done in welfare – we are eliminating it. During the last budget we did away with the welfare department and turned it into a jobs department. And everybody has to do something in order to receive a check. Everybody. When we are fully implemented in 1997, we will call it W-2. Everybody will work, and everybody will receive a check for their work, just like every other American across this country. That is common sense.

But in order to accomplish these things we had to go to Washington on bended knee to get waivers and kiss somebody's ring to say, "Please, please give us a chance to try something that might work." I have had waivers under Reagan, Bush and Clinton, 178 waivers to try something new. Why should states and governors need waivers to try new, innovative ideas in welfare that could help people help themselves? Isn't that what it's all about? Why should we have to go to Washington and kiss somebody's ring to do what everybody wants us to do and that is to change welfare in our society and give people jobs and hope and optimism? That's what it's all about, ladies and gentlemen.

That is why I am fighting so hard for the federal government to block grant welfare funding back to the States.

The House, under the leadership of Clay Shaw, has passed a good bill, HR-4, and Senator Dole has another wonderful bill. It is probably the best bill. I am hoping that the Senate will do what is right and give states the opportunity to do what you want us to do, to make government better and give people hope.

Medicaid is another example where government sense is not working. Government sense is something like the Boren Amendment. You had Senator David Boren here yesterday speaking to you, and he did a nice job. Back in 1981, the states were forced to pay everything at cost plus a profit. We tried to change that, and they passed the Boren Amendment. Washington failed to do anything with the Boren Amendment, and now states get sued. If we do not pay enough, we get sued by the providers and have to pay more.

It has cost my own state of Wisconsin $120 million. It has opened up states to numerous lawsuits. In short, it has proven to be one of the most costly federal regulations on record. Government sense from Washington – imposing a "one size fits all" mandate – ends up costing more and accomplishing the exact opposite of what it was intended to do.

In the meantime, states have been using common sense. We had to. Medicaid costs have been increasing at an average of 20 percent a year, and they make up about 20 percent of all state spending. This leaves state budgets with ever-escalating Medicaid costs that are almost bankrupting states. We have been able to use managed care and HMO's in order to reduce our payments in the state of Wisconsin to one-half of the national average. It's just common sense.

There is ample evidence out there that states can do a much better job managing Medicaid, like welfare, which is why I am fighting so hard to get Washington to recognize the importance of sharing authority. Give us a chance at the state level to make programs more effective for the individual citizens of our states – instead of a "one size fits all" mentality. The states know what to do. Give us the freedom to do it. I cannot emphasize that enough. Do not send us block grants loaded with rules and regulations. Do not hamstring us with a new bunch of Boren Amendments. Untie the hands of the states and let us get the job done.

Congress has proposed capping Medicaid growth at about 5 percent a year, for a net savings of $182 billion over the next seven years. There is no way that we can reach those kinds of savings if the states do not have the maximum flexibility to make it work. Government sense led to out-of-control Medicaid cost increases. Common sense in the states will mean a Medicaid program that will serve the people who need it for years and years to come.

It seems so simple to me – government sense does not work, common sense does. So why are we not seeing more common sense out there? Because we do not have enough people like you. Because change is difficult, it is frightening, and for those who have benefited from the way things are, change can be downright dangerous.

Let me give you an example. In the state budget I presented this year, we are taking $1 billion off of the property taxes, and we are doing it without raising any other income taxes or sales taxes. It is the largest tax cut in our state history. How did we do it? We made changes, we made cuts, and we made some tough choices. We took a good, hard look at what our state government does and what it can do without. These are the kinds of challenges we face as we work to replace government sense with common sense.

The author James T. Evans once wrote, "America is not a gift. It must be earned by each generation. It must be recreated by each member of each generation. If not, it all will be lost forever."

Every single one of you in this room believes that. That is why you are here. It is not going to be easy. Nothing worthwhile ever is. We have to be willing to take action and not just sit around wringing our hands saying, "But what if it does not work?" Can you imagine if all the people who created this great nation had felt that way? "Better not try something new, what if we fail? What if it does not work?"

That is why I am here today. I did not come to brag about Wisconsin, which I love to do, as you can tell. I came to tell you that it can be done, and there is a better way for all of us. You can reform welfare, you can manage Medicaid, you can make the tough choices, and you can balance the budget.

I look out at all of you and I see people of action from all over the country, from all walks of life. We are facing the greatest opportunity ever right now to completely reform and change government in this country. People must get involved. The special interests have had their way long enough, telling us we cannot do this and cannot do that. We have let them substitute government sense for common sense and replace community and neighborhood with centralized Washington bureaucracy.

We need to get back to some basics, back to community and family and individual responsibility, back to the days when the family budget took precedence over the government budget. That is why this is such an exciting time to be here, to be fighting for common sense, fighting to make change happen, fighting to make our nation a better place. Working together, I know we will earn the great gift we call America. I also know that if we continue our common sense principles – be you Republican, Independent, Democrat or United We Stand America – if we work together, ladies and gentlemen, we can make sure that America is stronger and better tomorrow than it is today.

God love you, and thank you so very much.

Congresswoman
Barbara Jordan

Immigration
Reform

*ROSS PEROT: We have a lot of heroes in Texas. We have a lot of peo-
ple that Texans love. But one of the most beloved people in our state is
a great lady named Barbara Jordan.*

*Former U.S. Congresswoman Barbara Jordan currently is the
Lyndon B. Johnson Centennial Chair of National Policy at the LBJ
School of Public Affairs at the University of Texas at Austin.*

*Early in her career, Professor Jordan practiced law in Houston and
she served in the Texas State Legislature. She was elected to the U.S.
House of Representatives, where she served until 1978.*

*She received her bachelor's degree from Texas Southern, her law
degree from Boston University, and she has received 31 honorary doctorate degrees.*

*While in the House of Representatives, Congresswoman Jordan was
a member of the Committee on the Judiciary, the Committee on
Government Operations, and the Steering and Policy Committee of the
Democratic Caucus.*

*In 1976 Time Magazine selected Representative Barbara Jordan as
one of its 10 Women Of The Year. And, that same year, she delivered
the keynote address at the Democratic National Convention.*

She serves on the board of directors for the Mead Corporation,

Texas Commerce Bancshares, Burlington-Northern and the Northrup-Grumman Corporation.

Professor Jordan is the recipient of numerous humanitarian and public service awards. She has a heart as big as Texas. It has been my privilege to know her for many years.

She was appointed to chair the Commission on Immigration Reform. It is a privilege to introduce Barbara Jordan, who will now discuss with us the problem of immigration reform.

Thank you very much, Ross. I appreciate your inviting me to come here and talk to you today about immigration.

I congratulate you on coming to Texas in August. I go to Washington from time to time, and they tell me it is hot there. I tell them, "If you want to know real heat, come to Texas." If you want to know heat in its actuality, chair the United States Commission on Immigration Reform. It is a hot button issue. The President appointed me as the Chair, and I am the only Presidential appointee on it. It is a congressional commission. It is a bipartisan commission. It has an even number of Republican and Democratic appointees representing every conceivable view on immigration and what to do about it.

The purpose of the commission is to make recommendations to Congress to reform immigration policy and to ensure that immigration serves the national interest.

Let me emphasize the bipartisan nature of our deliberations. The issue of immigration is not a partisan issue. Immigration is central to our American identity. The tradition of immigration continues. There are two Texans in Congress who are dealing with immigration – Lamar Smith, a Republican, and John Bryant, a Democrat. They have introduced a bill dealing with immigration reform, and they have tracked the recommendations of the commission.

Senator Alan Simpson and Senator Ted Kennedy have worked together for years to ensure bipartisan support of this issue. The President and his administration have taken a very highly activist view and stance in working to curb illegal immigration. It is going to take both the Congress and the administration to do it.

Let me tell you a bit about the commission. We were created by the Immigration Reform Act of 1990. Our mandate is to make these recommendations and to make them by 1997.

In not quite three years, the commission has held dozens of hearings all over the country. We have been in Los Angeles, Miami, Chicago, San Diego, El Paso, New York City, San Juan, Austin, Texas, Lowell, Massachusetts, Nogales, Arizona. In coming months we are going to Seattle and San Francisco and back to Texas in the winter.

We remain engaged in the mission which Congress assigned to us, but we have reached certain conclusions. I will sum up those recommendations for you.

We have concluded that a properly regulated legal immigration system is in the national interest. We support the basic framework of current policy. I said properly regulated, and I mean that. Immigration is not a right guaranteed by the U.S. Constitution to everyone anywhere in the world who thinks they want to come to the United States. Immigration is a privilege. It is a privilege granted by the people of the United States to those we choose to admit.

This is not a mere favor we grant to people because we are generous. We are a generous nation. We are saying that immigration is in our national interest. We admit that. It is in our national interest to unite families, to create economic growth and to protect those who flee persecution seeking freedom in this land of opportunity.

The commission recommendations are intended to continue the benefits of legal immigration while limiting costs, and there are costs. Good things are rarely free. These costs are often borne disproportionately by a few states, especially California, Texas, Florida, New York, Illinois, New Jersey, and Arizona.

The commission first recommended a comprehensive strategy to deter illegal immigration. We must control illegal immigration before it erodes our first commitment to legal immigration in the national interest.

The commission defines credibility in immigration policy by a simple yardstick. Those who should get in, get in. Those who should not get in are kept out. Those who should not be here are required to leave.

We, as a commission, denounce hostility toward immigrants. That is antithetical to our traditions and our national interest. We cannot sustain ourselves as a society if we condone divisiveness. We are a country of laws. For our immigration policy to make sense, it is necessary to make distinctions between those who obey the law and those who violate it. Therefore, we disagree with those who would label any effort to control illegal immigration as somehow inherently anti-immigrant. Unlawful immigration is not acceptable.

Many Americans believe this government cannot or will not manage immigration. Despite any recent improvements in border management and other immigration enforcement, the continued entry of illegal aliens fuels that perception.

The commission recommends a seven-part strategy to fight illegal immigration:

1. Better border management, including prevention of illegal entry and facilitation of legal crossings,
2. Reduction of the job magnet. We must face the fact, the reason illegal aliens come here can be summed up in three words, *they get jobs,*
3. Limits on the eligibility of illegal aliens for benefits combined with impact assistance to states and localities for unavoidable costs of emergency health care, other emergency assistance, education and criminal justice expenditures,
4. Prompt deportation procedures,
5. Preparation for migration emergencies,
6. Initiatives to reduce the causes of migration in the source country,
7. Improve the data.

One recommendation caused more debate than any other. The commission recommended the development and implementation of a better system to verify authorization to work, one that can eliminate fraud and discrimination and continue to protect our privacy and relieve businesses of unnecessary and counterproductive paperwork.

At present, employers look at one or two of 29 different documents to establish work authorization. The most common are driver's license and Social Security card, and both are easily forged.

We visited a park in Los Angeles where for $40 you could purchase counterfeits that would pass muster by any employer in this country. That is why we have such a problem of illegal immigration. Verifying work authorization is not akin to Big Brother, much as opponents of the idea would have you think it is.

We rejected out of hand any concept of a national ID card that Americans would have to carry and produce on demand. This is the United States of America; no one should be stopped and demanded,

"Papers, please." But frankly, verifying the right to work in the United States is essential to curbing unlawful immigration and the worst excesses of the underground economy.

The abuse of our economy by unlawful workers and those who hire them, the undermining of wages and working conditions we have fought so long to protect, the erosion of integrity in our Social Security system by illegal aliens – these are the things that must stop.

Speaking as someone who – one of these days, and not too far off – hopes to receive Social Security benefits, I want to be sure there is no one else out there using my number. That is why we recommend electronic validation of the Social Security number. We all provide that number to any employer. It is already used in tax withholding and Social Security withholding. Verifying that number, which most of us know by memory, would require no document, no single document, and it may not require a document at all. It should be no more difficult than it is now for you to use your credit card in making a purchase or an ATM withdrawal.

This system is not going to happen overnight. We must improve the databases of both the Social Security Administration and the Immigration and Naturalization Service. Wrong information does not help anybody. It will not happen, however, unless we recognize this process must start now, first through pilot projects, and then, if they work, through national implementation.

Earlier this year the commission made recommendations on legal immigration reform. After examining the question from every angle – immigration and population, immigration and the environment, immigration and the labor force – we concluded that our focus must be as an overriding issue to the national interest. We concluded that legal immigration is in the national interest if it is properly regulated. We propose reforms to ensure that it will be well regulated.

First and foremost, as a nation, we need to set priorities. We believe there are three priorities:

1. Reunification of nuclear families,
2. Admission of highly-skilled workers needed to increase competitiveness of U.S. businesses and workers,
3. Refugee admissions that reaffirm our traditional commitments to provide refuge to the persecuted.

The number of immigrants should flow from these priorities. What that translates into is a gradual reduction of admissions during the next five to eight years. The reduction should be gradual because we have some unfinished business to address.

For family-based immigration, the priority has to be the nuclear family. First, spouses and minor children of U.S. citizens. Second, parents of U.S. citizens. Third, spouses and minor children of legal permanent residents. Our aim is to ensure that every nuclear family member is able to reunite with his U.S. relatives within one year of application. That is not currently the case.

There are more than 1.1 million spouses and minor children of legal residents who now wait in line. Under current law these nuclear families, mothers, fathers and young children, will be separated for years. That is not in the national interest, and that is not right.

The commission recommends 550,000 family visas per year until we have eliminated that backlog. This should take about five or six years. Thereafter, 400,000 visas per year should be sufficient to admit all nuclear families expeditiously.

In effect, what we recommend is to stop the extended families, adult children, brothers and sisters, and redirect those visas toward expediting admissions of nuclear family members.

It is not that we believe immigration of extended family members are harmful, but we do not have unlimited numbers of immigrant visas. The commission believes we must direct the numbers toward our priorities. I do not think anyone in this audience would argue against the fact that our basic family value – a reunification of wife and husband, parent and young child, elderly parent with the child who can help in his or her old age – must take precedence.

Even nuclear family reunification is not without obligations on the part of those who benefit from immigration. The commission believes that those who sponsor new immigrants have responsibility for ensuring that their relatives will not become burdens on taxpayers. You and I should not have to pay for someone else's family reunification.

Sponsors now sign an affidavit pledging support for the new immigrant. That affidavit has moral force. That should be enough, but it is not. That affidavit ought to have legal force.

The sponsor must be legally responsible. We also recognize that circumstances change. If a subsequent illness, death or accident renders a sponsor unable to fulfill these responsibilities and the immigrant is aged or infirm, then he or she should be eligible for our safety net programs.

With regard to employment-based immigration, the commission concluded that there is a two fold need for policy reform. The first reason is to enhance global competitiveness, not only for American business, but also for the American worker. We reject protectionism for highly-skilled specialized workers. The American worker who is educated, trained, professional, and experienced will thrive on competition anywhere in the world. Moreover, the entry of these foreign workers creates economic opportunities for American workers.

To give one example, we heard testimony from a company that intended to develop a new product line that would create thousands of new manufacturing and sales jobs. The one person with specialized knowledge for this new product was foreign and had done his doctoral dissertation on the subject. With his expertise the company embarked on this new venture, saving months of planning and gaining a competitive advantage over its foreign competition. Had the petition for the admission of this person with specialized knowledge been denied, the opportunity would have been lost, and along with it jobs for many Americans.

Much as we support specialized immigration of this type, the commission finds no national interest in continuing to import lesser-skilled and unskilled workers to compete in the most vulnerable parts of our labor force.

Many American workers do not now have adequate job prospects, and they are not improving. With welfare reform, many more unskilled American workers will enter the labor market. We should make their task easier to find employment—not harder with an oversupply of unskilled foreign labor.

Also, in our skills-based immigration system, we should not have artificially high ceilings. We recommend 100,000 visas per year, about 10 percent above current demand. We recommend examining this level every three to five years, and raising or lowering it to match economic realities.

The commission is also examining the future of our refugee policy. Later this year we will make a full report on refugee programs as well as on migration emergencies. We will pay particular attention to our experiences with Haiti and Cuba last summer. We recommend that the target be placed into law for resettling at least 50,000 refugees a year in this country, with specific provisions for emergency increases as necessary.

We believe in sustaining the humanitarian leadership of the United States in the world where there are 25 million refugees. A commitment to resettle at least a certain number of these refugees should be written into law.

That is not to say that resettlement in the United States is the best option. Restoring the fabric of torn nations so that people can stay home is the best. That remains our best solution for the world's refugees.

Let me speak for a moment about ethnic strife. Look at Bosnia and look at Rwanda. We live in a world where the kind of country we have built here, this land, is an exception rather than a rule.

The United States of America is the most successful multi-ethnic nation in history. We have troubles, and I am the last person in the world who would say that we are perfect. As a nation we have achieved a kind of perfection because of our founding, universal principle that we are all created equal, regardless of race, regardless of religion, and regardless of national ancestry.

When the Declaration of Independence was written, the Constitution was adopted, and the Bill of Rights was added, they all applied almost exclusively to Anglo-Saxon men who held property on the East Coast. Not so today. That I am here today, female and black, is testament to that. This self-evident principle applies to everybody in this room – everybody in this room. This level of progress happens in America not by accident. Immigration played an important role in broadening our view of ourselves.

Our history has not been an easy history. There have always been those who despise newcomers. The history of American immigration policy is full of racism and ethnic prejudice – the Know-Nothings, the Chinese Exclusion Act, and country quotas are just a few examples. Even before the Revolution there was an eminent person like Benjamin Franklin who feared that the Germans going into Pennsylvania would not become English. The German immigrants did not become English, and they did not make Germans out of Pennsylvanians. Instead, they became Americans. And so did immigrants from Ireland, Scotland and other parts of Europe, the Chinese, the Koreans, the Mexicans, the Cubans, and the Haitians.

We must not forget this history because it is a key to our future. The United States has united immigrants and their descendants from all over the world around a commitment to democratic ideals and constitutional principles. Those ideals and principles have been embraced by persons from an extraordinary range of ethnic and religious backgrounds. This is partly because we are founded on religious and cultural diversity within a framework of national unity. We are a nation that seeks unity, not uniformity. This is what we seek.

There is a word for this process that I am talking about, and that word is *Americanization*. That word earned a bad reputation when it was stolen by racists and xenophobes in the 1920s, but it is our word and we are taking it back. It must mean what it says. *Americanization* means the process of becoming an American. It means civic incorporation, becoming a part of the polity, becoming one of us.

It does not mean conformity. We are more than a melting pot. We are a kaleidoscope where every turn of history refracts new light on that old promise.

Naturalization is an important and vital step in the process. Immigration obligations are imposed because we are committed to immigration in the national interest. Those who come – who choose to come here – must embrace our common core of American values.

There is a common core of our civic culture that imposes obligations on the rest of us. Immigrants must be encouraged and assisted in learning to communicate with all of us, to the greatest extent possible in our common language, American English. This does not mean abandoning the old ways, it means enhancing them.

We must renew civic education in the teaching of American history to all Americans. We must vigorously enforce the laws against hate crimes and discrimination. We must remind ourselves as we illustrate to newcomers what makes us America.

We are a nation of immigrants dedicated to the rule of law. That is our history, and that is our challenge to ourselves. We, on the United States Commission on Immigration Reform, are trying to be true to that history and to meet that challenge with specific recommendations which we will make and have made to the Congress, because immigration is so critically important to our future. We cannot evade the responsibility to make the necessary choices to reform immigration. It is literally a matter of who we are as a nation and who we become as a people – *e pluribus unum* – out of many, one. One people, the American people.

The Issues

Foreign Policy

Senator
Sam Nunn

The Responsibilities of the
World's Last Superpower

ROSS PEROT: Our next speaker is Senator Sam Nunn from Perry,
Georgia.

He attended Georgia Tech, Emory University, and Emory Law
School where he graduated with honors. He served in the Coast
Guard. He has two children and a wonderful wife Colleen.

Senator Nunn first entered politics as a member of the Georgia State
House of Representatives in 1968. Throughout his public career,
Senator Nunn has focused his efforts on controlling spending, reducing
the threat of nuclear war, streamlining the federal bureaucracy, devel-
oping a comprehensive anti-drug strategy, combating waste, fraud and
abuse in government programs and agencies, and strengthening
America's defenses.

Recently he has been involved in passing sweeping reforms in the
Defense Department to improve management and reduce waste. He
has developed new methods to reduce the risk of accidental nuclear
war, and he was instrumental in the passage of national service legisla-
tion. He has led bipartisan efforts to support dismantling nuclear
weapons in the Soviet republics. He continues to press for support of
the efforts by the Soviet republics to become democracies and develop
free market economics.

He is consistently ranked as one of the most effective Senators in Washington. He has been elected three times to the Senate by the people in Georgia by margins of 80% or more. He was unopposed in 1990.

The Almanac of American Politics describes him as one of the most powerful figures in American government, and one of the key players in American politics.

I think the nicest compliment I ever read about Senator Nunn came from a newspaper in Georgia. It said, "Public events shift and change, but unlike some who gained prominence in Washington, Sam Nunn keeps on being Sam Nunn." He is still in touch with his constituents.

Senator Nunn is with us today to discuss a vital issue: the duties and responsibilities of the United States of America as the world's last superpower. We are honored to have Senator Sam Nunn with us today.

Thank you. Thank you very much, Ross, and thank you to the dedicated citizens of United We Stand America for making this unique event possible today, tonight and tomorrow.

When you read American history, our founding fathers made every effort to design a system of government in which voters would be able to choose the wisest, most able and the most honest leaders. They were very concerned though about whether they were going to be able to pull it off. They were concerned about the vast territory. They were concerned about voters not having enough information, and they were concerned about travel time. They were concerned about direct elections in a vast continent with very little information. They shied away at the beginning of our Republic from direct elections at the national level.

Today we have direct elections, and we have massive communication where anybody in politics can speak all over the world. They can cover the United States in an instant, talking to every group. There is no danger today of not being able to communicate. Why then do we have so much disillusionment throughout America? I think the problem is there are so many charges and countercharges, so much partisanship, so many negative 30-second ads and sound bites, and I must say, media hype, that obscures, many times, the issues. This confusion divides and discourages our people.

Ross, when you brought out the charts on the deficit in 1992 and you had so many citizens gathered here and throughout the country who responded to that in-depth discussion of the real fiscal challenges facing America, the public proved that they were interested in in-depth issues. And the public proved they wanted something more than bumper sticker discussions. I hope this meeting today and tomorrow will establish that our citizens want to move beyond empty slogans on a range of issues that face America. Our citizens want to move beyond political posturing, media hype and bumper sticker mentality.

I believe – as you do, because you are here and you are interested and you are involved – that America's challenges must be met with dialogue and debate. It must be civic discourse and civic debate and civic participation, thereby assuring a much more in-depth understanding of America's challenges and America's choices. If that happens, and it is happening, I believe that you are going to be able to do something very important. You are going to be able to hold those of us in public office accountable for our actions.

You will be hearing from Senator Pete Domenici. Pete is going to discuss the efforts underway in the Congress today to balance the budget. I know he is also going to mention a subject close to my heart because we worked for years together on a bipartisan basis. He is a Republican and I am a Democrat, but we have come up with a plan to reform our tax code. I am not going to discuss it today, but it meets the description that Pete Peterson gave you. It is a progressive and fair consumption tax, and I hope that you listened carefully to Senator Domenici's explanation.

Ross and all the people putting together this conference found out the hard way how dangerous it is to invite United States Senators to anything because we never are able to predict our schedules. It is one of the perils of public office. But inviting Senators to speak has more than one danger. It goes back in history and it is still true today.

I am reminded of a story of the Senator from New York that was called on to introduce President William Howard Taft many years ago. This Senator's name was Chauncey Depew, and he gave President Taft a glowing, effusive introduction. As the President was beckoned to the stand by Chauncey Depew, all 300 pounds of him started coming to the podium. Depew looked at the President weighing 300 pounds with a great protruding stomach, and he said, "Ladies and gentlemen, our

President is pregnant with integrity." And, of course, the audience started laughing. He said, "Ladies and gentlemen, our President is pregnant with courage."

About that time the President took the podium and he said, "May I respond?" Rubbing his protruding stomach he said, "Yes, if it's a girl, we'll call her Integrity. If it's a boy, we'll call him Courage. But if, as I suspect, it's simply gas, we'll name it Chauncey Depew."

So Senators have dangerous messages, but Ross has asked me to address you today, as he just related to you, on the responsibility of the world's last superpower, America. What are the obligations of America in 1995 and the years to come? Let me give you a few from my perspective today.

Obligation number one is to recognize that the world has undergone revolutionary change, not evolutionary change, but revolutionary change. Vaclav Havel, who spent years in prison under the Communist dictatorship in Czechoslovakia and then became President of the Czech Republic, said a couple of years ago, but it is true again today, "The world has changed so rapidly, we don't even have time to be astonished."

What are these changes? The Berlin wall is down. Germany is united. Eastern Europe and the Baltics are at last free. They are seeking membership in the European Union and in the NATO alliance. The Warsaw Pact is gone. No more line of confrontation and danger confronts Europe and divides Europe.

The Soviet Union, a vast empire, has disintegrated. Russia, its successor state, is broke. The people are disillusioned, but they are struggling toward a market economy. Two steps forward, one step backwards, and sometimes the other way around. The struggle is on, and it is going to take a long time. They are also struggling for some semblance of democracy. It is up to them. Where we can help on the margins, we should, but it will primarily be up to them. We should be pulling for them in both respects.

China, a vast nation, has undergone tremendous change in the last decade. They do have a continued authoritarian government but with market reform. In some sections of China they have experienced the fastest economic growth rates of any country in the world at any point in history. It is inevitable their influence will increase in the years ahead. There will be questions of succession and questions of stability. We need to make sure we keep an eye on China.

In the Middle East something occurred that we never thought would happen – Israel and the PLO are in dialogue. The fact that they are reaching agreement on difficult issues is amazing progress.

In South Africa, a man who spent 26 years in prison because of the color of his skin and because of his quest for equality, is now President of that country with an approval rating of something over 60 percent by the white population of South Africa. How is that for a wonderful miracle?

Even the long suffering Irish appear to be moving toward a moratorium on the killing and terrorism that has plagued that divided country for so long.

Ten years ago we had two nuclear superpowers that confronted each other all over the globe – the United States and the Soviet Union. It was a world of very high risk, but also very high stability, due primarily to the dangers of escalation to nuclear war. It was a balance of terror. Thank God we are past that era and hopefully it will never return. The situation has turned literally upside down. The danger of nuclear war is very low today, but so is stability. It is as though our house has come through an earthquake relatively unscathed, but is now being eaten away by termites.

In a strange, ironic and tragic sense – as we see on TV, hear on the radio, and read in the newspaper every day – the world has been made safer, it seems, for racial, ethnic, tribal, class, and religious savagery and barbarity. Such tragedy has come to the people of Bosnia, Somalia, Rwanda, Haiti, Sudan, and others around the globe.

So, what is the first obligation of the United States of America as the world's last superpower? We must recognize that when empires disintegrate, challenges are inevitable, and all these challenges are not going to go away.

The second obligation is we must recognize that the United States is the only superpower on the globe today. We have many commentators today describing the atrocities taking place around the world. On television we see the horrible scenes of man's inhumanity to man. And we have many people and commentators asking the question, "What about the United States' military? Why don't we send in the military and stop the killing?"

That question is asked frequently, and I think a little perspective is in order. For 50 years our military strength was our defensive shield against aggression by the Soviet Union. Our offensive sword was our free society, our energetic and productive people, and our free enterprise system with its incentives and free flow of ideas. What about our military today? First, we must remain strong. The world is still a very dangerous place.

When we ask about what our military is doing today, let me just give you a few examples of what our military is doing.

First, we are the only nation in the world that can deter the use of weapons of mass destruction. That is a fundamental, vital interest that we continue to have.

Second, we are the only nation that can lead and coordinate the worldwide effort to avoid the spread of weapons of mass destruction to the Third World and to terrorist groups. We have that as our number one security challenge in my view, and I think it will be so for the next 5, 10, 15, even 20 years. Keep in mind, this is the first time in history that we have had an empire disintegrate still possessing some 30,000 or more nuclear weapons and over 40,000 tons of chemical weapons. No one even knows how much in the way of biological weapons exist. There are tens of thousands of scientists who know how to make these weapons of mass destruction. They are in great demand in Third World renegade-type countries and some of these scientists do not know where their next paycheck is coming from.

This is a very dangerous situation that will have to occupy, in my view, the top of our list of security challenges. We are the only nation that can, with our allies in South Korea, deter and defeat aggression from North Korea or come to the rescue of nations in the Middle East that are the world's primary source of oil. We are the only nation whose military presence can give the Japanese the confidence to obviate any urge they might have in the future to develop nuclear weapons and go on a real rearmament program that would frighten their neighbors. We are the only country that can give that kind of confidence to our allies and friends, the Japanese. We are the only nation that can help preserve the stability in Europe by the presence of American forces there, dramatically reduced in number, but still very significant in terms of their psychological and political impact. We are the only nation that can keep open the sea lanes of communication on which not only our trade, but the trade of the world, depends.

So our second obligation as a superpower is to recognize that these are our vital interests and our unique responsibilities. No other nation can play this role that is essential for world stability. We must keep this in mind as we resist – I hope in most cases – the pressure for U.S. military forces to become involved in civil war and civil conflict all over the globe. That is not our primary role as a superpower. Our allies also must recognize this as they assume a greater responsibility to deal with the world's turmoil. We are going to need help.

Our third obligation as a superpower is that while we must lead and will lead, we cannot do it all. We must strengthen our alliances in Europe – we did not win the Cold War alone. We were the lead player on the block – no doubt that without us it would not have been done – but we were not the only ones. We had a strong alliance named NATO. We had a country in East Asia that was growing and was very strong, Japan, that played a big role with its economic strength and its example. So, we had allies all over the globe. We must strengthen those alliances today not only in Europe, but in the Middle East and Asia as well. And, yes, we must calmly and diplomatically and very firmly insist that our allies do their part militarily, economically and politically.

Our fourth obligation as a superpower is to distinguish between what the United Nations can do and what the United Nations cannot do. The United Nations can carry out many humanitarian missions, and they can do pretty well at what we call *peacekeeping* – that is helping keep the peace once the parties arrive at peace, and once the parties no longer believe that it is profitable for them to fight a war. That is what the United Nations can do and has done successfully.

What the United Nations cannot do, and we are seeing that every day in Bosnia, is inject itself with lightly armed forces in the middle of a conflict where the parties continue to believe that war will lead to their aims and goals. That is what the United Nations cannot do, and that is what we must prevent the United Nations from doing again. The U.N. is not equipped, is not financed, and is not trained for that kind of responsibility.

Finally, our fifth obligation as a superpower is to remain a world leader. This is something that can only be done by strengthening America at home. We have the continuing opportunity and the continuing responsibility to demonstrate to ourselves and, yes, to the world, that our ideas of liberty and justice and our respect for human rights and human dignity can work in America, a nation more diverse than any other developed nation in the world.

Now, this will not be done by legislation. It will not be done by Presidential decree or even by military force, but rather by individuals practicing these virtues in their own communities and in their own daily lives. When the world looks at America today, the principal indictment and criticism of America is not the number of aircraft carriers we have or do not have in the Pacific, or the number of troops we have in Europe, or even the decision-making process surrounding Bosnia and other questions. These are not the only – or the principal – criticisms.

The rest of the world asks the United States very tough questions that we all should ponder in our duties every day. The questions are: How can the United States remain a superpower when one-third of the American children are born out of wedlock? How can America remain a superpower when one-third or maybe even more of American fathers are not willing to assume the moral, legal or financial responsibility for their children? How can America remain a superpower when millions of these children have never had a loving, caring bond with another human being? How will we respond and how will we handle it when these children enter the cycle of drug abuse, of school dropout, of teenage pregnancy and violent crime and imprisonment?

We are in that cycle and that cycle is getting worse. The world asks America today, "Will America be an example of dynamic diversity or a dream eroded because of drugs, because of crime, because of disease and because of despair?"

America's response to these challenges will depend on how we answer the question recently posed by our colleague in the Senate, Pat Moynihan, when he asked, "Will we be the first species that forgets how to raise our young?" That is a question for all of us today.

Let me close today not by pretending I have all the answers to these questions, but with three observations. First, the most important line of defense today for our nation is not a line through Europe or the line through the Middle East or a line in Asia. Our most important line today is the line of students going to the classrooms of America in our schools.

Second, we must reach out to the millions of neglected and abused children who desperately need someone who cares. Government must play a role, but it will not be the decisive role. We all understand this fact because we have seen government programs fail time and time again. This is a battle that will have to be fought primarily one child at a time on an individual basis.

Third observation: The real heroes today in America, in my book, are not our Hollywood stars, nor our sports stars, nor our political stars, nor even our business stars. Our real heroes are those who are giving their own time and energy, extending a hand to a lonely or abused child, teaching them to read, or even just pitch a baseball, or just listening, being a friend, showing them that someone on this planet really cares.

I recently heard a story on the radio that really, really hit home to me. It happened in that war-torn country we call Bosnia, in its capital, Sarajevo. But I think it has meaning in Dallas. It has meaning in Houston. It has meaning in LA, New York, Atlanta and all over our country.

A young reporter covering the conflict saw a little girl shot by a sniper. The back of her head was literally torn off. A man was holding her on the street in his lap. The reporter threw down his pad and pencil, stopped being a journalist for a few minutes, helped the man get the little girl in his car which was parked nearby, and started rushing her to the hospital.

The man holding the bleeding child said to him as he was driving frantically, "Hurry, my friend, my child is still alive." A minute or so later, "Hurry, my friend, my child is still warm. Hurry, my friend, my child is still alive. Oh, my God, hurry, my friend, my child is getting cold." When they got to the hospital, the young girl had died. As they were in the lavatory washing the blood from their clothes, the man who had been holding the child looked at the reporter and said, "This is going to be the most difficult job I have ever had, telling her father that his little sweetheart is dead. It's going to be heartbreaking for him."

The reporter was amazed. He looked up and said, "I thought she was your child." The man said, "No, but aren't they all our children? Aren't they all our children?"

Yes, the world is watching America. They are not just watching the President or the Congress or the political candidates. They are not just watching our military forces. They are watching our cities and our towns and our villages to see if we will stop America's cultural erosion. They are watching to see how much we value our own children.

So I would end by saying our most important responsibility as a superpower today in America is to our children. By saving our children, we save ourselves and we save America.

God bless you all. Thank you.

Political Party Leaders

Democrats

Thomas "Mack" McLarty

ROSS PEROT: *Our next speaker is Mack McLarty. He is a special representative of the President of the United States and a lifelong friend of President Clinton. He served as the White House Chief of Staff for 18 months.*

After serving as student body president at the University of Arkansas, Mr. McLarty was elected to the Arkansas House of Representatives at the age of 28. He later served as Chairman of the Arkansas State Democratic Party. He served as Treasurer for the successful gubernatorial elections of Senator David Pryor and President Clinton. Then he became the Chairman of the Board of Arkla Gas, one of our country's largest natural gas companies.

Besides his work with Arkla Gas, Mr. McLarty helped transform a five-generation family business, McLarty Companies, into one of the South's largest transportation companies. He and his wife, Donna, have two sons.

Mack McLarty brings good judgment and common sense to the White House in solving problems. I have had the privilege of working with Mack McLarty, and he is a man of absolute integrity.

Mr. McLarty did not fly on a government airplane to get to Dallas

*today. He flew on a commercial airline. He is a busy man, and he came
down to visit with the American people as the representative of the
President of the United States.*

Let us give him a big welcome.

R oss, thank you for a very warm, a very gracious, and a very personal introduction. As Ross noted, he and I grew up in communities only a few miles apart. Long before I ever came to Washington, I
developed a respect for Ross and his leadership skills.

Those of you with United We Stand America have helped focus the
national attention on issues at the very center of American politics, and
that focus is here to stay. As you very well know, these issues are difficult and complex, and addressing them in a serious way is long over-
due. More than anything else, they demand careful attention. A wise
person once commented, "Too often we enjoy the comfort of opinion
without the discomfort of thought."

My purpose here today is to visit with you about some of those topics. I thank you for that opportunity and I applaud you in seeking solutions rather than just pointing fingers at problems. While we do face
some real problems, quite truthfully, here in America we have a lot to
be encouraged about. The economy is up and the deficit is down. Over
the last two years we have had a very strong investment-led recovery.

As a fourth generation in a family business, I am encouraged about
the economic fundamentals. From an international perspective, I think
we can all be grateful that no missiles are pointed at the children of
our country for the first time since the dawning of the nuclear age.

I am pleased that our policies have helped lay a foundation for economic growth. We obviously need to remember that ultimately it is the
private sector that must grow the economy and create jobs for the people of our country. My hat is off to you here, and all of those in the private sector, because you created the jobs, sold the products, provided
the services, and invested in that new plant or equipment. You are the
ones who toughed out a recession and fought to penetrate markets and
are working to train your work forces for tomorrow.

There are serious problems remaining. All of you know this is
clearly a time of profound change. We all know there is much to be
done. We must face that, even as the deficit declines and the economy

as a whole flourishes, too many of our people simply are not feeling the benefits. Most families are working harder for less, often holding down two jobs. They are having less time with their families and feeling that they may not be able to pass on to posterity a rising standard of living. That is largely why we are all here today.

Beneath the sometimes archaic policy discussions and the heated rhetoric, there is a real desire by all of us here to promote policies that result in something very real and very positive – an economy that provides opportunities for working families, an economy that offers everyone an opportunity to make a positive, constructive contribution to society.

After all, what most people really want is very understandable – a good life for themselves and a better life for their children and their grandchildren. Let me be candid with you. There are areas of honest and honorable disagreement between the President and Ross Perot, but on the whole, I would submit for your consideration that the similarities are perhaps greater than you think. There is a fundamental agreement in many ways on some of the broad economic philosophy. I think both the President and Ross understand that to lay the foundation for a strong private sector, we must really close two deficits – a budget deficit and a deficit in education.

Let me start with the pivotal issue that United We Stand America did so much to raise the profile of in 1992 – the festering in the serious problem of the budget deficit. Let me promise you, the nation heard you. The President took only 27 days upon entering office before he went to the nation with a major, line-by-line, deficit reduction plan. Whether you agree with all the points in it, it has reduced the deficit and we did act. We still have farther to go, but we are off to a good start. Let me just provide the perspective for you and consider what has happened.

At the beginning of 1993, the deficit was $290 billion, the highest ever. By the end of 1993, it went down to about $255 billion. By the end of 1994, it had been lowered to $203 billion, and by the end of this year, it will be down to $160 billion.

In three years the deficit has nearly been cut in half, down three consecutive years. That is the first time that has happened since Truman was President. That is good progress – from $290 billion to $160 billion.

Both Paul Voelker and Alan Greenspan noted that the reduction has helped to lower interest rates and spur the economy. Thousands of Americans and American families bought new homes or refinanced their homes when interest rates went down. This not only made their todays better, but their tomorrows will be more financially secure.

Cutting the deficit from $290 billion to $160 billion by the end of this year is progress. I know what you are thinking – a $160 billion deficit is still far too large. On behalf of the President of the United States, let me say, "We agree." For the first time perhaps in this era, both the President and the congressional majority have laid out balanced budget plans so we can get to zero.

The main issue now is no longer whether we are going to get to zero, but how. I think if we use order and discipline and common sense – that got us moving in the right direction – we can move from $160 billion to zero. I think that it can be done without slashing education or technology or research. I think it can be done without compromising our children's future regarding unsafe drinking water or polluted lakes and rivers.

I think one area that unites the President with the budget that United We Stand laid out in 1992 is that both approaches believe we can balance the budget while still finding the necessary spending cuts. We need to invest more in education and the skills of our people. In a constantly changing economy, I think you know that education is the real key to opportunity, because in so many cases, what you earn depends on what you learn.

I know Ross feels that way from his work in leading educational reform in Texas in the 1980s. Then Governor Clinton implemented similar educational reforms during this same period.

My point is we need to make sure that as we balance the budget, we preserve and enhance the investments in education and training. Your plan showed that and our plan shows that. I think the majority of the American people believe we can do it and that we must do it. As Ross Perot wrote, "Where will this nation be 20 years from now if we do not continue to make important public investment?"

Let me quickly turn to Medicare and let me be very clear – to preserve Medicare for our future generations, the President has strengthened and will continue to strengthen the Medicare trust fund.

Despite the claims of some, the President's balanced budget plan – the administration's plans that we are putting forward – will leave the trust fund in better shape than it has been in 12 of the last 20 years. We can and we must address the Medicare trust fund; we are trying to do precisely that. But I think we can do this without the trust fund going bankrupt and without finding new savings by raising out-of-pocket costs for tens of millions of Medicare recipients. I certainly do not think we need Medicare savings that could drive nearly 500,000 elderly Americans into poverty to pay for a tax reduction.

So I would submit to you for your consideration that we can and we will reduce Medicare spending. Accompanying the reductions should be new long-term care options, more plan choices for beneficiaries, aggressive pursuit of fraud and abuse, insurance reform, and important new insurance affordability protection for small businesses and working families. For changes in Medicare, I would submit to you, we should use order and discipline and common sense.

Let me make one more point about the economy. We believe there is another path to rising income that our nation must take – expanded trade. Of course, in this area there has been disagreement between our administration and United We Stand America, and I am well aware of that. The fact is that the President believed in and fought hard for NAFTA and GATT. He believes that you cannot turn your back on the tide of global trade. Our best option to make the new global economy work for our people is to create high wage export jobs.

We disagree on these trade agreements and we respect and understand your views. Our goals of providing good jobs through exports are very much the same – a level playing field for America's goods and services.

Obviously, in fair competition, we believe America can prosper and win. That is what our trade policy is about. That is why we have fought successfully to open Japanese markets to our automobiles and auto parts. We need to try to continue to work together on this issue. Our belief is that economic opportunity must also be married with community strength and personal responsibility.

A friend of mine once served on an urban school board. I asked him, "If you could wave a magic wand and have one thing to benefit education, what would that one thing be?" Without hesitation he said, "Parents." In the 1940s some of the top problems in our schools were talking, chewing gum, and making noise. Today they are drug abuse, alcohol abuse, teenage smoking, and teen pregnancy. I certainly under-

stand my friend's answer. That is why whatever we do in education, training, and welfare reform, we must link opportunity with responsibility.

I would submit to you that work and responsibility are not
Republican or Democratic values; they are American values. No child
in this country should grow up without them.

In 1993 we proposed and passed a tax cut for 15 million working
families that rewards work over welfare. We also collected a record
level of child support. United We Stand America knows as well as any
organization, that real reform means changing the way we do business
in Washington. The voices heard should not only be those of the special interests, but those who speak for the public interest.

United We Stand America has helped champion the pressing need
for political and governmental reform – make no mistake about that. I
applaud you and I encourage you to keep it up. We must never let the
narrow interest drown out the national interest. That is why we should
press forward in a nonpartisan way for real campaign finance and
lobby reform.

President Clinton and Speaker Gingrich have both indicated a willingness to work together on this important issue. Our proposal has
been on the table. I think you would agree with me it is time now for
Congress to act. Until Congress does act, the President will continue to
move forward to change the system.

In other areas we have taken action to change government and try
to reform Washington. All of us want our government to be more efficient. We have reduced the size of government by about 150,000 positions, mostly by attrition. The total reduction plan will be about
270,000 positions, making government the smallest it has been since
the 1960s.

There is a big government reform measure though that should not
wait. The President has consistently called for it – a line item veto. A
line item veto would let the President cut the pork out of the budget. I
suspect we are all for that. This is not a partisan issue. Presidents
Reagan and Bush, as well as your organization, have supported this.
No matter what party the President belongs to, no matter what party
controls Congress, the line item veto would be good for America.

If you run into some members of the House of Representatives over
this weekend, you might ask them what is holding them back from
passing the line item veto this year.

Let me close very quickly with an issue that is close to my heart. In 1993, I came to Washington as a business person, as a father, and as an American who was fortunate enough to grow up in a small town with strong values and real dreams. I wanted those values and dreams to still be around for the next generation.

Today, I close by discussing an important contribution that I feel you can make in this year to come. You have performed a real public service by elevating real and difficult issues. Clearly our politics are being poisoned by the tone of the discourse that makes it almost impossible to discuss our problems in a calm, reasonable, and careful way. Too often the din of discord substitutes for the civic drama of thoughtful debates.

What is really at stake in this debate is not who is up and who is down or who is the best positioned. What is really at stake are the values that brought us here and the vision that will lead us forward. That is what is really at stake. What is at stake is the sense of community that Ross Perot and I grew up with in Texarkana and Hope. I suspect many of you grew up around this wonderful country with similar upbringings.

It seems to me at that time there was less of *them and us* and much more of *we are all in this together*. That is what we have lost – at least in some measure – in my judgment. Whether we get anywhere as a nation depends on if we will do what it takes to get that kind of sense of community back.

I want to call on you to consider participating in holding those of us in government to high standards. Do not let us get away with name calling. Do not let leaders divide our country by race or class or religion. Do not let people pretend they love our country while hating our government. If you do this, then I think United We Stand America will be recognized, not only for the good work it does on the budget and lobby reform and Medicare, but on something more important, more fundamental – helping to restore the soul of our functioning democracy.

Thank you very much for your contribution to the public debate. I am honored to be with you.

Senator Christopher Dodd

ROSS PEROT: *Our next speaker is Senator Christopher Dodd. He is the General Chairman of the Democratic National Committee. He is currently serving his third term as a Senator from Connecticut.*

Senator Dodd was born in Willimantic, Connecticut. He is the son of the late Senator Thomas and Grace Dodd.

After graduating from Providence College in 1966, he entered the Peace Corps, serving two years in the Dominican Republic.

He served in the U.S. Army Reserve from 1969 to 1975.

He graduated from the University of Louisville School of Law in 1972, and practiced law in New London, Connecticut.

Senator Dodd was elected to Congress in 1974, and served three terms. He was elected to the Senate in 1980.

He is a member of the Foreign Relations Committee, the Banking Committee, Housing and Urban Affairs Committee, Labor and Human Resources Committee, Budget Committee and the Rules and Administration Committee.

In 1983 he founded the Senate Children's Caucus.

Senator Dodd lives in East Haddam, Connecticut.

In his role as Chairman of the Democratic Party, Senator Dodd is going to explain to us tonight what the Democratic Party will do to prepare our country for the 21st century.

Let's welcome Senator Chris Dodd.

T hank you all very, very much. And thank you, Ross Perot, for that very gracious and thoughtful introduction. Let me, first of all, express my deep appreciation to Ross Perot and to all of you who have come from all across the country. I left Washington a few hours ago. As I know you heard from colleagues of mine, we were up late last evening voting. But I want to tell you that I am deeply impressed with this audience and the fact that you have been here all day. You are now listening to the seventeenth speaker this evening, and you deserve a special award.

I had a very wonderful friend who served in Congress, and he is not well these days, but maybe he is listening in Arizona. If he is, I would like to give him a big *Hello*. Mo Udall was one of the most delightful Members of Congress to ever serve – a great human being and a great Democrat. Mr. Udall said one time, when he was the seventeenth speaker, that everything had already been said, but not everyone had said it. And so, my friends, I am here this evening to add the seventeenth voice to this gathering today.

Last fall the Democrats received a rude awakening – a wake-up call, to put it mildly. Perhaps the only good thing I can say that came out of it is that I am now the only Democrat on Capitol Hill that gets to be called "Mr. Chairman" these days. I can say this because I am the chairman of the Democratic National Committee.

Let me begin by thanking all of you, as I said a moment ago, for inviting me here this evening. This is an important event for our country. Others said not to come and that maybe I should not be a part of this. Well, let me tell you, when Ross Perot called me on the phone, I accepted immediately. I welcomed the opportunity to appear before a group of Americans who care about the future of their country, and I thank you.

This also marks, in my view, one of the few times in recent memory that people of different political persuasions and stripes have been brought together in one place, not to debate and argue and bicker, but to talk plainly with one another about our dreams and visions and hopes for our country. I welcome that opportunity. Ross Perot made this happen, and he deserves credit for it. He believes tirelessly that government is the business of all citizens, not just public officials. I agree with him on that score.

People have become uninterested and disillusioned. To many of them, the challenges that we all face in this country seem too daunting, the solutions far too elusive, and the public debate far too defensive to enter the arena to try to make a difference. I love the fact that you are not part of that crowd.

To your great credit, you have decided that the system needs to be changed. On issues like deficit reduction, you have already made a significant difference in this country. That is a sign, in my view, of your patriotism; and I am proud as an American to be in your company this evening.

Let me also express my gratitude to Bob Davidson, the state director for Connecticut of United We Stand America, and my folks here from Connecticut. We met a few weeks ago and talked about this meeting, and I am grateful to them for giving me an opportunity to meet and have a good, respectful, reasoned conversation about our common agendas. I am confident that this evening and this discussion will be no different.

I not only want to speak with you this evening about the future that I see for my own party, the Democratic Party, but far more important, I want to speak to you as well about the future of our country. Because, fundamentally, I believe that what is good for our country is good for the Democratic Party.

Tonight I am going to do something that may seem like heresy to some, an act of political heresy. Except for this reference, you will not hear the word "Republican" cross my lips. Maybe that is not what I ought to be doing or what you might expect from the chairman of the Democratic National Committee.

I am a lifelong Democrat who believes in my party's values of opportunity, equal justice and compassion. Values that have made my party the most enduring political party in the history of this nation, and the same values that today are being sorely tested in the corridors of power. In the spirit with which this gathering has been convened, I say, "Let us put partisan politics aside for a few minutes. Let us raise our eyes from the partisan battlefield to a far higher vision for our nation."

Ross Perot invited me to speak with you this evening as the general chairman of my party. I must tell you that I am new to that role. I never aspired to be the general chairman of my party. My ambition was to follow Abraham Ribicoff, a great United States Senator, into the United States Senate. But let me briefly describe what the Democratic Party has to offer our country.

Today, you and I live in the strongest, most decent nation on earth. I happen to believe that my party has played an indispensable role in making it that way. I happen to believe that this country would be a shadow of its present self if the Democratic Party and its leaders over the past 50 or 60 years had not been there to fight for working men and women.

In the 1930s when proud men and women huddled on street corners, desperate for work, it was a Democratic president who gave them jobs, and far more important in many ways, self-esteem.

When men and women toiled for a lifetime and still worried that they would die in destitution, it was a Democratic president that advanced the radical notion that a proud and wealthy nation could give its senior citizens some dignity.

When restless soldiers returned from World War II and Korea, we in our party, the Democratic Party, took a chance on their drive and their ambition. The G.I. Bill helped to create the largest, most prosperous middle class in the history of the world; and I believe that we have reaped benefits far in excess of the cost of that investment.

When women and minorities found the door of opportunity shut in their faces in our country, the Democratic Party led the crusade to try to pry it open. And today we are holding it open still, for millions of our fellow citizens who ask for nothing more than an opportunity to make their mark. I am proud of that achievement.

When the elderly worried that the next illness would be their last, it was a Democratic president and his party that calmed their fears. Thanks to Medicare and Medicaid, millions of Americans now know that their health does not exclusively depend on their wealth.

We built an economy where the vast majority of our people have a chance to work and earn a decent living. We can be sure that families eat safe food and have clean air and water.

Have we made our mistakes? You bet we have. Have we been anything but perfect? Absolutely. I understand that. But I also happen to believe that there is a proud heritage in this party's history. Let me just as quickly add there is no reason in the world why I ought to ask you to listen to the ideas of a Democratic Party based exclusively on what we have done in the past, although that may give you some idea and some indication of the road we may travel in the future. What you want to know is not what we have done, but what promises we are going to make and are we going the keep those promises.

Looking to our future, I believe the Democratic Party offers the tools to help build a strong, prosperous, and free nation. We seek a broad prosperity enjoyed by all who labor to create it. We believe in the fundamental importance of work for its obvious economic value, but, more fundamentally, for its social and cultural value. A great nation, any great nation, must maintain a vigorous work ethic among its people. It is only by the efforts of each citizen that we will harness the energy of a changing world. We believe in economic security for all who have earned it.

In America today, you have a right to a lawyer if you get arrested. I do not believe it ought to be a radical idea in America that if you get sick, you have a right to a doctor as well. In the wealthiest nation on earth, all Americans deserve decent medical care. One should not risk bankruptcy just to regain his or her health. We believe that the strength of a nation depends on many factors, on the ability of its people to defend itself against outside aggression, on the knowledge and wisdom of educated citizens, and on respect for one another and for our common values as Americans.

Lastly, we believe that the function of government, as well as our party, is to give voice to those who cannot be heard. We have not listened, you and me, as carefully to these people as we should. And I think we should strive to do better. Fundamentally, the hopes of working families have been, and will continue to be, the responsibility, the main responsibility, of the Democratic Party.

Let me move quickly to the President of the United States, the leader of the Democratic Party. He understands that he is the trustee of our common aspirations. Remember, this is an Administration that arrived in Washington, D.C. only recently. He never served as a senator, never served as a congressman, has not spent decades in Washington, was the governor of a small state and 32 months ago had delivered on his doorstep a bulk of problems – an incredible deficit, problems of unemployment, a nation that was concerned about its future. I believe this president has done a good job. A lot is left to be done, but this president has done a good job.

We have seen our deficit come down by $600 billion. We have seen 272,000 jobs taken out of federal service. That will make the government the smallest it has been since John Kennedy was president of the United States. We have seen seven million new jobs created over these past 32 months.

In my home state of Connecticut, while we applaud the end of the Cold War, the people who work at Electric Boat, Sikorsky and United Technologies – people who contributed to the strength of our national security arsenal – have watched good jobs disappear in these last few years. Getting a job in a fast food chain or some low wage scale job is not the answer, but we are putting people back to work; and we must do much more.

We are fighting crime with 100,000 new police officers on our streets, and it is making a difference in our cities. Listen to the mayor of New York, and listen to others tell you what a difference that has made.

We have a president who is deeply committed to education as well, trying to see to it that we invest properly so that our young people will be the best educated generation that you and I have ever produced in the history of our country. That has been the record of this president. It is not just talk.

What I have always admired about United We Stand America is that you have not been caught up in the personalities of politics. This group, more than any other group that I know of, concerns itself with action and with issues. All I ask of you over these coming months is this – listen to what is said, but also watch what is done; and do not be caught up in the cult of personalities.

I have spoken briefly about what I see as the values and vision of a Democratic Party and our president, but I would like to take the few remaining minutes that are available to me this evening to discuss an issue that transcends political affiliation. I hope that amid all the voices that you are going to hear this weekend, that we will find time to consider not only America's problems, and there are many, but also its great strengths.

Today we hear much talk about what is wrong with our country, and it is appropriate and proper that we discuss those problems. But, frankly, I do not think we hear enough about what is right about America. Who would have imagined just a few years ago where we would be today – five years from the start of a new millennium. The Berlin Wall has come down. We have won a 45-year conflict in the Cold War, and today we stand alone as the world's sole superpower. The Soviet Union has been relegated to the pages of a history book.

We are leading as we have led for 200 years. The revolution of freedom has overtaken the world. We have helped to defeat not just the tyranny of Soviet communism, but tyranny as well in Latin America. In South Africa; a black man is president, and we, in the United States, are all proud that we helped to make that possible.

We are leading another kind of revolution, a technological revolution that is shrinking distances between people and expanding understanding among them. A revolution that promises to open new horizons of hope to millions who strive for a better life for themselves and their families.

Everywhere in the world nations endeavor to emulate our Democratic values. They take our Constitution as the framework of their own. They seek to follow our example of tolerance, and they envy our free and honest way of life. If on this very night you were to travel anywhere in the world and visit a United States embassy, you would find the lines forming already in hopes of getting a visa to come to America. The reasons that your forebears and mine came to this country are the same of people today. This is the country that stands out as an example to the world.

As we analyze our problems, it is important to analyze them in the context of the strength and the vitality that we possess as a people. This is our moment. We have been given an incredible opportunity to make a positive difference in the world. Whoever we are, wherever we come from, this is our moment – you and I. Whether you are a private citizen, a congressman, a senator, or a president, this is our moment to try and make a difference.

In New England in the seventeenth and eighteenth century, they used to write on the old samplers, "Leave the land in better shape than you found it." Today you and I as public citizens must leave this world, leave this country, in better shape than when we found it. That is our collective responsibility.

Over these last several days I have thought a great deal about what to say this evening. I have wondered what I would say this evening had Mr. Perot said, "We are only going to let you talk about one issue, one issue alone that you thought needed addressing more than anything else." What would that issue be? Certainly there are important ones, and I have heard much discussion today, good discussion, about what needs to be done.

I believe that the overriding issue is how to preserve the promise of government by the people and for the people. Because none of the other issues that press upon us, no matter how important – the national debt, economic growth, Medicare, education, the environment – will be solved if we do not break the cycle today of the way that we finance our campaigns in this country. That is the single most important issue in my view. And let me tell you, this is not an abstraction for me. I am the chairman of my party, but, first and foremost, I am a United States Senator elected by the people of my state. And I am most proud of that position. But let me tell you firsthand how debilitating it can be. The average candidate for the United States Senate must raise around $12,000 a week during their six years of office if they intend to run for re-election. One candidate from the State of California spent over $28 million of his own money to win a seat in the United States Senate. I do not believe I am exaggerating when I say I think that is obscene.

In the House of Representatives, the candidates routinely spend over $700,000 to vie for a seat every two years. In fact, last year members of the two major political parties raised and spent over $384 million for Congressional campaigns – $384 million in one election cycle. And presidential candidates – you will see some of them tomorrow – must each raise at least $20 million just to win their party's nomination.

My friends, instead of waging war against campaign money, we in the political arena are waging war for it. We are caught up in the political equivalent of a nuclear arms race. And like the nuclear arms race, the outcome can destroy the competitors and threaten our republic. In today's system, too many candidates win office based on the size of their campaign war chest, not on the power of their ideas. Once elected, too many are forced to spend too much time raising private dollars and far too little time solving the public's problems. Worst of all, those who see government as a tool of private gain rather than public good have strengthened their grip on our public institutions. Their influence permeates the machinery of government and places our nation at risk.

Consider, if you will, how the present system is undermining our future. Major polluters have been allowed by elected officials to rewrite the laws that preserve our air and water. Food producers have been allowed to block efforts to update meat inspection rules that are 90 years old, even though 500 children and adults die each year due to contaminated meat and 30,000 of our fellow citizens become seriously ill. And elected officials have, literally, invited companies charged with ignoring the health and safety of their workers to rewrite the very laws that they consistently violate.

Now, let me say in the strongest terms possible to you this evening, I am convinced that nothing is more important to our nation's future than enabling our companies to grow and prosper. We must not saddle them with vexing rules. But I am equally certain that we can have a strong economy and clean air. We can have a strong economy and clean water. We can have a strong economy and safe food. And, yes, we can have a strong economy and safe work places for our fellow citizens.

These days children, seniors, and working families are told that they must make do with less in order to balance the federal budget. Very few Americans I know are not willing to sacrifice to achieve that worthy goal. Certainly, deficit reduction must be meaningful and strong. It also needs to be fair. And yet we have seen a provision offered and passed in the House that will provide a $20,000 tax cut to people earning over $350,000 a year, the most affluent one percent of our population. And they have voted to repeal the law signed by Ronald Reagan that requires large corporations to pay at least some minimum tax every year. Is that what we mean by shared sacrifice?

My state, I will tell you, is one of the most affluent in this country. Not one of my constituents has called and asked me to support a tax cut of that magnitude when deficit reduction ought to be the number one economic goal in this country. They, like most of us, believe that the time to lower taxes is after, not before, we have lowered the deficit.

As you know, the term *lobbyist* comes from the word lobby. In the old days that is where lobbyists would wait if they wanted to see an elected official. Today, lobbyists no longer have to wait in the lobby to influence the legislative process. They have been invited into the back rooms to write the laws. And those who now write the checks now expect to write the laws as well.

I do not believe this is the kind of change Americans have voted for in 1992 and 1994. Throughout my time in Congress I have supported efforts repeatedly to change these campaign laws. Both political parties have squandered opportunities to reform the current system. The sad fact is that far too many people from both of our parties are not willing to get off the horse that brought them to victory.

Tonight I ask you, in these next two days, to make this a critical issue to be raised with all the candidates. We have missed opportunities. I will be the first to tell you that my party has missed opportunities, but the fact that we have made our mistakes in the past is no reason to make them again. I urge you to join the effort to reform the campaign finance system before the end of this Congress in 1996.

As I mentioned a while ago, this is a wonderful opportunity that we have been given to make a difference in our country. I have great respect for what this organization has done and you are making a difference in this country. I have expressed my views as a Democrat. I have great faith in the values of my party, but I truly believe it is the long-term interest of our country that must be paramount in the minds of each and every one of us.

Before coming to Dallas this week, I recalled the 1970s when I served on the Assassinations Committee that reviewed the assassination of John Fitzgerald Kennedy. I have great affection for Dallas and Texas, having been here many, many times. But it will be almost 32 years ago that we lost that young president. On that day in Dallas he was supposed to give a speech, but never got to give it. It was a speech to a group of Democrats that he was going to meet with, as well as people at the Mart. I went back last evening, and I read that speech of John Fitzgerald Kennedy. I am not exaggerating – it could have been written for today. And I want to share with you those remarks, the end of those remarks, that he was prepared to give in this city almost 32 years ago because I think it describes you. I hope it describes me.

Planning to speak before the Democrats of Texas, John Kennedy had written these words:

> This is a time for courage and a time for challenge. Neither conformity nor complacence will do. Neither the fanatics nor the faint-hearted are needed. And our duty as a party is not to our party alone, but to the nation and, indeed,

to all mankind. Our duty is not merely the preservation of political power, but the preservation of peace and freedom. Let us not be petty when our cause is so great. Let us not quarrel amongst ourselves when our nation's future is at stake. Let us stand together with renewed confidence in our cause, united in our heritage of the past, and our hopes for the future, and determined that this land that we love shall lead all mankind into new frontiers of peace and abundance.

My friends of United We Stand America, this evening I commit to you, as the chairman of a great political party in this country, that I will live by the words John Fitzgerald Kennedy would have given 32 years ago. I commit to you that I will engage in a civil debate on how we can improve the quality of life in our nation for all citizens. And I deeply, deeply appreciate the honor that you have extended to me this evening to be a part of this historic gathering, and I thank you for listening.

House Democratic Leader Dick Gephardt

ROSS PEROT: Congressman Dick Gephardt from Missouri is the House Democratic Leader.

Congressman Gephardt was born in St. Louis in the same congressional district he represents today. He grew up in modest circumstances, but had wonderful parents. His parents were devoted to their two sons, and made every sacrifice necessary to see that they got the opportunities his parents never had.

His father did not get to finish high school because of the Depression. He drove a milk truck, sold insurance door-to-door, and later sold real estate. His mother worked as a secretary.

Both parents sacrificed to send their sons to college. Congressman Gephardt graduated from Northwestern University, where he served as student body president, and he also graduated from the University of Michigan Law School.

Congressman Gephardt and his wife Jane have three children, Matt, Chrissy, and Katie. I have had the privilege of meeting his family. His children are outstanding. Jane is a wonderful mother and one of the most respected congressional wives.

Congressman Gephardt's mother is 87, and she is loved by everyone in St. Louis. She is still very active and swims 34 laps every other day in the YWCA pool. That's where Congressman Gephardt gets all that energy, I guess.

Congressman Gephardt was first elected to Congress in 1976. In his first term, he was appointed to serve on both the Ways and Means Committee and the Budget Committee – an unusual opportunity for a freshman Congressman.

In 1984, he was elected Chairman of the House Democratic Caucus.

He entered the 1988 Democratic presidential primaries and won in three states.

In 1989, he was elected House Majority Leader, and served in that role through 1994.

As the Leader of the Democrats in the House of Representatives, Congressman Gephardt will share with us his party's vision of leadership for the 21st century.

Thank you, Ross Perot. Ladies and gentlemen, it is great to be here tonight. I want to thank all of you for inviting me and all of the others speakers. I want to thank you for taking your time and expense to come here, and I want to thank Ross Perot for doing what he is doing in pulling this group together. I have known Ross Perot for a long time. He is a real American patriot.

I want to get right to it tonight and talk about what I think is the great challenge facing our country in 1995 and beyond. I guess I want to start by going back to the elections of 1992 and 1994. In both of those elections the American people, including everybody in this room, were calling out for change. In 1992, I think the American people felt that the economic problems of our country were not being addressed. I think the same thing happened in 1994. People felt that the major challenge of our country was not being faced.

What is that challenge? I believe that challenge is our standard of living, our income, our ability to achieve economic results for our families. I put it in terms of the American Dream. I put it in terms of the land of opportunity.

I go back to what Ross said about my parents. I grew up in the 1950s. I was born in 1941. My dad was a milk truck driver. My mom was a secretary. I never thought then, at age 87, she would swim 34 laps, as she does today. They were great parents. They told my brother and me every day that we could achieve anything if we worked hard. We had pride in ourselves, knowing anything that we wanted to achieve was possible.

They used to say in America, "It does not matter where you come from, who you are, the color of your skin, your religion, or your background. Whoever you are in this place, you have an opportunity." It is that feeling of opportunity that lies at the heart of the American experience.

I think people wanted change in 1992 and 1994 because that American Dream had begun to crumble for millions of Americans. For 16 years incomes have eroded. Our standard of living has slipped. Last month the Labor Department reported the largest decline of annual wages in our history, 2.3 percent. Not since the 1840s, when the invention of the electric loom threw millions of weavers out of work, have we seen that kind of a decrease in wages.

But the interesting thing is that decline comes at a time when the productivity of American workers went up by almost 3 percent. So while productivity was going up by 3 percent, wages were going down by almost 2.5 percent. The chart below indicates that while the productivity of American workers went up 25 percent over the last 20 years, their wages have stayed flat.

Worker Productivity Compared to Compensation 1973-1994

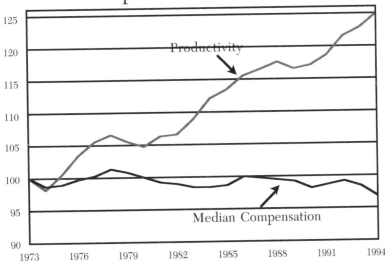

Listen to these facts. Between 1947 and 1972, the average American family felt a doubling of their income. In the last 20 years, average weekly wages declined by 19 percent in real terms. Over the last 20 years the median family income, no matter what inflation was doing, only went up by $66 over the whole period. That is about $3 a year.

People are working harder, even though some will say Americans are not working as hard as they used to. This is simply not true. American workers today are working about 82 hours more a year than they did 20 years ago, yet their wages are flat. When people are asked how long it would take to exhaust their savings, the average working family would see their current level of consumption – their standard of living – go down in two weeks if they were thrown out of work.

You ask, "Why is this happening?" Let's analyze that for a minute. The first reason it is happening is technology. Everything is changing. Everything that we do at work is changing because of computers and technology and the Information Revolution. It is as important as the Industrial Revolution was at the first part of this century.

When you go into a steel plant today, you do not see people handling the steel. You see people in white coats working computers because the organization of information is virtually controlling what is happening. People who have greater levels of education – we will talk about that more in a minute – are the ones who are able to cope with these means of dealing with work. This is an important place to look.

But, secondly, and I want to make this point very clear, I think our wages are being pushed down and held down because of the kind of competition we face today in the world.

I was in Indonesia about a year ago, and I visited European, Japanese, and American-owned plants. These are high-tech plants. These were not plants that were doing old kinds of things. They were making computers and microchips and televisions and all kinds of modern devices. I talked to workers who were pretty well educated. Most of them had high school educations. I asked them how much they made. They said a dollar fifty a day. A dollar fifty a day.

In China, Indonesia, Thailand, South America, Africa, all over this world, we face that kind of competition in terms of standard of living. If the competition is fair, and I am going to talk about that in a minute, that means our workers have to be 20 or 30 or 40 or 50 times more productive than the worker in Indonesia in order to compete. It is clear that trade and the problems in trade are part of this equation.

I took the position that, yes, we can have a NAFTA, but it must be fair. It must have enforceable provisions that say, "If we are going to compete with workers who are working for a dollar or a dollar fifty an hour, we have to be sure that they have a way to collectively bargain for their wages. We must be sure that they are living with the same kind of environmental regulations that we have in this society."

I did not believe the NAFTA that was passed did that. That is why I voted against it. I believe we need fair trade. I will talk about that more in a minute. Let me also talk about the trade problem with developed countries. We not only have a trade disequilibrium with our developing friends, we also have one with our developed friends. We have a trade deficit now that runs at about $150 billion a year. With Japan we have a trade deficit of about $60 billion a year, about half of our total trade deficit. American companies have only sold 400,000 cars in Japan in the last 25 years. Japanese companies have sold 40 million in the United States. Now, if that was on an equal playing field, if we had equal ability to sell and have access to their consumers as they have to ours, I would not object. But if you look at our trade deficit, it's almost

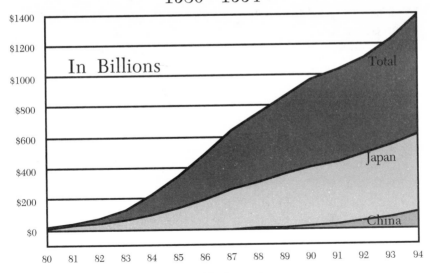

U.S. Cumulative Trade Deficit
1980 - 1994

one-and-a-half trillion dollars, half of it with Japan.

For every billion dollars of trade deficit, we lose about 17,000

American jobs. Now, you figure it out. Last year our trade deficit was about $150 billion. Let's round it off and say it was a hundred billion dollars. That is almost two million jobs.

I have no problem with that if it is fair competition and we are not competing and cannot get our workers to be productive enough to meet that competition. But I want our workers and our businesses to be on a level playing field, not on one that is unequal.

Now, let me end the analysis of the problem by pointing out that this is not just about money. This is about families and family values. From 1973 to 1993, the number of families where both spouses had to go to work went up by 40 percent. But their family income only went up by 7 percent. You know the stories. Dads are working, some of them two jobs. Moms are working, some of them two jobs. They are working overtime because they are trying to make up for that flat income, trying to stay ahead or just trying to keep where they are. It means they are not at home raising the kids. It means they are not at home to spend any time with one another so they can have an effective and successful relationship.

In the family where I grew up, even though my mom worked, she tried to get home to be there when I came home from school for lunch. She was there to talk to me, to work with me, to give me the values that have made this country great. The issue I am talking to you about tonight is not just money. It is quality of life. It is the success of the American family. It is the ability of the American family to provide for their children so they can be a strongly knit family that passes those American values down generation after generation. That is what we have at stake.

Now let's get to the solutions. There are six components of the plan that those of us in the Democratic Party, hopefully with the cooperation of many Republicans, will present in this next year.

First, trade policies that level the playing field rather than leveling the American worker. Second, a new approach to business in this country, one that rewards the people whose hard work and productivity are actually behind today's surging corporate profits. Third, a complete overhaul of an income tax system that currently favors the insiders, with loopholes that jump over the average family. Fourth, a new commitment to build the public works and the structures that we need to create jobs and to keep this economy strong. Fifth, a new commitment to health care reform to give families the health security they demand and deserve. And sixth, radical and fundamental political and campaign reform.

Now, first, I want to talk about fair trade, and I want to talk about trade with developing, and then underdeveloped countries.

With developed countries I want one simple thing, fairness. I want as good an access to their consumers as they have to ours. I have a really simple solution for you. I want to pass a bill that says to every country in the world – Japan, Germany, China, you name it – you treat us the way we treat you. It is just that simple.

Let me just tell you a story. Federal Express is one of our best companies. A few years ago they were having real trouble getting into Japan. They would land their planes, and they wanted to get their packages out by 10:00 a.m., to honor their pledge to their customers.

There was a problem, though. The Japanese said they had to inspect the cargo before it could be distributed. The problem was that they only had a few inspectors. So the planes would sit on the ground sometimes for a week before the packages could get distributed.

My bill would be really simple. It would say if that is good enough for Japan, then it is good enough for the United States. If they bring their planes in here, it will take us a week. I call it reciprocity. I call it just plain fair play.

Secondly, we cannot afford to compete with countries that do not recognize the rights of their workers and in fact, exploit their workers. We cannot trade on a fair basis with countries that say the environmental laws do not count and we will not enforce them in our country. I have a very simple deal. You have to have labor laws, and you have to have workers' laws, and you have to have environmental laws. They have to be in force for us to be on a level playing field and to be able to trade.

Next, I believe we must pay for performance. Now, let me tell you this one to me is probably the most important. If we are going to be 40 or 50 times more productive than the workers we are competing with, our workers have to be working with their employers in order to be that effective.

So I have a really simple idea. Let's get along, work together, and cooperate.

Let me tell you a story. I was at Magmum Copper in Arizona. In 1988 it was the least productive copper plant in America. They brought in a new manager. He took a case of beer along with the profit and loss statement to the union hall, slammed it down on the table, and said, "Ladies and gentlemen, if we do not get our act together, we are all going to be out of a job."

Something in 1988 happened to that place. They had had strikes; they had had violence; they had had a horrible relationship. But gradually they began to trust one another. They began to believe in one another. The managers began to empower the employees and ask them how to get things done. They put people on stock options and profit sharing. And do you know what happened? Rather than expending all their energy fighting with one another, since 1988 they have had a 64 percent increase in productivity. They are the most profitable copper plant in the United States today. The workers are the most highly paid workers in the copper industry in the United States.

We can work together. So you say, "How do we do it? How do we have Saturn, how do we have Motorola, how do we have Harmon International? How do we have Magmum?" The government cannot do it. It has to be done in the private sector. What we can do is hold up as examples the private companies that have done it.

There is a program in Australia called *The Best Practices* program. They have a ceremony every year to showcase the companies and the employees who have been working together with best practices. We can do even more. We could set up a code of conduct that people could voluntarily sign on to, to carry out these kinds of practices. We could create and condition every trade agreement on that nation's adoptions of a code of conduct or a similar commitment to their working people. We could put seals on the products of companies that have the code of conduct. And finally, we could have a new brand of stock that says this company really excels in working together with their employees to be highly productive in this highly competitive world.

We can do this. I call it the *X Factor*. I have seen it at Saturn. I have seen it at Motorola. I have seen it at EDS, Ross's company. I have seen it a lot of places. We can do it in America, because we are the best. We can be even better.

Third, we need a new tax system. Aren't you sick and tired of a tax system that does not work for anybody?

It is a mess of special interests. Everybody comes and says, "Oh, I gotta have a tax break for this or that." When they get a special interest break, everybody else's tax rate goes up. I have a tax plan that I think makes sense. Throw all the deductions out except one, the mortgage interest deduction, because it is the American dream to own a piece of the rock.

Second, if you do that, you can get a rate of 10 percent for 75 percent of the American people. Everybody earning $60,000 or less would have a 10 percent rate. If you do your withholding right, you would not even need to file a return. The only deduction left would be the mortgage interest deduction.

And finally, I am willing to urge that Congress pass a law that says before we ever raise tax rates we have to have a national referendum of the American people to do it.

Another important issue is infrastructure, a very boring subject, but an important one. Let me explain with one story. I was trying to get an interchange built in St. Louis on our outer belt, Highway 270 and Highway 55, right near a large, highly productive Chrysler plant. When I announced the effort to try to get it done, the head of the Chrysler plant called me and said, "What can I do to help?"

I asked, "Why do you care?"

He replied, "Well, let me tell you what happens. Traffic ties up there because the interchange is not adequate. We have a thing called just-in-time manufacturing. We cannot get the stuff in time, which means we have to shut the whole factory down at the cost of millions of dollars."

We have to rebuild the infrastructure of this country. We have a highway trust fund that has been great, but quite frankly, it is a little out of date. I say let us take two cents of the existing gas tax out of that highway trust fund. Let us put it into a new trust fund dedicated to state and local infrastructure bonds and let us let the state and local governments leverage that two cents tax year after year to build the structures they need at the local level to make their economies work.

My next to last vital issue is health care reform. I am not going to get into the argument about Medicare, except to say we will never reform Medicare unless we reform the whole health care system. We must have health care reform. I mean we must get rid of insurance companies who only want to compete by selecting only healthy people or who want to deny coverage to people who are, or who become, sick. Let us put them on a level playing field and make them compete for our health care resources.

And finally, political reform. I was interested in the Speaker's statement. I think we have a way to get lobby reform passed before the end of September. Let's take up the Senate bill in the House, pass it, and put it on the President's desk before the end of September.

The campaign reform we need must be radical. The big cost of campaigns is that they go on too long and contain too many TV ads. My solution is really simple. Make the campaign six or eight weeks long, that's it. Let's get rid of the TV ads and have more events like this where there is real debate about the issues.

Let me conclude with that which leaves me with great optimism tonight, the fact that you are here. The greatest danger to the oldest democracy in the history of the world – to the greatest country that has ever existed on the face of the earth – is indifference. The thing that scares me the most is when I hear citizens who are eligible to vote say, "I am not going to vote, because it does not make any difference. I am not going to participate, because it does not make any difference." Or they say, "My vote does not count. I am not going to go out and vote. I am not going to support someone's campaign. I am not going to take part in the process."

All of you are different. You have come here from all over this great country. You have paid your own way. You have been sitting here hour after hour listening to us tell our views. Whether everything each of us has said tonight is right or not, all of us are trying to keep this great country great. What I want to leave with you tonight is that what you do in your caring and in your participation is the key to whether or not this country has a brighter or darker future.

A few years ago I had the honor of sitting in a breakfast with Lech Walesa, the leader from Poland. During the breakfast, I asked him how he had started with his effort at *Solidarity*. He told me that he had worked in the Gdansk shipyard. He had felt, with some of his friends, that things were unfair at the plant. They could not bargain, they had no rights, and they could not speak out. They could not change the way the place ran. He said he finally convinced two of his friends to make a handmade sign that they tacked on a stick. They stood in the Gdansk shipyard one day protesting the conditions in the shipyard. He said, "Of course, the secret police came, since free speech was not allowed." They beat him up and threw him over the fence, out of the shipyard.

He said he remembered like it was yesterday, lying face down in the mud wondering what he would do next. He was afraid, he was afraid for himself and he was even more afraid for his family. He wanted to go home. But he said, "Something inside of me told me that I had to go back." And as all of you know, he got back up, jumped back over that fence, and began leading demonstration after demonstration until he had dramatically changed working conditions at his shipyard.

He told me that every day since then he has wondered to himself, "What would have happened had I not gone back?"

One man changed the history of the shipyard, changed the history of his country, and I say to you, he changed the history of the world. There is not a one of us in this room tonight who does not have more influence and more ability than Lech Walesa. If that one man could change his country and help defeat communism worldwide, there is no reason all of us together cannot change this country.

We must keep this American Dream alive for our kids and our grandkids. As long as you keep working, participating, coming to meetings, getting out for elections, and fighting for the people and the beliefs you feel strongly about, then you and others like you, will change this country and make it great and good and strong again.

Thank you very much.

Senator
Tom Daschle

ROSS PEROT: *Our next speaker is Senator Tom Daschle. He was born in Aberdeen, South Dakota in 1947. He graduated from South Dakota State University in 1969. He then went into the Air Force and served for three years as an intelligence officer in the Strategic Air Command.*

Senator Daschle joined the staff of former South Dakota Senator James Abourezk in 1972. He was elected to the House of Representatives in 1978 and to the Senate in 1986. In 1987 Senator Daschle was appointed to the Senate Finance Committee, an unusual honor for a freshman senator.

He was named the first Co-Chairman of the Democratic Policy Committee in 1988, making him the first South Dakotan ever to hold a Senate leadership position. Senator Daschle wrote the 1985 Emergency Farm Credit Act and authored 20 successful provisions to the 1990 Farm Bill.

He has authored landmark legislation to expand rural health services, introduced a bill to prevent companies from canceling retirees' health benefits without warning, and helped to lead the fight against fetal alcohol syndrome.

In 1991 Senator Daschle won an 11-year battle to compensate Vietnam veterans suffering from exposure to Agent Orange, and he is now pushing Congress to guarantee quality medical care to veterans suffering from Gulf War syndrome. I compliment him for that.

Last December he was elected Senate Democratic Leader, and he is currently a member of the Senate Agricultural Committee. Senator Daschle is married and the father of three children. As the leader of the Senate Democrats, Senator Daschle will share the Democratic Party's vision for preparing this country for the 21st century.

Please welcome Senator Tom Daschle.

Thank you very much. Thank you, Ross. As a South Dakotan and as a United States Senator, it is delightful for me to have the opportunity to be with you tonight.

As Ross was standing next to me, I was reminded again that he and I see eye to eye on a lot of things. It is great to be with him in this magnificent forum, and I congratulate him on his success this evening and throughout the weekend. This is an important event, and it is good to be here for a lot of reasons. You have had some tremendous speakers, and I have had the opportunity to hear some of them already. I hope that as a result of the dialogue and the opportunity that we have to discuss ideas, we can move this country forward.

As a South Dakotan, I have the opportunity to go home quite frequently. Not long ago I was home and I visited a grade school class. I was introduced by a nervous young boy who described me as an important public *serpent*. I think he meant *servant*, but there may be a message in there. Listening to some of the talk shows, you get the impression that people in government have serpentine characteristics, and I know you do not believe that.

When I was elected in 1978, I was elected by 14 votes. Some would say in my state, given our population, that that is about 60 percent. But we are a very proud state. When I came to Washington, the first thing that I felt I ought to do was to introduce myself to some of those people who had been here a lot longer than I.

One cold December afternoon I had the opportunity to visit with somebody I had heard a lot about. He was elected in 1934. He had a big bulbous nose and two big ears and a heart the size of a Mack truck. He had pictures on all of his walls, and two of them stood out as I waited for him to enter the room. One picture was a brown and white photo of two men standing in front of a biplane. I could not make out who they were, but down in the bottom there was no mistaking the signature. It said, "To Our Dear Friend, Claude Pepper, Orville and Wilbur Wright." Right next to it was a picture of a moonscape, and you really could not make out that person either, but there was no mistaking the signature. It said, "To My Dear Friend, Claude Pepper, Neil Armstrong." Here is somebody who had really seen history. And as we sat on that cold December afternoon I said, "What advice would you have for someone just starting out?" He thought for a minute and he said, "If there is any advice I have for you it would simply be this: Remember what you stand for, remember where you came from, and remember that in the end it is not necessarily whether it is an R or a D that is important, as strong a Democrat as I am. It is whether you are a C or a D, whether you are constructive or destructive in this process."

What we need are constructive people, making this country all that it can be. Criticizing what is wrong with this country is every American's right. If we fail to criticize our country, we fail our duty as citizens. But if we only criticize, if we make the mistake of equating cynicism with citizenship, then we will also fail.

America today faces huge challenges. What we need are fewer *destructives* and more *constructives*. We need less partisan squabbling and more constructive debate and solutions. And I know that you can be a part of that process.

The independent movement in general, and United We Stand America in particular, is helping to create the dialogue and find those solutions. We are here to talk about preparing America for the next century. In the few minutes I have before you, I would like to make four points.

First, to prepare for the future, we have to remember the past. Harry Truman once said, "The only thing new is the history you do not know yet." It was true in his time, and frankly, I think it is true today.

We have to remember what it was like to grow old in the dark fear of poverty and humiliation before Social Security. We must remember what it was like to be old and sick, choosing between health and home, before Medicare. We must remember what it was like before student loans opened the doors of colleges for children of farmers and factory workers, when going to college was as likely as going to the moon. We must remember what it was like when polluters pumped poisons into our drinking water and toxic chemicals into our air.

We must remember what it was like before the minimum wage, before rural electrification and the stock market crash. And we must remember that it was our advocacy of good government that allowed Americans to confront each of these problems and in many cases exceed our own expectations.

We have to remember our past. Today we face a new set of problems, and there are those who say that the best way to solve those problems is to ignore our history, to dismantle the successes of our past, to overlook government as a proven and powerful force for change. But I believe that would be wrong. We must fix what is broken, and we must rid ourselves of what we do not need. We must not destroy, however, what greatness we have accomplished.

Democrats believe that. We believe that our country must build on the greatness that we have achieved in 200 years.

Second, before we talk about policies, I think we need to remember our values. I do not know if you have ever had the chance to read a book that has been on the best-seller list for a while. It is a book that I recommend to you all. The book is called *Chicken Soup for the Soul*, and it has a lot of great stories about life in this country. On one of the early pages there is a story of a college professor who had a sociology class that he took into the slums of Baltimore. Upon entering the slums, they decided to study the cases of 200 young kids. These young kids had probably never left Baltimore, much less gotten out of that particular area in the neighborhood. This sociology class was asked to write an evaluation of each of those boys' future.

They interviewed them, they looked into their past and into their families. And in all 200 cases, they came to the unanimous conclusion that these boys did not have a chance. They are gone. They are seven or eight years old, but forget it, they are not going to be around 10 years from now.

That study was written, filed, and, like most sociology studies, it was put away. About 25 years later another professor came across the study as he was cleaning out the desk. He had his students follow up on those boys just to find out what happened to them. To their surprise, with the exception of 20 who had moved or died, the students learned that 176 of the remaining 200 had achieved more than ordinary success. They had become doctors, they had become lawyers, they had become professional business people, they were successful.

It blew away the class. They could not understand what in the world had happened. So they went back and interviewed them once more. They asked, "What was it?" Surprisingly, in each and every one of the cases, these now-professional people said, "You know, there was a teacher."

Well, this college professor decided to go find that teacher. She was old, but she was still very alert. The professor asked the teacher, "What was it? How was it? What was your secret to make those boys success-ful? Tell us." She smiled, she had a twinkle in her eye, and she said, "I just loved those boys. I loved them."

We cannot forget that. It does not matter how many policies and programs we have and it does not matter how much money we throw at those policies. If they are not grounded in basic values that Americans share, they are not going to work, period. We must recog-nize the importance of values as we legislate each and every day in Washington. That is what this country needs to be all about.

The third point I want to make is simply this: If we are going to get this country back on the right track, then we must give government back to the people. We have to open up government; and if people feel shut out now, we must open up to them in particular.

I remember a study a couple of years ago by a respected think tank. It was about what Americans thought of their government. One line in particular really grabbed me. That line simply read, "People talk about government as if it had been taken over by alien beings." Government was perceived as so big, so autonomous that most people felt powerless to control or even direct it.

Surely that is not what our founders had in mind when they spoke of this nation "of the people and by the people and for the people." That is not what millions of Americans fought for and even died to protect, whether it was in the Persian Gulf or Vietnam, or as we now celebrate its end, World War II. That was not what they had in mind.

Democrats made a start at bringing people back into the political process two years ago when we passed a simple bill that we called Motor Voter. It is a law that says we are going to make it easier for you to register to vote. We want you to have a choice, not a headache, when you cast your vote in this country.

Now some people want to drop the Motor Voter Act. They are lob-bying to have it repealed. How unfortunate, in my view, that would be.

We need to be constructive, not destructive, in the way in which laws affect how we vote.

We have waited long enough in this country for real campaign finance reform. It is time to break the grip of big money special interests on the political process. When a lawyer gives money to a judge hearing his case, we call it a *bribe*. But when a special interest gives money to a politician, we call that *business as usual*. That is wrong, and it is helping to fuel people's cynicism about government.

It is easier to find Elvis sometimes than it is to trace the trail of some PAC money, and that is wrong. We need real campaign reform. We need it in 1995, and you ought to help work to get us that piece of legislation this year. We also need real lobbying reform and a real gift ban in both houses of Congress, and we need that this year, in this session of Congress. The largest single voting block in the last election was the block that did not vote at all. That is wrong, and we must change it.

The fourth and final point I have to make is this: In order to prepare for the future, government has to give up its old shopworn infrastructure of the past. All around us our cultural and social and economic institutions are changing profoundly and rapidly. Government must change to reflect these new developments.

The government that worked in the Industrial Age cannot and will not work in the Information Age. The centralized bureaucracies we built in the 19th century to organize information and control decision-making will not work today. They are obsolete. We need to replace them with new structures that people can better access and better direct. President Clinton, Vice President Gore, and the Democratic Party have and will continue to make this a top priority because it must be done.

So those are my four points. Let us remember our history. Let us remember our values. Let us return government to the people and create a new structure for government that fits a new era. It is with that understanding that we must also remember our responsibility in this great democracy.

In 1989 I had the opportunity to travel with then-Majority Leader Mitchell, along with my wife Linda and others, to Germany right after the revolution. We had the opportunity to see East Berlin before it ceased being that Communism regime that we detested for so long.

One night before we left, we had the opportunity to talk with East Germans who had never known freedom or experienced democracy. I had a discussion that I have long remembered. Late one evening at a dinner, we talked about our two countries and the comparisons and the contrasts, and they told me about Peter Fetcher. They told me about what it was like for people like Peter Fetcher who wanted freedom so badly that they would have done anything, including give up their life, for just one minute of freedom.

They told me about the mine field you go through to get to the wall, 200 yards of mines. They told me about a 14-foot ditch filled with water and a 16-foot wall over which you had to climb to experience freedom. And they told me about Peter Fetcher, who got through the mines, got down the ditch, got up the wall, got on top of the wall, and just as he was about to declare his freedom, an East German guard shot him in the back four times. He fell on the other side, and he breathed free air.

They kept that part of the wall, and Peter Fetcher is buried there. But those East Germans said something that night that I would like to leave you with tonight. They said, "You know, you Americans take freedom for granted. You do not ever know what you have lost until it is no longer there. You never really can appreciate the magnitude of the gift that we have, and you Americans take it for granted."

But let me give you a piece of advice they told me that night. They said, "Freedom is something you either have to fight for or work at. We have had to fight all of our lives so that Peter Fetcher and people like him would never have to do what he did again, but all you have to do is to work at it. All you have to do is to make sure you never have to fight for it again. And whether or not you work at it determines whether or not someday you will fight for it."

That is what this is all about. We may not agree on every issue, but we recognize the freedom that we have, and we believe as deeply as they do that as precious as this democracy is, it is worth working at. You are doing it tonight. Thank you for doing it. God bless you all.

Political Party Leaders

Republicans

Haley Barbour

ROSS PEROT: *Haley Barbour is the Chairman of the Republican National Committee.*

Mr. Barbour is a seventh-generation Mississippian. He received his law degree from the University of Mississippi in 1973, and practiced law in Yazoo City, Mississippi for 13 years.

After having worked in both of the Nixon presidential campaigns at the state level, he served as Executive Director of the Mississippi Republican Party and the Southern Association of Republican State Chairmen from 1974 to 1976. Since 1974, he has been active in Republican campaigns at the state and national level, and since 1984, he has served as Republican National Committeeman for Mississippi.

Mr. Barbour took a leave of absence from his law practice as a partner in the firm of Barbour & Rogers in 1985 to serve as Director of the White House Office of Political Affairs for President Reagan. He also served as a Senior Adviser to the Bush presidential campaign in 1988.

He was elected to his first term as Chairman of the Republican National Committee in January 1993. Last November, under his chairmanship, the Republican Party won the greatest midterm majority sweep of the 20th century.

In January 1995, Mr. Barbour won reelection by unanimous vote to his second term as Chairman of the Republican National Committee.

He and his wife, Marsha, live in Yazoo City, Mississippi. They have two sons.

Mr. Barbour will tell us what the Republican Party plans to do to make the next century the greatest in our country's history.

———

Thank you very much. I appreciate, Ross, your saying that I was reelected to my second term unanimously. I won my first term in a landslide – on the third ballot!

When Ross called me a few weeks ago to invite me to speak at this conference, I asked him what he wanted me to talk about. He said my vision of the Republican Party in the 21st century. That is a great subject for me because that is what I think about all the time – what should a party be like in the future. So I am going to do something unusual, I am going to stick to the subject. For those of you whose brains and bottoms are not numb yet, let us talk about what a political party ought to be like.

Now, the first thing for sure is that you will not learn what a successful political party ought to be like in Washington, D.C. You have to look outside the Beltway to the states, to the grass roots where elections really are won and lost.

Thinking about Washington trying to teach us something reminds me of the great story about two young political consultants. They were in their twenties and they were killed in a plane crash. They went up to the Pearly Gates, and they were just fuming. They were mad because they thought they had gotten a bad deal. They complained and moaned.

Finally, Saint Peter said, "Look, fellows, I had a bad day, too. I tell you what, sounds like you did not get a good deal, so I am going to let you both go back for six months. You can go back as anything you want. You cannot go back as yourself, so let me know what you want to go back as."

One of them was a pollster, one of those kind of sober, serious guys. He said, "Saint Peter, I believe I would like to go back as an eagle." Saint Peter said, "Fine, you can go back as an eagle, but remember, you have to be back in six months."

The other one was one of those advertising natives, the cocky, frisky kind. He was grinning from ear to ear. He said, "Saint Peter, I know what I want to go back as, I want to go back as a stud."

He said, "Fine, you can go back, but both of you be back in six months."

Six months came and went and he had not heard hide nor hair from either one of these guys. Saint Peter called down to the Angel Gabriel. He said, "Gabriel, come on down. You have to find these boys. One of them is not going to be too tough. He is an eagle. He will be soaring over the Grand Canyon or the Golden Gate. The other one is going to be harder. He is a two-by-four in a condominium in New Mexico."

You see, Washington is a place where they do not even know what to ask for. A party that understands solutions is much more likely to be found away from Washington because this type of party listens and learns. It learns about ideas at work, about problem solving, about the difference between trying to say what people want to hear and really doing what needs to be done.

Trying to make everybody happy is a road map to failure. And "government by polling" is the enemy of leadership. That brings us to the crux of the matter for a political party: trust. Lack of trust is the greatest weakness of parties, politicians and the political system. Parties cannot regain people's trust simply by asking for it or claiming they deserve it. The party of the 21st century has to win trust the old fashioned way; they have to earn it. As Republicans, we were reminded by the voters in 1992 that to be trusted as a party you have to stand for something. We have to say what we stand for, and then we have to stand for it.

So my first goal for the party of the 21st century is to earn America's trust by being a party of principle and a party of ideas. I do not mention the lesson of 1992 lightly. Republicans did not lose the White House in 1992 because the people who voted for us in 1980 and 1984 and 1988 changed their minds about issues. They did not change their minds about taxes or spending, about deficits or crime or welfare. No, they changed their minds about us. They decided we Republicans were not adhering to what they thought they had voted for in 1980 and 1984 and 1988; that caused them to look elsewhere.

To regain public trust, a party must uphold and be willing to fight for a core set of principles. One that Americans rely on to be in the best interest of the nation and one that will produce the best chance for their families to have economic opportunity, personal security, religious liberty and freedom to pursue happiness. Not principles as government sees fit, but as they see fit. Never forget individual freedom and personal responsibility are at the core of what it means to be an American.

Being an American also means exercising your right to vote, being involved in politics, and participating in this great democracy. That is why it is so important to me that the Republican Party be a bottom-up party.

After 12 consecutive years in the White House, we became a top-down party, with decisions and ideas imposed from the top down. And frankly, the Perot campaign reminded us that if you do not give the people a chance to participate in our party, somebody will give them a chance somewhere else. The best thing is to be a participatory party even in terms of policy. People at the grass roots know best, whether they are parents or teachers or police on the front lines. That is why we have to give them a voice in what our party is saying and doing.

After I became chairman of the Republican National Committee, I established the National Policy Forum, a Republican center for the exchange of ideas. It is a public policy institute that has held dozens of forums across the country, allowing citizens at the grass roots to tell elected officials and opinion leaders about ideas they believe will work.

In two years, nearly 200,000 people have participated in National Policy Forum programs. Its first publication, *Listening to America*, included comments and thoughts from independents and Democrats as well as Republicans.

In its pursuit of the best policies for the country, the party of the 21st century wants to learn from the grass roots. It knows it has to listen to those beyond its own ranks. After all, neither party has a majority of the voters today. Just as we have to reach to the grass roots as a party, we also have to reach beyond the professional politicians. More than half of the freshmen Republican members of the U.S. House of Representatives have never before held full-time public office. They are citizen legislators. They do not intend to make Congress a career, and you can see the difference they are making. Of course, another reason they are making such a big difference is that most of them are not lawyers. As a recovering lawyer, I am allowed to say that.

A participatory party is also broadly based financially. In my first two years as Chairman of the Republican National Committee, our committee received approximately 75 percent of all our revenue in contributions of $100 or less – 2.6 million contributions.

The Political Action Committees gave the Republican National Committee less than one percent of our total revenues. Let me repeat that, PACs gave us less than one percent of our total revenue. Three-fourths of our total revenue came in contributions of $100 or less.

I am proud of those numbers. I am proud because the Republican National Committee is predominantly funded by small donors, by small business, not big business – by Main Street, not Wall Street.

Finally, a participatory party knows – as you who are grass root activists know – it is important to communicate not only with its leader and its elected officials, but also with the grass roots workers. We use every possible avenue to keep our people informed and involved.

Even Hillary Clinton one day publicly complained about our issue faxes, so we have taken her off our list. Our party communicates with our grass roots activists through cable and satellite television; through an award-winning magazine with a circulation of 600,000 households; through cyberspace via the Republican forum on CompuServe and, beginning next month, the Internet; through regional and state meetings, and by mail and fax. Communication is, and should be, our biggest operational expense. It pays off in participation and that participation makes it worth every dime. All in all, as you look at our communications programs, our financial structure, even our policy institutions, you will find the Republican Party is a participatory party, a bottom-up party, and better off for it.

Let us face it, being part of any party is worthless if you do not agree with it on the issues. All of us are interested in politics because of what we think government should or should not be doing: tax cuts or tax increases; more spending or less; or, genuine reform versus status quo. These are the reasons we give our time and energy and money to politics. Politics is policy and policy is politics.

This brings us back to what I mentioned earlier – that the party of the 21st century has to be a participatory party, a party of principle and a party of ideas. The hallmark of a party of principle is honesty – simply telling the truth. A party of principle does not try to tell you what you want to hear.

You should not trust a party that changes its story because of a shift in the political wind. You should not trust a party that practices government by polling. To deserve your trust, the party of the 21st century must give people something to vote for and then keep its word. It must be a party of principle.

In 1994, Republicans did something unique in American political history. We, as the minority party, ran a national issues campaign in a mid-term election offering the people a positive, alternative agenda.

As in the past, the party out of power had simply run against the White House saying what was wrong with them. We could have done that, simply running against Clinton, and Lord knows there is plenty to work with. But we did not. Instead, last year, House Republicans, through the Contract With America, said to the country, if you vote for us, this is what we will do. And the people responded. They embraced our ideas of smaller government, lower taxes, less spending, fewer regulations, genuine welfare reform and other much needed reforms.

Republicans made the 1994 election about ideas. It was a national issues election where the voters rejected big government and liberalism in favor of smaller government and more freedom. There was no question about what the 1994 election meant. Even Stan Greenberg, President Clinton's pollster, whom they paid $4.5 million for polling data, said in one of the great understatements of the year, "This was not a casual act on the part of the voters." Amen.

Voters knew exactly what the Republicans stood for, and that is the mark of the party of the 21st century. A party worthy of your trust, or anybody's trust, sets out its positive agenda in a straightforward manner, makes the campaign about issues and wins a mandate from the people.

Republicans did exactly that in the 1994 election. As Ross said, "It resulted in the greatest mid-term majority sweep of the 20th century." The verdict of the voters gave Republicans a mandate for reform – for budget reform by eliminating the deficit without raising taxes; for genuine welfare reform, requiring able-bodied people to work and eliminating incentives for illegitimacy; for tort reform, putting common sense back in a civil justice system that has run amuck; for regulatory reform, ensuring that we effectively protect our health and our safety and our environment with the least burden on economic growth and job creation; and for a crime bill, establishing an effective death penalty and understanding that criminals, not society, are the problem.

Our mandate was for Congressional reform, and we are keeping our promises. On the first day, the new Republican majorities began reforming the way Congress does business. As a result, the House has – for the first time ever – been audited by an outside accounting firm, something Congress requires annually of every major public corporation.

Congress now, for the first time ever, must abide by the laws and regulations that the rest of us live under. And for the first time ever, the new majorities, the new Republican majorities, have cut Congress' own budget by 10 percent.

The Republican Congress, in its very first appropriations bill, set an example by cutting its own budget to 10 percent less than the previous year. These are cuts that President Clinton says he may veto. Frankly, I thought cutting the Republican Congress was the one budget cut of which President Clinton would approve.

We made, and are keeping our contract, to balance the budget in seven years without raising anybody's taxes. Indeed, our budget provides for much needed tax relief for families and for economic growth. Thirty-seven million American families would see their income tax reduced, and 4.7 million families would have their total income tax liability eliminated.

Republicans passed the first balanced budget resolution in 26 years. Let me repeat that; the new Republican Congress passed the first balanced budget resolution in 26 years. Now we are passing appropriation bills that meet that balanced budget goal.

I think it sends a powerful message that we cut Congress' budget first. Congress and the government cannot expect the American people to participate in balancing the budget unless Congress cuts its budget first.

Second, we cut foreign aid $1.6 billion below the previous year, and $2.8 billion below what Clinton requested for this year. We cut foreign aid 20 percent; and we have eliminated AID, the Agency for International Development, the principal foreign aid agency of the government. Believe it or not, President Clinton is threatening to veto the foreign aid cuts.

We also voted to eliminate hundreds of agencies and programs in areas other than Congress and foreign aid. We are making real cuts, that is, spending less than the previous year. In other areas spending is staying flat. Defense spending is flat for the next seven years. In fact, something you do not hear, outlays in next year's defense budget are cut by $6.5 billion, or 2.4 percent below this year.

Finally, spending for some programs goes up. Social Security goes up, exactly as planned. It is untouched. Most others go up, too, but at a slower rate. School lunches and even welfare spending goes up, but not as fast as Clinton has proposed. Medicaid, the health program for the poor, goes up every year. It is important to note – because we said it in last year's campaign – that overall, federal spending is going up 3 percent a year and we are still balancing the budget.

I am not surprised you do not hear much about spending going up. Washington is the only place in the world where spending increases are called cuts. That is how the supporters of the ever bigger welfare state have funded the failed welfare state for so long, despite the fact that most Americans think government is already too big for its britches and we are not getting our money's worth for our tax dollars now.

Now, between Ross' book – if you haven't bought this book, I urge you to – and Debbie Steelman's presentation about Medicare earlier, there is no reason for me to go into detail about Medicare, but I do want to make three points. First, the bad news is if we do nothing, Medicare will be bankrupt in seven years.

Republicans are not going to let Medicare collapse in bankruptcy; it is just too important. The good news is that we can save Medicare from bankruptcy while Medicare spending continues to increase. Under our budget, it increases 54 percent over seven years. Medicare spending will increase $1900 per beneficiary, per year over the seven years. Spending will increase from $4800 per beneficiary now, to $6734 per year for every Medicare beneficiary. No one is talking about cutting Medicare. No one.

The third point is this – everybody should be working to save Medicare from bankruptcy. Some in Congress publicly refuse to even make a proposal to save Medicare. They would rather stand in the weeds and attack the Republicans with the lie, "Republicans are cutting Medicare to pay for tax cuts for the rich." As you all know from everything you have heard today, that's bull feathers. Bull feathers.

When President Clinton proposes $192 billion in Medicare savings and $110 billion in tax cuts – as he does now – you do not hear the Democrats say Clinton is cutting Medicare to pay for his tax cuts.

Medicare is a prime example of how the public has a right to demand politicians deal with them honestly. If there is a problem, admit it, and then get on with solving it.

The party of the 21st century will tell the truth, and it will tell the truth even when its friends and allies disagree. Maybe it would have been better short-term politics for Republicans to have switched on NAFTA and beat Clinton. But to be a party of principle, you have to be for what you are for, to earn people's trust.

What you say today has to be consistent with what you do later. Many of you who disagree with us on NAFTA, on this or that single issue, voted for Republican candidates last year because you agree with us on most issues on where our country should be headed and government's proper role in getting there.

We do not claim we have all the answers and we do not claim there is not a lot more to do. Take term limits. Term limits failed in the House even though 85 percent of the Republicans in the House voted for it. Eighty-two percent of the Democrats voted against it. Term limits are the best means of campaign reform, and we are going to keep bringing it back up until it passes.

Let me close by saying that most Americans share our belief in smaller government. The Democrats, starting with the President himself, believe if we will only give government enough of our money and enough control over our lives and businesses, then government can solve all of our problems. So, regardless of the issue, government is their answer.

Republicans respectfully disagree. We are for smaller government. We are for smaller government because we believe individual freedom and personal responsibility are preferable to more government power and more government responsibility.

It is more freedom, not more government, that gives all Americans the opportunity to make the most of their God-given talents, their freedom, and their willingness to work hard to use those talents. That is what is special about Americans, that we have been endowed by our creator with certain inalienable rights. Among these rights are life, liberty, and the pursuit of happiness, not the guarantee of happiness, not the entitlement to happiness. Government cannot do that.

Freedom is the first principle of the party of the 21st century, and the policies we pursue, the programs for which we fight, are central to the goal of giving Americans more freedom and expecting from them an equal measure of responsibility.

If you believe in this philosophy and want to be part of the party of the 21st century, know you are welcome, that your voice will be heard, and you need pass no litmus test to get involved. The party of the 21st century has an open door, and as its chairman, I say, "Come on in."

Thank you very much.

Speaker of the House of Representatives Newt Gingrich

ROSS PEROT: *Speaker of the House Newt Gingrich is the son of a career soldier. In addition to being the Leader of the House of Representatives, he also represents the 6th Congressional District of Georgia.*

During his boyhood he lived all over the United States and in France and in Germany. He received his bachelor's degree from Emory University and both his master's and doctorate degrees from Tulane University.

He taught history and environmental studies at West Georgia College, before being elected to Congress in 1978.

Speaker Gingrich served as the House Republican Whip from 1989 to 1994, and he became the Speaker of the House of Representatives in 1995.

Speaker Gingrich and his wife Marianne live in Marietta, Georgia. He has two married daughters, Kathy and Jackie.

Newsweek *describes Speaker Gingrich as a "Revolutionary centrist."*

The New York Times *describes him as "A thoughtful analyst who gushes with ideas."*

The Wall Street Journal *called him "The most pivotal Republican in the land today."*

Speaker Gingrich is the author of the Contract With America.

Earlier this year, he worked around the clock to pass legislation implementing the Contract With America. *Although not every bill has been passed, he did keep the promise that all 10 measures would be voted on within the first hundred days of the new Congress.*

Join me in welcoming Speaker of the House Newt Gingrich from Georgia.

L et me say first how excited I am to be here with my fellow revolutionists who are committed to changing America.

I think Ross Perot has done America a favor by writing a brand-new book called *Intensive Care: We Must Save Medicare and Medicaid Now.* I want the entire country to realize that here is a serious study of what we need to do to get this country back on the right track in two of our most important areas. I wish that every American citizen could take a look at this book before we get into the debate this fall.

And, Ross, I want to thank you for your continued civic leadership of this country.

Coming out of the 1992 campaign, many citizens decided they would stay active and would work in United We Stand America. We had a Sixth District United We Stand America group. Dick Taylor, the executive director from Georgia, Henry Collins, the Chairman emeritus, and Ann Merkel, the current Chairperson worked regularly with me and my staff to make sure we knew what was going on.

Let me tell you what that led to. In 1994, the message we heard very clearly all spring and summer was that there are millions of Americans who want real change and they want Washington to quit behaving like an empirical capital that lorded over them.

We wrote – with Dick Armey, who has an interesting idea about getting the IRS out of your life; John Kasich, who has an interesting idea about getting to a balanced budget so we don't cheat your children; Tom DeLay, our whip; and a number of other people – a Contract With America. We thought it began to move us down the road we needed to travel.

The Contract was totally positive. It did not attack President Clinton, it did not attack Democrats. It just said, "You vote for us and we will keep our word. We will do what we pledge; it is a contract."

I will never forget election night. About 2:00 a.m. the word had gone out in a great shock that I would be the next Speaker of the House. Two Washington reporters came up to me and said, "Well, what are you going to do now?"

I said, "Well, we are going to pass the Contract."

They said, "No, no, the election is over. What are you going to do now?"

And I said, "We are going to pass the Contract."

And they leaned closer. They said, "Come on, what is your hidden plan?"

And I said, "Well, I know the Contract With America is our plan!"

They never quite got it.

So we came to Washington on the opening day. We met for 14 hours in the longest opening day in American history. We were a brand-new team that had never before been in charge in 40 years. The only member of the House Republican Party who had ever served in the majority was Bill Emerson of Missouri. He was a page in high school the last time there was a Republican majority. We passed the Shays Act, which said that any law which applies to the rest of America applies to the U.S. Congress, and congressmen have to obey the law.

We promised to begin cutting congressional committee staffs, and we did cut them by 30 percent to keep our word to you. We began to shrink the number of committees. We are right now in the process of privatizing one building and two parking lots. We just privatized the barbershop. We are going through a series of things that, for Washington, are so radical they do not believe they are happening.

Every week, we bring in the Washington reporters and they write, "Well, last week was pretty good, but this next thing is going to be really hard." And, "Yes, for seven months they have done it, but this next thing will be really difficult."

Let me tell you the truth, it is going to be really hard. When we go back this fall, we are going to continue to fight to balance the budget, as John Kasich and Pete Domenici reported. We are going to continue to fight to save the Medicare trust fund, which in April, the Clinton administration trustees reported would start going broke next year and would be bankrupt in seven years. We are going to continue to fight for real welfare reform, emphasizing work and family. We believe that the American people want that kind of change. We believe we are hired by the American people to implement that kind of change.

Let me also be totally candid. We failed on one item in the *Contract*. We had promised to vote on Term Limits. We brought it to a vote. Eighty-five percent of the Republicans voted yes; 82 percent of the Democrats voted no. We had a simple majority. It takes 218 to be a majority, but a constitutional amendment requires 290 votes. We had 230. When the vote was over, I stood up on the floor as the Speaker and said, "I want to promise the American people that passing Term Limits will be an issue in 1996." If we are still a majority, the first substantive vote in 1997 will be on the same topic. We will bring Term Limits to the floor again.

A reporter came by to see me today and asked about a third party. I said we have a third party, it is the House freshman Republicans. There are 73 of them. They are all militant. They are all committed. They all think they were elected by a coalition of United We Stand America and Republicans. They all go back home pledged to real reform; they think Dick Armey and I are a little soft and a little old. They keep pushing us to be real revolutionaries. I am here on behalf of those House Republican freshmen. I want you to know that you should not relax or rest for a moment, either.

We had a very unusual event recently. We went to the District of Columbia High School for a town hall meeting. We had a thousand residents of the District, about 900 of them African-Americans, who came out to talk about our national capital. Because frankly, as Americans, we ought to have the best capital city in the world. We should not settle for anything less than the best capital city in the world. I have said repeatedly that Washington, D.C., is the prime example of why we have to replace the welfare system. Cities like the District of Columbia are the reason we have to rethink public housing, the reason we have to dramatically change education in the inner city. It is not so we can run a cheap welfare state; I have no interest in running a cheap welfare state that destroys lives. My interest is to create a society of opportunity so that every child of every background in every neighborhood in America has a full opportunity to pursue happiness.

There were 45 people in a row who asked questions and made comments. They were very polite. I think they were partly stunned at the experience. A young woman stood up in the middle of this town hall meeting, and I was standing there answering questions, a conservative

Republican from Georgia. The young woman said, "Why should we trust you?" And I want to repeat this to you because I want you to know where we are coming from. I said, "You shouldn't. Don't trust anyone you loan power to. Watch them. Make them accountable. Make them tell you before they run what they are going to do; and if they don't keep their word, fire them. But do not trust anybody you give power to."

So I come here to say to you that we need your involvement. Washington will not change unless the American people, again and again and again, insist on change.

I want to talk just for a few minutes about two items that I think are vital in terms of the changes we need. I want to talk about Medicare, and then I want to talk about campaign and lobbying reform.

First, we use a planning model, a vision of strategies and tactics. We think through our vision of where are we going. Then we set up our strategies – this is America; there is always a future; you can do better; you never stop, you go. Vision – what is your vision of the future? what kind of country do you want? what are your strategies to get there? We then ask, "What kind of projects? – a definable achievement." Think of it as a building block.

Next, we think tactically – "what are we going to do every day?" For example, I want you involved, because my vision is of an America where citizens make a difference. The tactics ought to be talk radio, letters to the editor, going to town hall meetings, writing your congressman, things that bring you to bear on your political system. I want people involved.

We then practice: listen, learn, help, and lead. We go out and listen to people. We learn from them. That is why I was in D.C. at a town hall meeting taking notes. Then we try to help people. In a free society, if people know you will listen to them, you will learn from them. And you will help them. Frankly, they want you to lead.

Now, in that framework, let us take Medicare first. On April 3, the Clinton administration trustees wrote a report. They said that the Medicare trust fund, next year for the first time in history, starts running out of money. In seven years, under the current system, it will be bankrupt. These were the actuaries and the technical people. We took that seriously. Not only is it a problem for my 80-year-old mother-in-law; not only is it a problem for my mom and dad; not only is it a problem for every current senior citizen; but, 10 or 12 years later, when the baby boomers start to retire, if this ship of state is not in order, the ship is going to sink. It is not designed today to handle the scale of people who are going to start retiring around 2010 or 2015.

You have probably never heard a politician talk about that far in the future. They usually talk about the next election. They tell you what they can get away with so you will vote for them one more time. This does not get anything solved.

We are just the opposite. We think if we do not keep our word to our children and grandchildren and we do not do the job for our country, you should not reelect us. We think we ought to be honest and upfront, tell you the truth and solve the problems.

We are designing, and we will unveil in September, a tremendous new approach to Medicare. It starts with this proposition – any senior citizen who wants to keep the current system, can keep it. If you are 75 or 85 or 95 years old, we are not going to force you to change. We do not believe the government should coerce you. We are going to keep the current system and nobody has to be frightened.

We do believe there needs to be a lot of choice. We think a market-place needs to be created where senior citizens have the right to choose. We believe better health care can be offered through a variety of choices. A medical savings account plan is an excellent example of choice which will improve the current system.

I just want to give one set of numbers so you are armed and pre-pared when you go back home. This year Medicare spends $4,800 per senior citizen. Under our plan, over the next seven years, Medicare will spend $6,700 per senior citizen.

Now, most of you probably do math well enough that you know if you are at $4,800 here and you are at $6,700 there, that is called an increase. Now, I want to go really slow here for a minute because we have a lot of reporters who are listening, and you have to go through this slowly for them. I do not want to be negative, but you might even have one or two liberals show up who claim that going from $4,800 to $6,700 is a cut. Now, this is not because they are bad people; this is just an early sign of the educational dysfunction that has hit our society.

We are going to provide $1,900 a year more per senior citizen over the course of our program. We are going to work with all the people who deliver health care. We are going to deliver good health care for more than we are currently paying per individual. It is a good increase.

But let me tell you the second part, which is very important. We are working on a plan to enlist senior citizens to help us check on what happens to the money. We just had a report in Georgia last Sunday of a doctor who had personally billed $7 million a year for seeing patients; this is called theft. We will never develop a bureaucracy smart enough to keep up with the crooks, because the crooks have the incentive to work at night and on the weekends, and the bureaucrats go home. So what we are thinking through is a system where if senior citizens look at their Medicare bills and find waste, fraud and abuse that saves a thousand dollars or more, they keep 10 percent of the savings.

Let me put to rest a charge you will hear from liberals who seem to want to protect the Washington bureaucracy rather than protect the senior citizen. What we are doing on Medicare is directly related to the trust fund. If we had zero tax cuts, Medicare would have a problem with the trust fund. If we forgot about balancing the budget, Medicare would have a problem with the trust fund.

The fact is the Medicare trust fund is spending more than it is taking in starting next year. You do not have to believe me or any Republican elected official, just get a copy of Ross' book. He has the charts and he shows step by step what happens. Look at the facts. Then let us have a dialogue among our citizens, as adults, concerned about our country, concerned about our parents and grandparents. We need citizens, trying for a change, to do the right thing instead of just making partisan points.

Now, I want to talk very briefly about lobbying and campaign and other reform.

I shook the President's hand in New Hampshire because I thought the gentleman who got up at that picnic and said, "You really ought to take lobbying and campaign reform and money in politics and deal with it all at once," had something very important in mind. I do not care whether you take the money as a campaign contribution, as a personal gift, or as a dinner, it is wrong.

If you take the money through some other device directly or indirectly, it is equally as wrong. For example, if the people who like you happen to own three newspapers, and those three newspapers run editorials every day that happen to favor you, I think this is an abuse of power. In America, there are many ways to have power, and as a history teacher I am a serious student of how to solve the problem of those who abuse power when they have it.

I think we are in as grave a danger as the Roman Republic was after the Punic Wars. I believe the dangers to our society are the sheer power of money and influence on a world scale. And not just Americans, but people who show up on Tuesday who made a billion dollars in Hong Kong, or a billion dollars in Frankfort, or they made a billion dollars in Colombia out of the drug trade. I think the danger to our society of unbridled power gradually crushing the spirit of freedom is very, very real.

Let me share with you what I have learned. I came to Congress as a reformer. My first speech, when I announced in April of 1974, was about reforming the Congress. I lost twice. I kept campaigning. When I arrived as a freshman, one of the things I did in my first year was move to expel a convicted felon serving in the Congress who was voting while he was out on appeal. I made the assertion that when you have been convicted on 29 counts of stealing $70,000 and you are waiting to go to jail, that you have lost the presumption of innocence. This was a very radical position. I insisted on the first vote in over fifty years on expelling a member of Congress – not because I was trying to make a point for myself, but because I was trying to make a point about cleaning up the Congress.

In 1987 I filed charges against a sitting Speaker of the House. His cronies filed charges against me. My wife and I spent a year and a half and $144,000 in legal fees being investigated. At the end of the investigation, the only thing they found wrong was that we had not written down that I had co-signed my daughter's mortgage on her house. I was glad to announce I co-signed my daughter's mortgage. She later sold the house, so I do not even have that now.

The fact is this – I watched Jimmy Carter try to reform the system, I watched Ronald Reagan try to reform the system, I watched George Bush try to reform the system, and now I am watching Bill Clinton. President Clinton had a Democratic House and a Democratic Senate for two years. They could not pass reform.

I take this seriously. We have been focused all summer on saving Medicare. I am going to start next week writing a paper on how to think through the problem of money and what it does. Money at every level, not just campaign money, not just politicians' money, but about the totality of the power of money in America.

What are we going to do to save our society? I think this is a topic too serious to play narrow, cheap political games with. I am not going to be drawn into games about important reform issues. I just want all of you to know that I more than agree with the President and I am willing to say here tonight that if we have a Commission on Campaign Finance and Lobbying Reform, I think Ross Perot ought to be on that Commission, period.

What I am not going to do is have the President and me each submit three names to set up a partisan commission. A commission of only partisan members would report next year and the reforms would die. That is not hard. Failing is not hard. Succeeding is hard. Something some of our friends in Washington do not get.

So, I want you to know that I came here tonight to pledge to you and to Ross Perot that we are going to take on this issue. We are going to raise the tough questions. We are going to follow those questions wherever they lead, because our freedom as a country and our tradition of over 200 years is too important to let it be bought off in a wave of money from a variety of sources that we do not understand and cannot even follow.

Let me say this in closing. I am proud that all of you are here. I am frankly proud that Ross has stayed in the game and has put up a fair amount of money. He has been active and has taken some hits, but because he loves his country enough, he stays the course. We do not always agree. We agree about 85 or 90 percent of the time, but he has had the courage to keep doing it, and you have had the courage to come here.

When you go back home, you look at your children and your grandchildren, you look at your friends and your neighbors, you look at kids down the block. You know, politics is not the kind of cynical, cheap, tawdry business the news media likes to report about. The media should not take the simple, easy way of lowering everything to the lowest possible denominator.

In a wonderful letter, Catherine Drinker Bowen, who had written a history of the Constitutional Convention, wrote to a fellow historian and she said, "You know, all these liberal critics are attacking my book because it's romantic." She said, "I have to tell you, I don't know how to write about America without being romantic."

This is a great country filled with good people. This is the greatest hope the human race has ever had. We have been endowed by our Creator with inalienable rights. Our challenge is to rise to the occasion. Our challenge is to reach out for those children you are going to see. We must remember what we do in public life; what we do in campaigning; what we do in talk radio; and what we do in letters to the editor, is the necessary bridge to the next generation having freedom.

I came here tonight to thank you, to tell you that we sure need you, we need your help. Folks like Zack Wamp who has a great new election reform plan. You are going to hear tomorrow from Linda Smith and Sam Brownback. Bill Archer is going to be here to talk to real change. We need your help, not for us, we need your help for our children. Because together we are the future of this country. Success will be based on our effort and our courage. We must succeed so that all the children and grandchildren can inherit the kind of freedom that we have had as Americans. Thank you. Good luck and God bless you.

Senator
Trent Lott

ROSS PEROT: *Our next speaker, Senator Trent Lott, is the Senate Majority Whip. He is the number two Republican in the Senate. He is the first person to hold the position of Whip in both the House of Representatives and the Senate. He was elected House Republican Whip in 1980, and served in that position until 1989.*

Senator Lott was born in Grenada County, Mississippi. He is the son of a farmer turned shipyard worker. His mother was a school teacher. He received his undergraduate degree and law degree from the University of Mississippi.

His public service career began in 1968 when he became the administrative assistant to Congressman Colmer. He was first elected to the House of Representatives in 1972, and he was reelected seven times. He was elected to the Senate in 1988. While he was in the Senate, he served on the Armed Services Committee, the Commerce Committee, the Science and Transportation Committee, the Budget Committee, and the Joint Committee on the Organization of Congress. He is the current Chairman of the Armed Forces Services Subcommittee on Strategic Forces, and Chairman of the Commerce Subcommittee on Surface Transportation and Merchant Marine.

Senator Lott and his wife Tricia have two children. Senator Lott is with us this evening to share the Senate Republican view of their party's leadership to take this country into the 21st Century and make it the greatest in our country's history. Let us give Senator Lott a big Texas welcome.

———————————

Thank you very much, ladies and gentlemen. It is a great pleasure to be in Dallas with you tonight. Thank you, Ross Perot, for the invitation to be here, and thank you for all the work that you put into making this conference possible.

I would like to begin where House Minority Leader Dick Gephardt concluded by thanking all of you for being here. This is what our Republican forum of good government is all about. It is about people being involved. It is about participation. The fact that you are here tonight – the fact that you care about your country and are interested in hearing speakers talk about the issues in the House and the Senate and what our vision is for the 21st Century – is a great credit to you. We need more Americans like you all who are willing to pay the price to be involved and to travel across this country to come together and talk about the future of our country. I thank you for being here.

United We Stand America is involved all across this country, including my state of Mississippi. You know we are asked to talk about the vision of leadership that we have as elected officials in the Congress for the 21st century. Before you can really appreciate what your vision should be for the future, I think you need to look back just a little bit and learn from history. Then, we can talk about where we are now, so that we are best able to look toward the future.

I know how many of you feel. For 16 years in the House and six years in the Senate I served in the minority – 22 years struggling in the minority. I worked against, I spoke against and I voted against big government, wasteful spending, tax increases, more and more controls from Washington, campaigns getting worse and worse, and in many, many, many respects, the loss of moral values. It was a very depressing experience. But we are fortunate because there are people like you who are willing to get into the arena and fight for what you really believe.

And now, after 22 years, I have spent the last seven months in the majority, and let me tell you, it feels great. Some people say, "What difference does it make?" It is hard to see the difference that has taken place, but it is taking place. I can tell you as the Majority Whip in the Senate, we are slower in the Senate than they are in the House, but we are going to get the Contract With America done in the Senate before the end of this year.

Debating the defense authorization bill for our country yesterday and today demonstrates the big difference that I see now that I am in the majority. I believe national security is one of the principal responsibilities of our federal government. For years liberals said, "We should disarm, we do not need this, we do not need that. Let us just cut back. We do not have to worry about the Soviet Union anymore because it has imploded." Liberals seem to have forgotten why the Soviet Union does not exist anymore.

America has been strong and vigilant, and because we kept our guard up, we won our victory against Communism. But yesterday and today, in vote after vote, the liberals would get up and they would rant, and they would rave, and they would howl; and then we would vote and we would win. That is the difference being in the majority makes.

So we need to think a minute about how we got where we are. For far too long we just said, "Let Uncle Sam do it. We are not going to worry about it here in our hometown of Dallas or in our state of Rhode Island or in Mississippi. We will let Washington do it."

Well, Washington did it all right. Washington did it to us, and we have given up many rights and privileges and opportunities for the future. It is time that we stop and change the status quo in Washington. That is what you voted for in 1994, and that is what we are going to give you this year and next year as we begin to turn that tide around.

I hate to run down a list, but I need to do it, and I will be brief. We know where we have been. We do not like it. We want people to be involved and to change it. We are involved in changing it, and let me tell you what, we have been doing that this year.

First, we thought that we should begin with Congress. Congress should cut its own big appetite and get it under control first, so we have cut our legislative appropriations bill this year by $200 million. That is the first appropriation bill.

The first bill we passed said, "How in the world can we explain to the American people that we pass laws they have to live under, but that do not apply to us in Congress?" And the first thing we said was, "We are passing congressional coverage. We are going to live under the same laws that all Americans live under." And you know why I really want to do it? Because once we have to do it, I believe we will see how bad these ridiculous federal laws have been, and we will begin to change some of them.

The next bill was the unfunded federal mandates' bill. We said, "It is time that Washington stopped telling states and the localities and individuals, 'Look – you must do this. Oh, and by the way, how you pay for it is your problem.'" We passed a bill that said if the federal government says you must do it, the federal government should pay for it. If we cannot afford to pay for it, you should not have to do it.

For years I have been advocating the line item veto. I was for it when Jimmy Carter was President. I was for it when Ronald Reagan was President. I am even for it when Bill Clinton is President. We need the line item veto, and we are going to get it. Before this year is out, this Republican Congress is going to give President Bill Clinton the line item veto and see if we can save some money with it.

As the Majority Whip, my single biggest disappointment this year is the day we lost the balanced budget constitutional amendment by one vote. I tried every way I could to count those votes and get 67, but they just kept adding up to 66. If any of you out there can find one more Senator, just one more Senator, we can put a Balanced Budget Amendment in the Constitution. Then we will not only get a balanced budget resolution this year, we will get a balanced budget and we will keep it because the Constitution will mandate it. We need your help with that.

After the vote we said, "Look, we did not get the votes, let us just go out and balance the budget. That seems like a good idea – put it in the Constitution if we can, but if we cannot, just go do the job." As John Kasich, an exciting young man, told you earlier today, for the first time in years we passed a balanced budget resolution that will get us there by the year 2002. Some people said that is too quick. When I went home to Mississippi, I was visiting with a Congressional Medal of Honor winner in Hazlehurst, Mississippi. He said, "That's good, but why is it taking you so long?"

We passed that balanced budget resolution and in the next 60 days we are going to pass that reconciliation bill that enforces what we said we were going to do. We are going to get a balanced budget in place. We are going to do the job, and then we are going to reduce the debt of this country. You do not hear much talk about that.

One of the things that I advocate is tax cuts – tax cuts that give you growth and tax cuts that give you fairness. You tell me why it is fair that we should have a marriage penalty for people so that if they get married and live together; they pay more taxes than they do if they live apart. How about an IRA for a spouse living and working in the home? Fundamental fairness. Everybody else can have an IRA. How about giving that spouse in the home a chance to save a little for retirement? It is about fundamental fairness.

Explain to me how we ever got in the deal where senior citizens who want to keep working when they are 66 or 67 lose their Social Security benefits, but not if they are 64 and not if they are 71. It is ridiculous and we should get rid of that.

We should have a capital gains tax rate cut. You know why? Because it will bring growth in the economy and will create jobs. When you give a capital gains tax rate cut to people who own 60 acres of timberland in Mississippi, you know who benefits first? The pulpwood hauler in a raggedy old truck and slick tires who hauls that timber out of the woods – that is who gets the job. That is why in balancing the budget we want to also have some fairness in the tax code and some opportunities to create more jobs and to have growth in the economy. We need your help as we try to do that this year.

We need legal reform. It is high time that we get some control on bogus lawsuits in America. We are going to work on that and we are going to get that as much as we can in Congress this year.

One of the things I feel so strongly about is regulatory reform. Have you noticed all the rules and the regulations that come out of Washington? Sixty-three thousand pages worth of new regulations last year. It affects your lives. It can be the alphabet soup of the EPA or the IRS or the FDA. The list is endless. It is time that we get some regulatory reform and get some of these regulations off the books. Ask these questions:

- What is the cost?
- What is the risk?
- What is the need?

We need to stop this avalanche of paperwork and rules and regulations that come out of Washington. We need to put the decisions back in the people's hands in the private sector – in business and industry in America. We are going to do that this year.

We need your help to do that. Again, in the Senate, we have missed getting a regulatory reform bill by one vote – only one vote. We have to get 60 votes to cut off the filibuster – or to invoke cloture, as we call it in the Senate. Right now we have 59 votes. Can you get us one more Democratic Senator? We have all 54 Republicans voting for regulatory reform. We have five Democrats who are willing. But what about your senator – check on your senator. Is he or she willing to vote for real regulatory reform? If not, tell your senator what you are going to do about it next year when the election comes.

I know we have all talked about Medicare reform and welfare reform. We need them. We need them both. We need Medicare, so we need to preserve it, improve it and protect it. I make a pledge to you that we are going to fix Medicare. We are going to allow people to get what they need. And I tell you why I am going to make sure of that – my mother, who will be 83 years old next week, depends on it like a lot of you and a lot of other senior citizens. We are going to fix Medicare. We are not going to mess it up, and you can count on that as we go forward this year toward the completion of our program.

We have talked about welfare reform. You have talked about it. Political figures have talked about it for years. It is high time we do something about it. Once again, Speaker Newt Gingrich and the House of Representatives did a great job on welfare reform. It is our turn in the Senate.

When the Senate returns to session on September 6, we are going to get the job done with your help. We are going to require your work. We are going to give people an opportunity to get off welfare. There will be additional training, but the main thing is, again, we are going to get welfare out of Washington and we are going to turn it back to the states to be innovative, have reflection about it and get the job done. That is what we are doing.

You have to admit, that is an incredible list of things that we are trying to change. It is not business as usual in Washington. We are trying to change the direction of our country. We are trying to give your liberties and your freedoms back to you at the state, local, and – most importantly – the individual level. We will continue working on that.

But now I think we need to look to where we want to go in the 21st century. How can we get to a country that is even better than it is today? I am not one of those who believes that America has seen its best days. Oh, no, we are just beginning. I agree with the Ronald Reagan/Jack Kemp optimistic philosophy that we do not have to have a smaller pie and smaller pieces in America. We can make it bigger and better, but we have to think about it. We have to have meetings like this. We need a vision, and we need real leadership as we look to this next century. How do we get it? What should that involve?

The first principle I believe we must adhere to is to move decision making out of Washington, D.C.; move it back to the states and counties and cities and households. This is not just a rhetorical adherence to state rights. The fact is that, for too long, too much power has been concentrated in the federal government in Washington. We must move it back to the people where the genius of this republic really exists.

Our second principle, as we move government back to the states and individuals, is to reduce the size and scope of government across the board. It will not do any good for the case of freedom if we just move Big Brother down to the state legislatures. We must reduce the overall size and the overall dependence on the federal government. We need to strengthen these functions, but we have to design ways for them to cost less so your tax burden will be less.

Now, the third principle is this – it is very important that as we move government closer to the people and make it smaller, we must make sure that we strengthen the core essentials that the federal government does offer.

There are some basic reasons for the federal government, as Thomas Jefferson, Benjamin Franklin, George Washington and the rest of our great founding fathers would have said. We must secure our borders against illegal and unlawful entry, and we must secure our borders against illegal drugs. The President should worry a little bit about drugs, not just cigarettes.

When was the last time you heard any talk in Washington about the War on Drugs? It is as if it does not exist. But if you go out and check in America and the rural towns and the schools and in the cities, the drugs are tearing our hearts out. We better get serious about it, or they will destroy us from within.

We must also open our markets for American trade around the world. I want free trade, but it has to be fair trade or we cannot live with it.

We must ensure our national security. Yes, the Soviet Union is gone – hallelujah. But North Korea is still there, and crazy people in Iraq, and growing threats around the world, people with missiles – not just local Scuds – long-range ballistic missiles. America should not repeat history again. We should not drop our guard as we have already done three times this century.

Yes, we can be smaller, lighter, even cheaper than we were. We have to be careful, though, that our men and women have decent facilities to live in and that they have the equipment and the weapons to fight and win any war that they must fight for America's interest around the world. Oh, by the way, not under orders of the United Nations, please.

I am not going to vote to put my son or my daughter, any of my loved ones, friends, or any of your children under the command of the United Nations, or even NATO, unless there is a clear American interest and a preplanned knowledge of what we are going to do – not in Somalia, not in Haiti, and not in Bosnia, either.

What we need from leadership in the 21st century is a leadership that is based on fundamental moral principles that look to God for guidance. Our forefathers did. We need leadership that is committed to individual freedom and responsibilities with an opportunity for every American, regardless of religion, sex, race, or any other limitations. This is America, and by pulling together, we can have a magnificent 21st century.

Let me conclude by this, my favorite quotation that I have used for years, because it so strikes at the heart of what you are all about and what I believe in. It is a quotation from Peter Marshall when he was chaplain of the United States Senate. In one of his last prayers, he said, "Oh, God, give us the strength to stand for something lest we fall for anything."

I stand for a government of the people, a government out of Washington, a government that turns back to our strength – and that means you. The people in America are the ones who make America great. We need your help and we are counting on it, and with it we are going to have a magnificent 21st century.

Thank you all very much and God bless you.

Presidential
Candidates

Governor
Lamar Alexander

ROSS PEROT: *Governor Lamar Alexander is a Republican presidential candidate and the former governor of the state of Tennessee.*

He was born in Maryville, a small town in the mountains of Tennessee.

He came from a strong family. Even though they had little money, they made great sacrifices to see that Lamar had a good education. He had a library card from the time he was three years old, and started taking music lessons when he was four.

Governor Alexander says that when he walked the four blocks from his house to Maryville High School, the streets were filled with neighbors who were so interested in his well being that he couldn't have gotten in trouble, even if there had been much trouble to get into.

He says that at school his teachers taught him a lot more than algebra and music. They taught him the importance of telling the truth, the greatness of this country, the value of hard work and being on time, and the difference between right and wrong.

Governor Alexander and his family attended the Presbyterian Church. He writes, "If the church doors were open, we were there: Sunday morning, Sunday night, Monday night Boy Scout meetings, Wednesday night prayer meetings, Thursday night choir practice."

He was an Eagle Scout.

Governor Alexander graduated Phi Beta Kappa from Vanderbilt

University and received his law degree from New York University. He served as a law clerk in the U.S. 5th Circuit Court of Appeals. He worked as Senator Howard Baker's Legislative Assistant.

Lamar Alexander was elected Governor of Tennessee in 1977 and remained Governor until 1987.

In his first campaign for governor, he literally walked 1,000 miles across the state of Tennessee, visiting with the people.

Governor Alexander served as Chairman of the National Governors Association in 1986.

From 1988 to 1991, he served as President of the University of Tennessee. From 1991 to 1992, he served as U.S. Secretary of Education for President Bush.

He is the author of four books.

Governor Alexander and his wife, "Honey," live in Nashville, Tennessee. They have four children.

We are pleased that Governor Alexander could be with us this morning.

Ladies and gentlemen, Governor Lamar Alexander.

Thank you very much. Ross, thank you for the invitation. My campaign is going very well. I measure my progress by what I am doing these days. I am walking across New Hampshire and driving across Iowa. I measure the progress by the number of honks from the trucks that go along and by the number of beef burgers that we serve in Iowa. At least no one has said to me what they said to Mo Udall when he ran for the presidency. He walked into a country store in Georgia, stuck his hand out and said, "I am Mo Udall, I am running for President." And the store owner looked at him and said, "Yeah, I know that. We were just laughing about that yesterday."

Most of the news media whom I have met so far have started off by asking me one question, "Why are you here?" So let me see if I can answer that question. I am here because the revolution that Ronald Reagan helped to begin and that Ross Perot helped to nourish and encourage and that elected the Republican Congress in 1994, that revolution is stuck in Washington, D.C. I believe it should come as no surprise to any of us that it is stuck in Washington, D.C., because the revolution is primarily about changing the way Washington, D.C., does its business.

I believe it will take a Republican President from the real world to work with the Congress, to help our country move into the next century and to get that revolution unstuck and back on track. I believe further, that if we in our party, the Republican Party, decide to nominate an Inside-the-Beltway candidate, we run a grave risk that what happened in 1992 will happen again in 1996 – we will invite a third-party candidacy, President Clinton will be reelected, and the revolution will fail.

I do not believe that that is in our country's best interest, because my view of the world is much different from Bill Clinton's view of the future. I believe that our country badly needs a Republican president who can capture more than 51 percent of the vote and lead this country into the next century and get that revolution unstuck and back on track.

So I am here today, in answer to the reporters' questions, to try to earn your respect and to earn your support and to enlist you in something that I hope is much larger and even more important than a presidential campaign. I am here to offer you a choice, the choice of a Republican candidate from the real world – someone who has actually balanced budgets; someone who has actually started a company in private life, which today has 1,200 employees; someone who fought along with Ross Perot years ago for real change in education; someone who believes in freedom from Washington, D.C. and in a citizen Congress; and someone who thinks the most important two words in our discussion of America's future are *personal responsibility.*

In case anyone doubts for a moment that the revolution Reagan started and Perot encouraged and that elected a Republican Congress is stuck in Washington, D.C., let us just look at the scorecard. The economy is still sluggish. The Balanced Budget Amendment is not passed. We do not yet have a line-item veto. There are still million dollar pensions. We do not have term limits. No one is serious about abolishing the U.S. Department of Education. We do not have a capital gains tax cut. Republicans cannot agree on how many new rules from Washington to put on welfare.

So I think we need to talk about how to change things.

Last week in Marshalltown, Iowa, someone asked me before lunch, "Why don't you tell us how you are different. How would you get that revolution unstuck?" Let me try to do that in my minutes this morning.

First, I believe the election is about the future. That is another reason that I am here this morning. The agenda for this conference is on exactly the right subject – what kind of America will we have in the year 2000?

There are many people, I think, who do not understand that that is the issue. This is not an election about political hot buttons or about who can make the longest list of people we do not like or who we are mad at. It is not a contest to see who can get a bill in and out of a sub-committee in the United States Senate. It is not about electing the president of Washington D.C. or a thank you for a long-serving Senator. This should be an election for one purpose – the future, what kind of country are we going to have in the year 2000. Because in 1996, you and I are selecting the first President of the next century. The person we elect next year will serve during the entire year 2000. So I am different first because I understand this is about the future and that everything else is just noise.

I am different in the second place because I am from the real world. I have been a governor and a university president. I have helped to start a business, which today has 1,200 employees. We did that in 1987. My wife and I and a fellow named Bob Keeshan, better known as Captain Kangaroo, started a company that helps large corporations provide child care services for their employees.

I have had the privilege of going to Washington. I have been there twice – once for President Nixon, once for President Bush. You might say I have been there long enough to be vaccinated but not infected. I came home.

The real world where I came from began in Maryville, Tennessee, which was described by one newspaper as a little town at the edge of the Great Smoky Mountains where Mr. Alexander grew up in a lower middle-class family. That was all right with me when the newspaper said that, but I discovered, when I called home the next week, that it was not all right with my mother. She was literally reading Thessalonians to gather strength with how to deal with this slur on the family. "We never thought of ourselves that way," she said. "You had a library card from the day you were three and music lessons from the day you were four. You had everything you needed that was important." And I had a grandfather down the street who had run away from home when he was 11, became a railroad engineer, and came back. He used to instruct us growing up, "Aim for the top, there is more room there."

We had nosy neighbors who kept us out of trouble, algebra teachers who taught us about the Constitution and churches that were open. We had a father who would take us to the courthouse to meet the Congressmen and who taught us to look up to this country. That was the way we grew up. That was our promise of American life, aiming for the top.

We thought we could be the railroad engineer. We thought we could be the principal, like my dad, or the president of the Kiwanis Club or the President of the United States. That was the way we looked at America's future.

Now I know there are a great many children today growing up who do not look at it that way. I stood with some children in East Los Angeles who were writing poems, "Farewell To The Morning." That was their view of the future. I am running for President because I would like to change that.

The real world in which I grew up was a world in which we knew some things were right and some things were wrong – and we were not afraid to talk about it. We knew and know that it is absolutely foolish for the government in Washington to spend $600 million more a day than it brings in. We believe it is wrong for Washington to pay drug addicts $446 a month in Social Security disability benefits. We believe thousand-page education bills written in Washington, D.C. will not educate the children of Dallas or Nashville or any other town in this country.

We believe that two words that will almost never get guns out of school are *federal law*, and two words that almost always will are *personal responsibility*. We believe that racial discrimination is wrong and that racial preference is just as wrong. We believe it is wrong to burn the flag, and that 1.5 million abortions a year is a tragic number. We believe that if Congress can start its day with prayer, then surely we can find a minute of silence in a school day when children who wish to can voluntarily pray.

I am ready to go to work to help this revolution get back on track – to get unstuck.

Where I come from makes a difference in where I stand. Let me give you an example or two. First I hope you will understand that because I have actually balanced state budgets as the Governor of Tennessee, I do not think we ought to be giving any awards to

Congress for balancing the budget. I think it is their job. I would not give them an award for balancing the budget any more than I would give a Boy Scout a merit badge for telling the truth. That is what we should expect them to do. If all I had ever done was balance the budget of the State of Tennessee, we would still be at the bottom in family income. Congress ought to do it – quit moaning about it and get on with it.

Number two, I have had plenty of experience making executive decisions as a governor, as a businessman, as a university president, and as a cabinet secretary. This experience is most of what you need to deal with foreign policy and national security issues. We need a President who can make an executive decision. Ronald Reagan was not a world traveler or the China expert, and his most important early foreign policy decision was when he fired the air traffic controllers. He sent a message to Khadafy and to people all around the world that here was a President who could make a decision and stick to it.

We need a President who will stop the free fall in defense spending. We need a President who knows that you should never point the gun unless you are prepared to pull the trigger. We need a President who will never send our armed forces into battle under United Nations command. We need a President who understands that we are the number one superpower in the world, but we should never become involved in anyone else's civil war unless we are prepared to commit more than sufficient forces to pick one side and win that war.

The most important words to me in getting our revolution unstuck are jobs and growth, number one, freedom from Washington, number two, and personal responsibility, number three.

I know that growth works because I have seen it work. When I became Governor of Tennessee, we were third from the bottom in family incomes. We had never built a car. Now we are the fastest growing state in family incomes and the third largest automobile producer. It did not take any magic potion to cause that to happen. We simply tried to create an environment in which the largest number of new jobs could grow. That meant we had to defend the right-to-work law, reduce the debt, reduce the number of state employees, change the banking rules, and reduce regulations. It meant we had to keep the fifth lowest taxes, and it meant a focus on education.

That is where I met Ross Perot. He was trying to change the schools of Texas when I was in a fight with the National Education Association to put in place the only statewide program in America that pays teachers more for teaching well. It helped our children, it helped our teachers, and it helped create jobs.

When the big Saturn plant came to Tennessee, they asked, "Why would you come here?" And the President of Saturn said, "Because they pay teachers more for teaching well, and that's the kind of incentive environment in which we would like to try to build American cars that compete with the best Japanese and German cars."

I would take the same attitudes to Washington, D.C. As the President of the United States I would create an environment in which the largest number of new jobs can grow. I know a little bit about that because I have helped do that. A flatter, fairer, simpler federal income tax would help. A big cut in the capital gains tax would help. Rationalizing our export and tax policies so we do not encourage our manufacturers to go overseas would help.

When we began this country, there were only three federal crimes. Now there are 3,000, and there are 300,000 regulations that are enforced by criminal sanctions. That is an outrageous expansion of the central government in this country, and it ought to be stopped.

We will never get our country back on track and our revolution unstuck without a focus on education. I would move all the elementary-education and secondary-education decisions back to you – out of Washington – and back to families and classrooms and to parents. Then I would become the chief spokesman for radical change in our schools – school choice, pay more for teaching well, open the schools, and higher academic standards. That is what we need in the President of the United States.

I have been fighting for 20 years for more freedom from Washington, D.C. That kind of discussion began with King George. And then Ronald Reagan in 1964 said we had two enemies – Communism abroad, big government at home. He talked about the evil empire. Now we have an arrogant empire. I guess we could say, "One down and one to go."

Last summer I drove around this country and spent the night with people. I wish I could have taken you there with me. One place, with Father Jerry Hill, is not far from here – in the Austin Street Shelter in Dallas. He will not even take a federal grant anymore. "Why should I fill out forms all day Friday," he says, "to justify what I do Monday through Thursday?" He is absolutely outraged that the government in Washington is paying $446 a month in Social Security disability benefits to men who he is trying to help get off drugs and back on their feet.

Here is a real world example. Two days ago at a stop on my walk that day through New Hampshire, I met a young couple who had just come back from the Human Services office. They had been encouraged to separate so they could get more welfare benefits. That happens every day in this country, and we can put a stop to that. But the President wants to reinvent welfare in Washington, D.C., and the Republican senators, to my disappointment, want to reinvent it the Republican way.

What the election of 1994 said, what I believe Ross Perot's candidacy said, what Ronald Reagan said since 1964, and what I would say is this – we do not need to reinvent welfare in Washington, D.C. One more time, we should end Washington, D.C.'s involvement in welfare and send all of the decisions and all of the money home.

That is how the revolution becomes unstuck. Send it home. We do not need Washington telling us what our prison sentences ought to be. We do not need Washington passing 1,000-page education bills about our schools.

We need to change the culture of Washington.

I believe in term limits. I am against million-dollar pensions. Last year I used to say, "Cut their pay and send them home," and I still believe it. I believe a six-month citizen Congress – even if it were a Republican Congress – would be a better Congress. There would be fewer messages from there to here and more messages from here to there.

And now one last thing. The most important two words, *personal responsibility*. Here is where I need your help. I can make an executive decision, balance a budget, and fight for freedom from Washington. I proved that I can help jobs grow. But together we could do something about personal responsibility.

I can set a good example, so can you. I can lecture Hollywood, so can you. I could do more than you could if I were privileged to be your President. I could stop Washington from undermining personal responsibility, which is what it does when it spends $600 million a day more than it brings in or when it pays drug addicts $446 a month. But you can do more than I can about rebuilding our families, our neighborhoods, our churches and synagogues and our schools.

I had much time to think while walking across New Hampshire and driving across Iowa, and I have been thinking this – we have never lived in such a period of unparalleled opportunity. We have many problems, but we have more capacity to change them than any other country. We are the only superpower. We have one out of every five dollars. We have almost all the great colleges and universities in this world.

It was our Statue of Liberty in Tiananmen Square. It was our song, "We Shall Overcome," they were singing in the streets of Prague. It was Bibles, mostly from this country, that were smuggled into the former Soviet Union. It is our ideas of democracy that are spreading around the world.

I have been thinking about this while walking across New Hampshire. We should spend much less time thinking about what the country owes us and who we can blame for what goes wrong. We should spend much more time thinking about how we can accept the personal responsibility for the consequences of our own actions. If we did that, we would have this country back on track and this revolution unstuck in no time.

I am here to invite you to join us. I would like for us to go into the next century aiming for the top. I would like to see more children writing poems about "Aim For The Top" than "Farewell To The Morning." I would like to see someone who is writing a cover story about this country write about a rising, shining America.

If you believe that the arrogance of Washington is the problem and the character of our people is the answer, then I would invite you to come on along. Together we can get Washington off our backs. But even more important, we can get ourselves back into our families, our neighborhoods, our churches and synagogues, and our schools. That is what made this such a remarkable country in the first place; that will do it again.

Thank you.

Pat Buchanan

ROSS PEROT: *Our next speaker is Republican Presidential candidate Pat Buchanan.*

Mr. Buchanan was born and grew up in Washington, D.C. He came from a large family – 9 brothers and sisters. He was the Valedictorian of his senior class at Gonzaga Catholic High School. He graduated with honors from Georgetown University, and received his master's degree in journalism from Columbia University in 1962.

He was Senior Advisor to President Nixon from 1966 to 1974. He traveled with President Nixon as a member of the delegation to open up the People's Republic of China, and he accompanied President Nixon to the final Moscow-Yalta summit in the summer of 1974.

Mr. Buchanan also served as Assistant to President Gerald Ford, and was the White House Communications Director for President Reagan from 1985 to 1987.

He was a member of President Reagan's delegation on both his first and second summits with Mikhail Gorbachev.

He has written a number of books, the latest one titled, Right From the Beginning.

He has been a nationally syndicated newspaper columnist, co-host of CNN's Crossfire, *and host of Mutual Radio's, "Buchanan and Company."*

In February 1993, Mr. Buchanan founded The American Cause, an educational foundation dedicated to the principles of freedom, federalism, limited government, traditional values and a foreign policy that puts America first.

Pat, being on Crossfire, *I know that you are used to the heat – but I am not sure that anyone ever gets used to the heat that we are having here in Dallas. We are glad that you could be with us in Texas today.*

———————————

Thank you for that introduction, Ross. Please let me introduce you to the individual I intend to nominate to replace Hillary Rodham Clinton – Shelley Buchanan.

Folks, when I made the decision to run for President of the United States, one cynical journalist came up to me and said, "Pat, are you serious about this?" I said, "Am I serious? I have given up my spot opposite Michael Kinsley on *Crossfire*. That is a tremendous sacrifice. I gave up my radio talk show – I gave up my newspaper column – I even gave up my book contract." I said, "It is not as impressive as Newt's, but I gave it up. So, what does that tell you?" And he said, "What that tells me, Pat, is it gives me my lead – *Unemployed, angry white male may seek presidency*."

Well, I have been unemployed for about 16 weeks now. That makes me hard core, but I am looking for a job. Let me tell you something, there is a difference between me and the other folks looking for this job – a difference that Ross and I have in common. Together, we stood up against NAFTA. We stood up against GATT. We stood up against the World Trade Organization. And we stood up against the $50 billion bailout of Mexico.

People ask me, "Pat, why are you against NAFTA?" I said, "There are lots of reasons why I'm against NAFTA. You do not force Americans making ten bucks an hour to compete with Mexican workers who have to work for a dollar an hour." I said, "We should not get into a deal with a government like that. We will rue the day we did" – and we did rue it.

One year later, Mexico devalued the peso. What happened? America's trade surplus disappeared. We now have a $15 billion trade deficit with Mexico, which means 300,000 American jobs were lost this year. Illegal drugs are coming across the borders. Illegal immigration is soaring.

What do we get in addition to that? We are required to pay $50 billion to the government of Mexico. For whose benefit was that, my friends? It was not for the benefit of the working Americans on Main Street. It was for the benefit of the investment bankers on Wall Street – and we all know it.

Politicians of both parties sold us out up in Washington, D.C. They took Citibank, Chase Manhattan, J.P. Morgan, and Goldman Sachs off the hook – and they put us on it. I will tell you this – you have my word. When I get to the White House, NAFTA will be canceled. Also, there will be no more $50 billion bailouts of socialist regimes anywhere in the world.

"Why do you oppose GATT," they ask. I tell them, "Because I think it is un-American to force a single mom in a textile plant in South Carolina making $10 an hour to compete with Asian workers who have to work for 25 cents an hour."

That is not what America is all about. Why are we doing this to our people? The wages of working Americans have gone down 20 percent in 20 years right here in the United States.

Back in 1992, I went to a paper mill in the North Country of New Hampshire. It was Christmas, and every one of these guys had lost their jobs. They were about my age – middle age – middle class guys.

As I walked through the line shaking their hands, one man looked up at me, and with tears in his eyes, he said to me, " Save our jobs." For three hours, I continued driving through the North Country and I could not think of a thing I could have said to that guy – because he was not going to get another job. This man had worked at that paper mill all his life. Sometime later, I read in the Manchester newspaper that the United States Export/Import Bank had just guaranteed a great big loan for a new paper mill in Mexico.

What are we doing to our people, my friends?

I traveled on to Red Oak, a tiny town in Iowa. I was on a radio show with a young lady. And she said to me, "Do you know what happened to the Eveready plant down the road, Mr. Buchanan? Three hundred jobs, and they are shutting it down." I said, "Why?" She said, "They are taking the plant to Singapore. It doesn't cost as much."

What are we doing to our country?

When I was a little boy, my four uncles went off to World War II. They called it the ETO – European Theater of Operations. All four came home, but one uncle does not have a leg now – he has a Silver Star.

They came from the Mon Valley of western Pennsylvania – Towns like Charleroi, Donora, Monessen. They are ghost towns now.

These men came home to the steel mills and the coal mines. Our government then built up the steel mills of Germany and Japan. These countries then exported steel to the United States and these fellows lost their jobs. They live in ghost towns.

What are we doing to our country?

My wife's hometown is Detroit. It was the forge and furnace of the great Arsenal of Democracy. Now, it looks like Beirut.

They say, "Look at the Dow Jones." I say, "Look at your country, my friends."

There is another reason I oppose GATT. It is the wholesale surrender of America's national sovereignty to multilateral institutions and global organizations. While in Boston last year, I went on out to Lexington and Concord. I stood on the green in Lexington where American boys, in their teen years, stood up against the greatest Army in the world and were cut down. Then I went on down to Concord. I saw where they stood up again and drove the British back.

What were they fighting and dying for? They were fighting and dying to get the British out of our country. They were fighting and dying to achieve what George Washington said we should always maintain – that America would be sovereign – be free – be independent – and retain her liberty from all these world organizations from London and Brussels – from anywhere.

Look how far we have gone, my friends. When those 16 young Americans were shot down in the so-called friendly fire incident in Iraq, the vice-president of the United States issued a formal statement saying, "The parents of these young men and women can be proud they died in the service of the United Nations."

These 16 Americans did not take an oath to the United Nations. They took an oath to the Constitution of the United States – to you and me. And when I get to the oval office, never again will young Americans be sent into battle except under American officers and to fight under the American flag.

Let me tell you another story. Before I ran for President, I had a party at my house. A lot of friends came over. One fellow had a bracelet on. And I said, "Is that one of those POW bracelets?" He said, "Yes, it is." I said, "Let me see it." So he took it off, and handed it to me. The name on the bracelet was Captain Humbert Versace – only I knew him as Rocky Versace when he was a sophomore at my high school. He was executed by the VC ten years later.

Last week, I read that our government backed a world bank loan of $265 million to Hanoi, which is still a communist regime. This means Rocky's mother is guaranteeing loans to the regime that murdered her son. You and I are doing the same thing. You and I sent Rocky Versace to Vietnam. That, my friends, is your New World Order.

I want to say today to all the globalists and internationalists – in Tokyo, New York, and Paris – when I raise my hand to take the oath of office, your New World Order comes crashing down.

It is time we begin looking out for our country and our people first for a change.

Look at foreign aid. Each year we send $12 billion abroad in foreign aid. Fifty billion dollars goes to Mexico. World Bank loans go to communist China.

If we cannot balance our budget, what are we doing sending American dollars abroad to balance the budgets of foreign countries? It is astonishing. We have to cut our budget. We cut it for veterans, we cut it for old folks, we cut it for the elderly and for farmers – then our government ships $12 billion abroad. I tell you, when I get to the White House, foreign aid will come to an end and we will start looking out for the forgotten Americans right here in the United States.

Let's talk about illegal immigration. I heard what the governor of Texas had to say about the Mexican people being good, hard-working people with good values. He is right, but they have a bad government. We cannot continue to allow soaring illegal immigration – that is running at about a million and a quarter to a million and a half people per year who are apprehended. A country that loses control of its borders is not really a country anymore.

The Constitution of the United States obligates the federal government to protect the states from foreign invasion. Our government is derelict in this Constitutional duty. If we can send an Army halfway around the world to defend the borders of Kuwait and Saudi Arabia, why can't we defend the borders of the United States?

I will build a security fence. We will seal the borders of this country cold. We will stop the illegal immigration in its tracks if I am elected. You have my word on it. I will do it.

People say, "Pat, how will you do that when they have Proposition 187 and the people of California voted for it – but the next day a federal judge got up and overturned Proposition 187. So, how are you going to do it?" I said, "I have got a solution for these federal judges. We are going to impose term limits on every federal judge we have."

Let me talk very briefly about a divisive issue – Affirmative Action. It is like Right to Life. Right to Life is divisive. You know where I stand on that issue. Let me tell you where I stand on Affirmative Action. I have opposed Affirmative Action and racial quotas all my life. Let me tell you why. What is America supposed to be like? What is the ideal? The ideal of America is a country where it does not make any difference where your father came from – no difference where your grandfather came from. This is supposed to be a country where men are judged by their character – not the color of their skin. This is a country that is supposed to believe in equal justice under law and special privilege for none. I believe in the idea of no discrimination. This was wrong in the past. I do not believe in preferential treatment.

Remember that time – that horrible time – when we woke up in 1983, and there were 260 Marines dead in Beirut? Nobody said, "So many Asian-Americans, so many African-Americans, so many Hispanic-Americans." There were 260 Americans dead. If we can be united in death, let us be united in life, as one nation, one people under God, again.

Theodore Roosevelt, one of our greatest presidents, said we have to get away from this idea of "hyphenated Americans." Justice Scalia said the government in the United States should recognize only one race, that is, American.

This is why I promise you that I will tear out this whole diversity program root and branch – Affirmative Action, discrimination, and all racial set-asides – they will all be gone. You can rely upon it.

How about balancing the budget? You know, folks ask me, "Pat, where are you going to balance the budget? How do you do it?" I tell them, "The founding fathers left us a road map. It is called the Constitution of the United States. It is called the Tenth Amendment." What does that Amendment tell us? It tells us power is not given to the federal government. Power belongs to the states; power belongs to the people.

Let me tell you a story. Just before President Bush left office, $2

million was given to a California university to study and produce guidelines for the teaching of education to American children from fifth to
twelfth grade. It was a well-intentioned grant.

Do you know what they came back with? Six hundred pages of
guidelines to teach the children of America about this marvelous, great
and glorious country. In those guidelines, there was no mention of Paul
Revere's ride that ignited the American Revolution. There was no mention of Robert E. Lee; no mention of the Wright brothers; no mention
of Thomas Edison, the greatest inventor of all time; and no mention of
Jonas Salk finding a cure for polio. But, there was a directive to study
some radical feminist convention that occurred in Seneca Falls, New
York in 1841. I never heard of it. Have you?

What are they trying to do? They are trying to capture America's
children. They are trying to inculcate and indoctrinate America's children in their contempt for American History.

We are Americans. We do not need some character in the
Department of Education in sandals and beads telling us how
America's children should be educated. This is why we should shut
down the Department of Education and give the money back to the
states and back to the people.

A couple of years ago, I gave a little speech in Houston that I did
not think would be long remembered because I spoke just before the
great communicator himself, the Gipper. The press remembered it.
What I said in that speech was this, "There is a cultural war going on
for the soul of this country." And there is, brother, there is.

You have heard about it now in the Department of Education study.
We see it when they take down God and the Ten Commandments out
of the public schools. They replace Easter with Earth Day. It is not
only in the schools. It is in the museums. What are they doing to our
museums? On the 50th anniversary of the victory in the Pacific won by
the best generation of Americans ever produced, World War II was
presented as a racist enterprise by Americans to destroy a unique
Japanese culture. What are they doing?

Those were our fathers and uncles that fought that war. These men
fought it because of Pearl Harbor – they fought it for Bataan,
Corregidor, Midway, the Coral Sea, Okinawa, and Iwo Jima. That was a
generation of heroes. Look in our museums of how they are portrayed.
Tell it to the victims of the Bataan Death March – to the victims of the

rape of Nanking. The Administration up in Washington said, "We have to change the name of VJ Day because they do not like it over in Japan." We have to call it "Victory in the Pacific" Day. Whom do they think we were fighting out there – whales and porpoises?

Look how far they are going, my friends. They took the name of Custer off Custer National Battlefield at the Little Big Horn. I asked one liberal friend, "Why did you do that?" He said, "The Indians did not like Custer, Pat." I said, "I know that. That is why they shot him full of arrows."

George Washington's birthday, I grew up in that time. On that day there was a special sale. You went down to the stores, and you got a little, teeny TV set for a buck. That day was set aside to honor the greatest man of the 18th Century. What is it now? They took Washington's name off Washington's birthday. It is now Presidents Day so we can all pay homage to Millard Fillmore, Franklin Pierce, and Bill Clinton.

When I get up there, it will be Washington's Birthday all over again, folks.

I want to thank Ross Perot who invited me to this wonderful conference. I also want to say this about Ross. He and I did something back in 1992. Our leaders had walked away from us in 1992. They had taken a new course they had said they would not travel.

When they did, I stood up to the leaders of my party – the whole establishment of my party. I ran against them in the primaries of 1992. I fought as hard as I could and I got beat. When both parties had nominated their candidates, Ross Perot got up, and ran as hard as he could. He fought against both of them. He fought for what he believed in, and he got beat.

I am here to tell you now – our time is coming, our time is coming. I am back. I am trying to return my party to the ideas and ideals in which many of you and I have believed in all our lives. I cannot do it without you. I need your help. Join me.

We will take back our party. Together, we will go up the federal road – and we will take back Washington, D.C., and we will take America back to the things we believe in.

Thank you very much.

Senate Majority Leader Bob Dole

ROSS PEROT: Senator Bob Dole is the Senate Majority Leader, and he is also a Republican presidential candidate.

He grew up in Russell, Kansas in very modest circumstances.

At one point when oil wells were being drilled in the area, his family lived in the basement of their farmhouse and rented the upstairs to the oil well crews. His father bought milk and eggs from the farmers, and sold them to the retailers. He later worked in a granary.

Senator Dole worked from the time he was a small boy, milking cows, pulling weeds, selling goods door-to-door, and working behind the soda fountain at the local drugstore.

He attended the University of Kansas. He served in the Army in World War II as a Lieutenant in the Tenth Mountain Division. Only in America would a farm boy from Kansas be taught to fight in the mountains and snow!

He was severely wounded in 1945 in Italy and was decorated twice for heroic actions. After the war, Senator Dole earned his law degree from Washburn University in 1952. He then worked as a lawyer in Russell County and served as a Kansas state legislator.

In 1961, he was elected to the U.S. House of Representatives from

Kansas. In 1968, he was elected to the U.S. Senate and is now serving his sixth term. In the past, Senator Dole has served as the Minority Leader of the Senate, as the Majority Leader 1985-86, and as Chairman of the Senate Finance Committee. He has also served as Chairman of the Republican Party.

Senator Dole was the Republican nominee for vice president in 1976 with President Ford. He was a Republican presidential candidate in both 1980 and 1988.

His wife, Elizabeth, serves as President of the American Red Cross and she served as the Secretary of Transportation in the Reagan Administration.

One of my most vivid memories of visits to Washington was being in Senator Dole's conference room and seeing a photograph of a man in overalls. His strong, lined face looked like a figure out of a Norman Rockwell painting. I asked who it was. It was Bob Dole's father.

That picture hangs in Senator Dole's conference room as a constant reminder of his roots and the importance of the hard-working, middle-class in America.

We are indeed pleased that the Senator could be with us this after-noon. Please join me in welcoming the Majority Leader of the Senate of the United States, Senator Bob Dole.

Thank you very much. Ross, I am very honored to be here. I have been watching on television. I think I watched a couple of hours last evening and heard a number of good speeches. I took a little bit of each, put them together and here I am.

I know we are all here to try and figure out how to fix America. I want to tell a couple of little stories that take just a minute or two before I give you my views.

I remember going to Utah Beach last year for D-Day ceremonies. Many of the veterans took their kids and their grandkids with them. They are young people who never really thought much about America, much about leadership, much about World War II, or any of the wars since that time, whether it was Korea, Vietnam, or the Gulf Crisis. They never thought of their fathers or grandfathers being 18, 19, or 20 years old. I thought during those very moving ceremonies, these young people are learning for the first time what sacrifice was all about, and what American leadership was all about. I could see in their faces the beginnings of this awareness.

Sitting there watching the ceremonies and listening, watching the tears flow down the cheeks of the men and women and the grandchildren who were there to pay a tribute to men and women who made the supreme sacrifice, I said to myself, "If only all of America could be here, if only all of us could see what America has meant to the world." Because when America is engaged – whether it is morally, spiritually, materially, or economically – good things happen. We were slow getting into World War II, but when we did, good things happened.

That is the face of America. That is the America that I grew up in. That is the America that some of you might have grown up in.

Then I flash forward, say 45 years, and as a Republican leader in the Senate I am greeting someone from Czechoslovakia or Hungary or Poland, somebody who has become a leader of their party or a leader of their country. They became leaders when Communism collapsed or the Berlin wall collapsed. These new leaders have been elected by the nearly 500 million people in Eastern Europe and the former Soviet Union, who for the first time in their lives, have tasted freedom. They have the right to vote, the right to travel, and the right to go to church – freedoms we take for granted.

They have come to talk to us, not as the cynics have said for foreign aid. Rather these people of all ages have come to talk to Republicans and Democrats so they can learn to be like America. These people, many of whom who had been locked up and been in prison for speaking their minds, do not want money or technical assistance. They want to be like America. You can see it in their faces as the tears stream down their cheeks.

I want to relate where I am coming from with these two stories. America is the greatest place on the face of the earth. Let us not make any mistake about that. Nowhere on earth is better than the United States of America.

That is where I come from. I am not perfect. I have been reading some of the press saying, you should not go down there to this so-called *panderama*. But this is an opportunity to speak to real Americans from all over America. That is how I view it. I hope that is how you view it. I read the other day that you are the fly in the ointment. Well, we need more flies, if that is the case. You are making a difference. I have had a chance to visit with Ida Terry from Kansas, she is making a difference.

Many of you are frustrated with the political process. In fact, I guess everybody here is frustrated with the political process. But you did it differently. You did not sit on your hands and just complain or write letters to the editor, to members of Congress or to state legislators. You felt there was a real sense of urgency and you decided to challenge business as usual.

In 1994, for the first time in 40 years, you gave my party a majority in the House and the Senate. If we use that majority as we should, you will continue to give us that support. I listened to my friend Thomas Daschle last night. I listened to Chris Dodd and I listened to Trent Lott. I listened to a lot of speakers – Republican and Democrat.

They are all good people. We have differences in politics. Politics is a very competitive system. It is like anything else. We are fighting for your mind and your spirit and your ideas. When we stop, when we are out of ideas, or when we do not keep our word to the American people, then that is the time to throw us out .

I want to say right up front, yes, the federal government is big, but the federal government does many good things. I imagine many people in this audience, like me, were able to go to college on the GI Bill of Rights. So keep in mind that there are some good basic functions the federal government provides, but in so many areas the government has overstepped its bounds.

The government has become too big, too intrusive, too undemocratic, too insensitive. We need to rein in the federal government to make it smaller. Just as importantly, we need to reconnect the government with the common sense values of the American people. The government has grown too distant. It steps on our values. That is not what government is all about, so we want to rein it in, we want to reconnect it.

Finally, as I stated earlier, we are America. We are the greatest nation on the face of the earth, and we need to reassert American interests around the world whenever and wherever challenged.

I am not talking just about military action. I am talking about leadership – moral, spiritual, economic, and in some cases where our interest is threatened, it will have to be military leadership.

So reining in the federal government, as Ross has said, "Putting the owners of America back in charge, is job number one." We are trying to do that job.

We have made some progress. We are applying the same laws to Congress that apply to you. That is the first thing that happened in the 104th Congress this year. We think that was a step in the right direction. Even though term limits failed in the House, we are going to bring up term limits in the Senate. We are going to have a vote because we promised you we would have a vote. We are going to keep our word to the people of America.

As I watched President Clinton and Newt Gingrich shake hands up in New Hampshire about a month ago, I said to myself, "they have a great idea." Let's have a commission to reform the campaign finance system. I suggested that idea three years ago. We can do it if we let outsiders take a look at it and make the right decision and then make Congress vote it up or down. We will then have a good campaign reform system that will get rid of the special interests. We have not given up and we hope you have not given up. The *Boston Globe* had an editorial yesterday that the House ought to follow the Senate's example. We dealt with lobbying reform, we passed a law two weeks ago on lobby reform and a gift ban. We have one thing left, campaign finance reform.

I have one more idea. We have to take the whole political system off the backs of taxpayers. For 20 years our political parties, Republicans and Democrats alike, have financed their $20 million national conventions at taxpayer expense. Just let me tell you one thing. If I am elected President, the next Republican convention will be financed entirely by the members of my party and not the taxpayers of America.

While we are fixing things, we have to take a look at the Constitution. I carry a copy of the Tenth Amendment in my pocket. It is not very long. It is only 28 words in length, and here is what it says. It says, "The powers not delegated to the United States by the Constitution, nor prohibited by it to the states are reserved to the states respectively, or to the people."

You just heard Governor Thompson say in a very eloquent speech, "Give the states a chance, give governors a chance, give state legislators a chance." They are elected by the same people who elect us. We can trust our state governments. We can trust our state legislators on welfare reform and many other programs. Let us give power back to the states and back to the people where it belongs.

We in Washington, D.C. are not the only ones with compassion.

Everybody in this room has compassion. We are not the ones who know how best to fight crime. We are not the ones who understand how to educate our children. We believe they are better handled and operated on the state and local level where you can have a voice, where you can make a difference. Not all power and all wisdom is vested in Washington, D.C.

I think we are on the right track. Let us get back to what made America great in the first place, faith in the wisdom of our people, and the belief in the power of freedom. That is what it is all about.

As we put people back in charge of government, we need your help. Our second big challenge is putting America's financial house in order. My biggest disappointment this year was the loss of the Balanced Budget Amendment by one vote. I hope Ross has one more conference and invites the six Democrats who voted for it last year and against it this year, and you all persuade those six Senators to change their minds. What is wrong with a constitutional amendment for a balanced budget? It should be in the Constitution, so we cannot change it every day. We need your help.

I heard Pete Domenici tell you that we are going to get a balanced budget. We are going to make many tough choices. We are not going to preserve the big spending status quo. I hope we can count on you to help send this message: When it comes to balancing the budget, you better lead, follow or get out of the way. That is our message to those who would stand in the way of balancing the budget.

We also want to fix the tax code and eliminate most of the IRS. That would not cause any great heartbreak. Today's system, with 437 IRS forms and over five million pages of rules and regulations, is too complex. The instructions for the EZ form are 31 pages long. We should start over with a blank sheet of paper and design a tax code that is simple, honest, and fair to all people. We are going to do it. We are going to get it done. We have Jack Kemp as chairman of the commission working on a better system for economic growth and taxes. We need to make taxes flatter, fairer, and simpler.

One of the biggest challenges facing America today is the growing gulf between the values held by our people and those held by our governing and cultural elites. When I spoke out against Hollywood movies and music that celebrated sex and violence, it touched a chord with parents all across America. Democrat, Republican, and Independent

Americans are concerned about the loss of any lingering sense of shame. We are concerned about standards of decency in our popular culture. Americans feel government and the entertainment industry are working against them instead of with them in raising their children. The American people are not morally confused. It is our government and our cultural elites who are.

Travel across the country, ask the people this, "Do you want to continue subsidizing illegitimacy?" The answer is no. Ask them, "Are you happy to send your children to school where condoms are passed out and where educators run down America and refuse to respect our values?" They will answer no every time.

You have demonstrated the power you have. I hope you will take a look at some of the TV violence on cassettes and in the movies. You can make a difference as you have made a difference in the past.

Finally I want to say this about leadership. I am an unabashed patriot. I like to see the flag. I like to see the capital lighted up at night. I am as proud of America as anybody here, and you are all very proud of America. You want us to fix it. You have given us a challenge. We are trying to keep our word.

We are one vote short on a Balanced Budget Amendment. We are one vote short on regulatory reform that costs the average family $6,000 a year. But we have not given up. If you do not give up, we will get those things done on the domestic side.

There is one more thing I want to touch on. I want to talk about American leadership abroad. The last 30 months we have seen a difference in our prestige around the world. I know foreign policy generally does not show up on the radar screen, because Americans supposedly do not care about foreign policy. Well, you do care, if you are an American you care about our defenses. You care about our prestige around the world, because America is a leader. We are the leader of the free world. We may not want to pay the price, but who else would pay the price?

I would just say that, as I said earlier, I am not perfect. But I have been tested and I have been tested and I have been tested. I believe if I have one asset, and you can ask any Democrat or Republican in Congress, Bob Dole has kept his word. They may not like my word, but I kept my word because in our business, pretty much like your business, all we have is trust. If people do not trust us and if we do not keep our word to our colleagues or all Americans, we might as well move on. There is no place for us providing leadership in America if you cannot trust our word. That is why I would like a chance to lead America on one more mission and in the direction you helped us chart in 1994. We have begun the journey. We still have miles to go.

It would be my great privilege to march by your side in the last great crusade of this century to put our nation's future back in your hands to free our people once again to build an America as big as our dreams, as strong as our hearts, as great as our history demands. That is what America is all about. That is what this election in 1996 is all about.

Thank you very much. Thank you very much, Ross.

Senator
Phil Gramm

ROSS PEROT: *Senator Phil Gramm was born in 1942 in Ft. Benning, Georgia, the son of an Army Sergeant.*

His father suffered a crippling stroke while he was a small boy. Senator Gramm's mother worked two jobs to take care of the family. She worked as a practical nurse and also worked in a cotton mill for $28 per week. Senator Gramm's father read to him from his wheelchair – books such as The Iliad, The Odyssey, *and* The Outline of History.

He attended the Georgia Military Academy. He received his bachelor's degree and doctorate of economics from the University of Georgia. He worked part time in a peanut warehouse to help pay for his college costs.

In 1967, Senator Gramm became an economics professor at Texas A&M University. He won election to Congress in 1978 from Texas as a Democrat, and he was reelected in 1980 and 1982. He switched to the Republican Party in 1983, and ran for the Senate in 1984.

In 1990, Senator Gramm was reelected to the Senate from Texas and received the highest percentage of votes received by any Senate candidate in a general election in over 30 years.

Senator Gramm is married to Dr. Wendy Lee Gramm, and they have two sons in college, Marshall and Jeff. Senator Gramm serves on the Budget Committee, Appropriations Committee, and the Banking,

Housing and Urban Affairs Committee in the Senate. He is one of the authors of the Gramm-Rudman Balanced Budget Bill.

Please welcome the Senior Senator from the state of Texas, Senator Phil Gramm.

———

Thank you very much. I could not help but be moved in listening to Meredith Bagby and realizing that when there are so many who have trouble finding something right with America, let us not forget that America produced her.

Ross, I want to say I am very happy to be here tonight. Ross Perot and I are largely in agreement on who ought to be the next president of the United States. We both believe he ought to be a Texan. We both believe that he ought to be something more than just another pretty face. We both believe he ought to be plain spoken and not beat around the bush. It is just beyond that point that we disagree.

I came home to Dallas today to ask you to join me and to join the Republican party in changing America. You joined us in 1994 in saying to our Congress, "Stop the taxing, stop the spending, and stop the regulating." With your help and with an outpouring of support for change in America, we elected a new Congress and the taxing and the spending and the regulating have stopped.

We are still one election away from changing the course of American history. We are still one election away from getting our money, our freedom, and our country back. That one election is beating Bill Clinton in 1996.

As a young member of Congress, I was the author of the Reagan budget in the House of Representatives. I was a foot soldier in the Reagan revolution. And as president, I want to finish the Reagan revolution. I want less government and more freedom. I would not want the government we have in Washington, D.C. today, even if it were absolutely free. And I have some bad news for you, it is not free. In fact, as of last Thursday, it cost $1.6 trillion a year.

I believe the government in Washington has too much to say about how your income is spent, about how your business is run, about how your land is used, and about how your children are educated. I want to take that power away from Washington. I want to give it back to your family so that you can once again make those decisions every night around your kitchen table.

I want to balance the federal budget the way you balance your family budget, by setting priorities. And when "No" is the right answer, I will say, "No." Let me let you in on one of the poorest kept secrets in Washington, D.C. "No" is often the right answer in Washington, D.C.

When you are on the wrong road heading in the wrong direction, have you ever noticed that speeding up did not help you? I am very proud of the fact that last year at the darkest moment in the health care debate – when it really looked like Bill Clinton was about to convince America that it made perfectly good sense to tear down the greatest health care system the world has ever known to rebuild it in the image of the post office – when Republican pollsters were saying to us, "The last thing on earth you want to do is look into a TV camera and say 'I am against the Clinton health care plan, flat out against it'" – and when 20 Republican senators had signed on to a big government compromise that would have taxed your private health insurance, set up a national health board in Washington that would have set up health care purchasing cooperatives all over America, and would have started a new medical entitlement bigger than Medicaid for you to pay for – I am very proud of the fact that I stood up and said, "The Clinton health care bill is going to pass over my cold, dead political body."

And may I just make note of the fact that my political body is alive and well and with you in Dallas. The Clinton health care bill is deader than Elvis. And who knows, Elvis fans may be right. He may be back, but the Clinton health care bill will never be back.

Now, I know that Ross, the consummate schoolteacher, gave you all a notebook to write in. I want you to get out your pencil and I want you to write this down, "As President, I will make balancing the federal budget my number one priority and I will not run for reelection if I do not get that job done." And let me tell you how I am going to do it.

Some of you have heard me talk about the Dickie Flatt test. By the time this campaign for president is over, every person in America is going to know the Dickie Flatt test. Here is how it works. The federal budget is written so that Washington rounds to the nearest $50 million. If an expenditure is $49 million, it does not even get on the books.

You tend to lose contact with reality when you are writing a budget like that. Only Ross Perot knows what a billion dollars is. I try to make it real in the following way. I try to look at every government program, and I try to think of some hard-working, honest-to-God, flesh-and-blood American. I often think about a printer in my old congressional district from Mexia, Texas, named Dickie Flatt. I think about him because he is one of the hardest-working, best people I know. His print shop is open till 6:00 or 7:00 p.m. every night. He is open until 5:00 p.m. on Saturday. And whether you see him at the PTA, the Boy Scouts, or the Presbyterian church, try as he may, he never quite gets that blue ink off the end of his fingers.

Let me tell you what I am going to do as President. I am going to look at every federal program and I am going to think about the millions of people like Dickie Flatt in this country who get their hands dirty working for a living. I am going to ask a simple question, "Are the benefits we are getting by spending money on this program worth taking the money away from Dickie Flatt and the millions of people like him to pay for it?"

Let me tell you the answer to that question. The answer to that question is generally "No." And when the answer is "No," I will say, "No."

We are going to give Bill Clinton the line item veto at the end of this year. He may use it on a little piece of pork or a little strip of bacon. But I want you to know that before I will let the government in Washington mortgage the future of our children, I will use the line item veto on the whole hog. I do not want less government just to balance the federal budget. I want to let working families keep more of what they earn.

In 1950 when I was growing up, the average family in America with two little children sent one dollar out of every fifty dollars they earned to Washington, D.C. Today that same family is sending one dollar out of every four dollars to Washington, D.C. I do not believe Washington is doing as good a job spending your money for you as you would do if you got to keep more of it. I intend to change that.

As some of you know, I offered the Contract With America tax cut as an amendment to the Senate budget to cut government spending, to cut taxes, and to give every working family in America a $500 per child tax break.

President Clinton attacked me and attacked my amendment. He said that my amendment cut spending for children – which came as a shock. I responded by saying, "This is not a debate about how much money we spend on children, but it is a debate about who is going to do the spending."

Bill Clinton and the Democrats in Washington want the federal government to do the spending. I want the family to do the spending. I know the government and I know the family and I know the difference. And there is a big difference.

I want to cut the capital gains tax rate this year. I want to index it. I want to index it for inflation this year. I want to start lifting the confiscatory burden of inheritance taxes that causes poor, small businesses and family farms to be sold each year.

As President, I want to control spending, cut tax rates, and go to a flat tax. Now, I know if the President were here he would get up and say, "But if you cut tax rates, rich people are going to exploit the situation by investing their money. If they are successful, they will earn profits."

Well, welcome to America. I am tired of people trying to divide Americans based on their income. Socialism and the politics of class warfare have been rejected in Eastern Europe. They have been rejected in the former Soviet Union. They are being rejected in China. It is time in the 1996 election that we reject envy and socialism once and for all and forever in our great country.

One thing is very clear to me, and that is President Clinton grew up in a different America than I did. When I was a boy riding in the car with my mama and we rode past the nicest house in town, never ever once did my mama stick her finger out the window and say the government ought to raise their taxes and give us some of their money.

But my mama did something that I bet many of you share as an experience with me. Often when my mama would ride by a very nice house in town, she would say to me, "Phil, if you make good grades and if you work hard, you can have a house like that." I like my mama's America a lot better than I like Bill Clinton's America, and I want it back.

I think if we are going to be honest with ourselves in 1995 – whether we look at the economic crisis, the deficit, the tax burden, or the regulatory burden, or whether we look at the moral crisis, illegitimacy, crime, the destruction of the basic values and virtues that built America – we have to conclude that if we stay on the same road we are traveling, we know if we do not change the policy of our government, and if we do not change it dramatically, and if we do not change it soon – in 20 years we are not going to be living in the same country that we grew up in. That is the bad news.

The good news is that we do not have a problem in America that we cannot fix. The good news is that if we can force our government in Washington to make the same kind of tough, real world decisions that we make every day in our businesses, that we make every day in our families, we can make America right again.

How many businesses represented in this very room have in the last year had to make a decision at least as tough as freezing government spending at its current level for three years, or limiting the growth of government spending to no more than three percent a year for seven years? That is what it takes to balance the federal budget. Yet there are hundreds of people in this room and tens of thousands of people in Dallas tonight who in their business this very year have had to make decisions a lot tougher than that just to keep their doors open.

How many people in your neighborhood have had to make tougher decisions than that in their families when something really bad has happened, when somebody's lost a job or when a family has lost a parent?

I remember the day my father was buried. When we got home from the funeral, my mama sat us all down around the kitchen table and explained to us that our life was going to be different in a way that we had not thought about. We were going to have less income.

My mama started working double shifts. My brother started buying all the groceries and doing all the cooking. It was wonderful at first because all he could cook was hamburgers and French fries. When that got old, we discovered the frozen chicken pot pie.

My brother wrote all the checks, paid all the bills, decided who we had to pay and how much we had to pay. They never came to take us away.

I did all the housework, did all the dishes. I swore that when I went off to college, I would never wash another dish in my life. I learned a great lesson from that, and that is, if you say you are not going to do something, the Lord is going to make you do it. He is going to make you do a lot of it. And like every good husband should, I have washed many a dish since that day.

Here is my point. We changed – we grew closer, we grew stronger, because in America families and businesses live in the real world and they have to make tough choices. Our government in Washington has not lived in the real world in 40 years. If I become President, that is going to change.

I want to try to do something now that I do not think anybody else who has spoken here today has done. It seems to me it is something every candidate for President ought to do. If it is a little tedious, bear with me.

I want to tell you what I want America to look like when my programs as President are fully in effect. You know, one of the last days of the first term of the next President will be January 1, 2001, the beginning of the new millennium. Let me try to outline for you what I want to join and work together with you to produce and what I want America to look like on that day.

On January 1, 2001, your life will be better and your future will be brighter because the federal budget will be balanced. The 50 cents out of every dollar that we save that is siphoned off today to pay for government deficit spending will be available to build new homes, new farms, new factories, to generate new jobs and good growth and new opportunities.

On January 1, 2001, the federal government will be spending just 18 cents out of every dollar earned in America, down from the current 22 cents out of every dollar. Now, what does that mean to your family? Well, what it means is that the $3,900 per family that is being spent in Washington today will be spent by you and your family on January 1, 2001. That is what it means.

On January 1, 2001, our Flat Tax will be in effect and you will be able to file your income tax on a postcard. And because we will repeal the inheritance tax in the year 2001, not one family farm or one small business will have to be sold to pay inheritance taxes to the federal government.

By January 1, 2001, able-bodied men and women now riding in the wagon on welfare will have been asked to get out of the wagon and help the rest of us pull. We will have stopped giving people more and more money to have more and more children on welfare. The illegitimacy rate will be falling as fast in the year 2001 as it is rising today.

Those who can and should help themselves will be doing it. They will be learning to love it again. Those who need our help will get it in programs tailored in their own states, run in their own communities in conjunction with local churches and with charitable organizations.

It always makes me mad when I go to my mama's house and see the bars she has put up on her windows. By the year 2001, I want those bars down. I want my mama to be able to walk around her neighborhood on the darkest night and not be afraid. I want the people she is afraid of today to have bars on their windows.

By January 1, 2001, your family will be safer because we will be grabbing violent criminals by the throat and not letting them go. To get a better grip, the seven percent of criminals who commit 70 percent of the violent crimes in America will be in prison where they belong. We will have stopped building prisons like Holiday Inns. The color televisions will be gone, the air-conditioning will be gone, the weight rooms will be gone. We will turn our federal prisons into industrial parks and prisoners will work ten hours a day six days a week. They will go to school at night. When criminals have served their full sentence and they get out of prison, they will have learned a skill by working to pay for the cost of their incarceration. They will know how to read and write. They will be drug free. They will not be in any hurry to go back to prison.

America will not have an *education president* on January 1, 2001. We will have something a lot better. You will be *education parents* again. By January 1, 2001, there will be no federal Department of Education. The $32 billion every year that Washington spends trying to tell you how to run your schools will have been taken away from them. Half of it will go back to parents as an education tax credit so you can spend your own money educating your own children. The other half will go to local school boards so those locally elected school board members, local teachers, and local parents can set education policy in America again.

By January 1, 2001, America's 40-year experiment with Washington imposing values on our people will be a bad, but fading, memory. I want to be very clear on this point, having opposed Bill Clinton's attempts to impose his values on the American people, I will never attempt to impose my values on you. In fact, there is only one person who has ever lived who I would trust to impose his values on America. When He comes back, He is not going to need government to impose his values. Until He does come back, the values of our families, refined by their individual faith, will permeate up from our homes through our neighborhoods and through our communities to become the nation's values. Our government in Washington will respect those values.

In taking the oath of office, I will put my hand on a Bible and I will swear to uphold, protect, and defend a Constitution that I know enshrines equal justice under law. When my hand comes off that Bible, I will pick up a pen and I will end by executive order quotas and set-asides in the executive branch of American government. I will veto any bill that requires quotas and set-asides. I will fight for equal and unlimited opportunity for every American, but there will be special privilege for none. There is only one fair way to decide who gets a job, who is promoted, and who gets a contract – and that is merit and merit alone. If I become President, we are going to have a merit system in America again.

By January of the year 2001, we will have rebuilt our national defenses. We will be recruiting and retaining the finest young men and women who have ever worn the uniform of this country. We will provide them with the best training and the finest weapons that we can build. We will guarantee that even in a world where the lion and the lamb are lying down together, that America will always be the lion. On January 1, 2001, nowhere in the world will Americans be serving under U.N. command.

The election for President in 1996 is not just a contest between candidates and between parties. It is a choice between two very different visions for America's future.

In Bill Clinton's America on January 1, 2001, our government in Washington looks pretty much like it looks today, except it is bigger, it is more expensive, and it is more powerful. But 40 years of failure is enough. Bill Clinton will be remembered as the last president of a liberal era who believed that big government knew best. Bill Clinton is yesterday's president wedded to yesterday's government.

I will be tomorrow's President, and I will take America back to the future by reaffirming, as our founders did, that ordinary people with opportunity and freedom can decide their own destiny and the destiny of the world.

Now, I know that some people are going to say, "Gosh, in listening to Phil Gramm's 2001, it sounds an awful lot like a Norman Rockwell painting." Why not? After all, Norman Rockwell painted America as we wanted it to be, as we knew it could be. I see Norman Rockwell paintings everywhere in the fabric of our families and in our country. I see a Norman Rockwell painting in the history of my wife's family.

My wife's grandfather came to America as an indentured laborer to work in the sugarcane fields in Hawaii. When he came to America, he did not have one penny. He spoke not one word of English and he did not know a single person in America. He came here with a dream. He came here with deep faith and he came here with willing hands.

Twenty-five years later his son, my wife's father, got on a freighter coming from Hawaii to the mainland with $25 he had won in an essay contest with the dream of going to college. He went back to Hawaii as an engineer and became the first Asian-American ever to be an officer of a sugar company in the history of Hawaii.

And his daughter, my wife Wendy, under President Reagan and President Bush, became Chairman of the Commodities Futures Trading Commission where she oversaw the trading of all commodities and commodities futures in America, including the same cane sugar that her grandfather came to America to harvest so long ago.

Now, I am not sure that even Norman Rockwell could have captured that story in painting. We have a right to dream great dreams because we are Americans. If American history proves anything, it proves that what we can dream, we can do. Our founders dreamed that they could start the world over, and they did it in America. With God's help, we can make our dream, the American Dream, a reality now and forever.

Thank you very much, and God bless you.

Alan Keyes

ROSS PEROT: Our next speaker is Mr. Alan Keyes. He is a Republican candidate for the 1996 Presidential nomination. Mr. Keyes was born in New York City. He received his undergraduate and doctoral degrees in government affairs from Harvard University.

He is the author of a nationally syndicated newspaper column on current affairs. He is the host of "The Alan Keyes Show: America's Wake-Up Call," a nationally syndicated radio show.

He was the United States Ambassador to the United Nations Economic and Social Council from 1981 to 1987. He later served as Assistant Secretary of State for International Organizations. Following government service, he became President of Citizens Against Government Waste, and he was the Founder of the National Taxpayers Action Day. He served as Interim President of Alabama A&M University in 1991.

Mr. Keyes is married to Jocelyn Marcel Keyes. They have three children.

Mr. Keyes, thank you for coming to Dallas to talk to us today.

Thank you. It is good to be here. It is good to see that in the face of your enthusiastic response that the people who believe we have

lost the spirit of American initiative, the spirit of American self-government, the spirit of American self-reliance are dead wrong. The people
of this country are determined that this shall be the government that it
was intended to be. Not a government of the government, by the
bureaucrats and for the politicians, but a government of the people, by
the people and for the people, and they are gathered here.

I do not think that we have faced this critical a moment in American
history since this republic began. And I say that advisedly. If you look
back over the course of our history, we have had a lot of crises. The
great crisis of the American Revolution, the Civil War, the Depression,
and the World Wars. We have been through an awful lot. But our
founders predicted time and again that, if the final threat ever came to
the freedom of America, it would not be because of some exterior foreign invasion. It would be because somewhere along the way we lost
the will, we lost the character, we lost the wherewithal to govern ourselves and retain our freedom.

I think you can see all around you in America today that there are
signs that that crisis is upon us. We have a government that over the
decades, on the claims of war and the claims of peace and the claims of
every kind of crisis that they can find, has extended the bureaucratic
control – its control over our resources, its control through regulation in
every aspect in our lives. Some people have come along who seem to
believe that it is the business of government to substitute for the work
and the will and the energy and the responsibilities of this great people.

That is not how this country was built. It is not how we got here. It
is not how we sustained its liberty during the 19th Century, or moved it
to a position of world leadership in the 20th Century. I do not believe
that the challenge of politics in America is about the confidence we
can have in our rulers. I believe it is about the confidence we must
have in ourselves. If we are willing once again to assert that true confidence, then I think that we can put this country back on its path
toward glory.

Several years ago when I was at Citizens Against Government
Waste, I can remember reading a report of a Congressional debate
where a senator said that the deficit problem at that time was not a
problem that had people demonstrating in the streets. This was his way
of saying that he did not think the American people really cared too
much about whether it was going up or going down or what was hap-

pening to it. I am thankful that, in the course of years since then, we have managed to do one or two things to perhaps change his mind.

One of the things that I was instrumental in putting together was National Taxpayer Action Day. I took that as a challenge. I said to myself, let us prove that, in point of fact, this is an issue people will get into the streets over. In the course of a few months – it only took us about three-and-a-half, although everybody thought it was impossible – we at CAGW organized the demonstration in every Congressional district, in cities and towns all over America. People in large groups came out to demonstrate their concern over what was happening to all our money, and to demonstrate their understanding that there is not a single dollar this government spends that does not represent the work, the sweat, the dreams, the aspirations of some American family. They have no right to disrespect our dreams. They have no right to disrespect our sacrifice.

We had promoted an agenda, many points of which are today on the agenda of United We Stand America – the agenda of government discipline through a balanced budget. The Congress keeps telling us that we have got to wait until they figure out where to cut and then they will get responsible.

This reminds me of having kids in college. When you send them an allowance and they spend it all, they call and ask for more. At some point you get upset and decide you have got to put an end to it. What do you do? Do you sit down and write them a letter or make a phone call to say, "Son, if you are willing to make up a list of all the things that you are going to cut back on next semester, then after I get that list, I will decide how much to cut your allowance." Then you sit and wait with bated breath for that list to come.

No, what you do is say, "This is what I am sending you. This and no more. When you have spent it, hit the books, because that is all you are going to have time and money to do – study."

Well, I will tell you, I think it's time we sent that same message to the federal government. Did you get that letter in the mail where the federal government said, "If you will specify where you can cut your family budget, then we will raise the taxes?" Do you remember that letter? I don't remember that letter.

They raise our taxes and let our family budgets take the consequences. I say let them cut taxes, let them pass the Balanced Budget

Amendment, let them acknowledge the discipline that should be at their environs and let them take the consequences of that because that is their responsibility.

The key to deficit responsibility is simple. Do not let them fool you with all this talk of giving us their list of cuts. They cannot spend what they do not get. So do not give it to them in the first place. Today fiscal responsibility reflects what has been an enormous expansion of governmental power and spending in the course of the last several decades. They did it on every excuse they could find. Now, some of them have been pretty good excuses.

There were the wars we had to fight and the things we had to do to defend the freedom of this country. Somebody in Washington and at various levels of the public sector, discovered that this war thing was really a good deal. They decided that they were going to make war on everything in sight. We had the War on Poverty, and the War on Crime, and the War on Drugs, and war on this and war on that. It is amazing how – at the end of a lot of these wars – what we find is the poverty is worse, the crime is worse, and drugs are worse than they had ever been. And, we have less freedom than we had before.

I think it is time we began to realize that sometimes this "war on this" and "war on that," has just been an excuse to make war on the pocketbook and decision-making authority of grassroots Americans. We need to call it to a halt.

We have reached the era where the people of this country, if they wish to save freedom and self-government, are going to have to stand up and with one voice reclaim the real and special purpose and mission of this people. That special purpose and mission is not to put together the best government in the world. That is not the great genius of the American people. As our founders said, "Our genius is not government, it is self-government." Our genius is not putting together programs and bureaucracies. Our genius is in allowing the people of this country, through their investments, their respecting their wealth, and their creativity, to shape the destiny of this nation. It is our job, not the government's job, to do that.

When we did our first Taxpayer Action Day, the first one had as its slogan, "Time For A Clean Sweep." Our second slogan was "Take Back Your Power." You know, they still ring pretty true to me.

It is time that we stand up and abolish all of the vestiges of the ideas that aggrandized government power and bureaucratic control, and sweep this nation clean. It is time that we stand up and with one voice declare that we are going to do what we are supposed to do – take our power home. Not go to Washington and use it well, not go to Washington and use it to solve all the problems of the world. I tell you, when a politician stands in front of me here and outlines his 12-point program to solve the problems of America from Washington, D.C., you know one thing, that he is not telling you the truth.

There is not a single major problem this nation faces today that can be solved from Washington, D.C., and you and I both know it. There is only one reason to go to Washington today, and that is the reason we have got to keep foremost in our minds. You go to Washington to break up the power game. You go to Washington to bring those resources and take them home – back to the families, back to the businesses, back to the grass-roots, community-based institutions where they belong – so that we can get on with the business of making this country what it is supposed to be. That is our challenge as a people.

In this generation, as in every generation of Americans, we have got to decide whether we are still fit to meet that challenge. Now, that is a tough decision. It has been put to all Americans down through the years. You see at various points that critical question is put before us. Our founders made it clear that we were embarked on a mission to vindicate the capacity of mankind for self-government. Down through the years all the philosophers and the writers and the people who thought they were so smart had said that ordinary folks could not govern a nation. They had to leave it to the few, they had to leave it to the rich, they had to leave it to the powerful, they had to leave it to the smart ones that knew it all. They believed that ordinary folks did not have the capacity to deal with their own affairs, they did not have the virtue.

For the last 200 years we have been embarked on the business that our founders set us about – the business of proving them wrong, of proving that ordinary people are, indeed, capable of building up what has become the most extraordinary nation in the history of the earth. But you know that extraordinary nation, I think sometimes we misunderstand it.

I listen to folks talk about American politics these days and they talk about the American Dream, and I listen hard. What I hear from them is that this is a dream of material prosperity, a dream of economic success. It is a dream about what kind of job you have and what kind of car you drive and all of that. And if you are not quite going to live in the house that you thought you were going to live in, or have the car you thought you were going to have, then you are deprived of the American Dream.

I have really started to wonder about this. I go back to the beginning and it seems sort of strange that a lot of those people who came over to this country from old Europe, for instance, they actually left situations that were, in terms of material comfort and finances, better than the awful risks they found. They came to a wilderness. They didn't even know whether they would have enough to eat. The people who broke out to the Western Frontier went from developed cities in the East to areas of the West where all they had the opportunity to do was to work themselves to death against harsh climates, against uncertainties. I do not know that it made sense for them to do that if what they were looking for was an easy road to prosperity.

I read that American saga and I do not see people who went in search of just material things. I see the people who wrote down in their charters that what they sought was an escape from an old world which dictated their conscience and established their merit based on who their parents were or what their ancestry was about.

That is one of the reasons I oppose this whole Affirmative Action business. We are not supposed to be judged based on what our ancestors did or what they suffered. We are supposed to be judged as individuals, based on what we do, based on what we are able to achieve, based on what we represent as individuals.

And when you tell me that somebody's skin color or somebody's gender is going to determine their prospects in this world, that is turning the clock back way farther than just a few decades. It is turning the clock back hundreds of years. Back to a time before this nation stood up and declared that all men are created equal and endowed by their creator; not by their ancestry, not by their skin color, not by their gender, not by the Congress, not by the Constitution, and not by the laws. They are endowed by the almighty hand of the Creator, God, by their intrinsic worth that every human power must respect.

The truth is that, as you look back at the history, look back at the wars, look back at the battlefields, you will not find patriots facing death with certainty and with courage because they wanted another car in their garage or a fatter paycheck.

They faced those sacrifices for the sake of that dream of human dignity, for the sake of that dream of real and effective freedom, represented not by the claim that you do what you please, but by the pride that you have the capacity to do as you ought. Not because they order you, but because you choose to do what is right out of your heart and love of that which is righteous. That is what the dignity in this country offers. It offers it to each and every one who is willing to meet the challenge of that freedom.

What this means is that those principles, those things that constitute our common identity as a people, are not just about our material prosperity. They are about our moral identity. They are about our common allegiance to those great principles of moral right and truth that allow each of us to stand up and claim that not the government, not the tax man, not the bureaucrat, but that we ought to be in control of our resources and in control of our destiny because that is our God-given inalienable destiny. That is the truth on which we stand.

You know, I love the title of this organization, United We Stand America. But you do have to wonder sometimes on what do we stand united. You know what we stand united on? You look over the great American people, you will see many different races, colors and kinds and creeds. We have gathered them from all over the globe. We have gathered them of every description, every nationality. They have come here to make this nation work. They have been brought here either in chains or in hope, but always in the end under the star of the same destiny.

We have all come to America. How do you take such diversity and make it run? You make it run on the basis of our common allegiance to those principles of justice watered with the blood of our patriots and sons and daughters; watered with the struggle and the sacrifice in the pride of all this great people over the decades of our existence. That is our moral truth.

But you know what that means. That means that that allegiance to those moral principles, it is on that ground that we stand united. Not just in the cause of limited government, not just against increased taxes, not just against government waste. We are not a people who define ourselves in terms of what we are against. We define ourselves in terms of those values, those principles, those dreams and realities of human dignity that we have stood for and struggled for and fought for and died for in the history of this land.

I have fought for all of these fiscal issues, and we must continue to fight together to see them through. But there is not a single fiscal problem, not a single thing on which we are wasting our dollars in this country today that will be resolved if we let our character be destroyed. We will never balance the budget. We will never capture the problem of the deficit if we do not balance our hearts, if we do not tackle the moral deficit that is destroying our families, corrupting our children, and destroying their lives.

We must face the truth about the abortion doctrine, and we must face it now, and we must face it with the courage to say that it is an issue, and that it is certainly an issue that refers to those great principles I was talking about. And that it is an issue that we are not going to run away from. And that is why before every audience in this land that I speak to, I say that if you think you're going to solve your money problems by going to the Congress and getting all kinds of amendments through and leaving your country standing on the corrupt grounds of the licentions concept of freedom epitomized by the abortion doctrine, you are wrong. That principle will have to be rectified or this nation will not solve its fiscal problems or any of its problems. And with that thought in mind, we have to think through exactly what's involved there. That great doctrine said all men are created equal and it made a reference to God.

A lot of people are embarrassed by that. They think that you should forbid American politicians from talking about God from political platforms. You know that would mean we are forbidden to quote the Declaration of Independence. I have got to quote the Declaration, and I have also got to think through what it means. What it means is that, in drawing the line between human and non-human, and in respecting the rights of all human beings, this is not our judgment. This is not the judgment of any man. It is not the judgment of any Congress. And it is not the judgment of any woman, whomsoever.

My mother did not determine that I am a human being. Our Declaration says that God Almighty made that determination long before she got here. I will tell you straight up front, you may wish to back away from the little bits and pieces, the little buffet-style smorgasbord, and take what you like of the American principles and leave the rest, but it does not work. I, for one, remember the last time that the American people gave to human powers the right to draw the line and to put the non-humans on the one side and kill and repress or oppress them. My people were on the wrong side of that line. I will not let it happen again, not to my people and not to the great unborn.

So let us say this: "United We Stand on the great principles of our Declaration. United We Stand on the great truth that our freedom comes from God. United We Stand in respect of that authority which requires that we use our freedom responsibly. United We Stand as a people which acknowledges that freedom is our birthright; but that the responsibility to protect it, to enhance it, and to pass it on to future generations, is our discipline. It is our mission. It is our challenge as a nation.

Let us make that the top priority of this nation's life and of the generations to come – that we shall not give the government the power to control our resources or the power to discipline our lives. With these two agendas, fiscal and moral, marching hand in hand, we will restore America to what it is supposed to be – the shining beacon for all mankind of our capacity to live under a charter of law in respect of the will of God. We will be examples of what freedom can accomplish when mankind respects its origin. That is the great mission of its nation. Do not let it go. Do not let it go. Do not fail to hold that banner aloft. We shall move into the 21st century knowing that freedom will prevail.

Thank you very much.

Senator
Richard Lugar

ROSS PEROT: Our next speaker is Senator Dick Lugar from Indiana. He was educated in the public schools, graduated with honors from Denison University in Granville, Ohio and he attended Oxford University as a Rhodes Scholar. While at Oxford he went to the American Embassy in London and volunteered for active duty in the Navy at the completion of his studies.

Senator Lugar served as an intelligence officer to the Chief of Naval Operations Arleigh Burke under President Eisenhower.

After his tour of duty, Senator Lugar returned to Indianapolis to help his brother run the family's ailing farm and machinery business. While managing the business, he was encouraged to run for the school board and he did.

In 1967, he ran for and won two terms as Mayor of Indianapolis. He helped Indianapolis emerge as one of today's most successful cities. Senator Lugar was known for his outspoken support of transferring power from the federal government to local communities.

In 1976 Senator Lugar was elected to his first term in the Senate. He has served as the Chairman of the Senate Foreign Relations Committee and the Senate Agricultural Committee.

He is currently the Chairman of the Foreign Relations Subcommittee

on European Affairs, a member of the Select Committee on Intelligence,
and a 1996 presidential candidate.

Senator Lugar and his wife, Charlene, have four sons and seven
grandchildren.

Senator Lugar, we are delighted you could be with us today.

Thank you. Ross Perot, members of United We Stand America, and guests, I thank you for sponsoring this great forum to discuss the most important issues we face as Americans.

In my presidential campaign travels, I found that many Americans are frustrated with the economy and with our political process. I have proposed important changes, including abolition of all federal income taxes. I would abolish federal income taxes on individuals, businesses, capital gains, gifts, and estates, and would liberate the American people from deficit spending and the Internal Revenue Service.

We are unfortunately locked into a low growth economy by a dismal national savings rate and Federal Reserve policy. The only way we have a hope of properly funding Medicare and Social Security in the future is to get the economy growing dynamically. And the best way to encourage savings, investment, growth and productivity gains and higher wages is to give back to Americans the right to control their own money.

Under my plan, what you make is yours. There will be no federal withholding, no IRS audits, and no reporting paperwork. You alone will decide what to do with your money. You can pass that money on to your family. You can pass the family farm or the family business to your loved ones without federal tax. You will be taxed only when you buy retail goods and services at a time and an amount of your choosing.

Americans are also frustrated with the political procedures. United We Stand America members have often charged that politicians choose to pander and not to lead. They sign pledges when it seems expedient and break them just as regularly.

When I announced for the presidency, political pundits in Washington said that I was intelligent and a good, honest family man who should be President. However, they said I will not be President because I do not use wedge issues, negative campaigning, or cynical pandering – all which supposedly excite and move voter opinion.

Well, I reject the idea that Americans are not ready for a President who will lead positively and constructively.

I will talk to you today about an issue that some Washington pundits will claim is totally off the radar screen of public opinion polls, and, therefore, perhaps the proof that Lugar will never be President. But they are wrong on both counts.

Listen carefully because I have come to Dallas, Texas, to alert the American people to a most dangerous national security problem, a challenge we must meet successfully.

On April 19, 1995, terrorists demolished the Oklahoma City federal office building killing 168 men, women, and little children. Two and a half years earlier, international terrorists attacked the New York City World Trade Center. Had that explosion succeeded in undermining the structural foundation of that 110-story building, 30,000 people would have died.

From the tragedies of Oklahoma City and the World Trade Center to the first act of nuclear terrorism requires but one small step. Suppose that instead of minivans filled with hundreds of pounds of the crude explosives used in Oklahoma City and New York, terrorists had acquired a suitcase carrying a grapefruit-sized 100 pounds of highly enriched uranium. Assuming a simple design, a weapon fashioned from this material would produce a nuclear blast equivalent to 10,000 to 20,000 tons of TNT. Under normal conditions, this would devastate a three-square-mile urban area. Most of the people of Oklahoma City would have disappeared. In the case of New York, the tip of Manhattan, including all of the Wall Street financial district, would have been destroyed.

I have good news as we enter the twilight of the century – thousands of U.S. and Russian strategic delivery systems are now being elimi-nated as a result of the Nunn-Lugar legislation. These Soviet missiles, until recently, were primed to destroy most of life as we know it in our United States after only 30 minutes of flight time.

But warheads removed and dismantled from missiles in Russia now pose greater dangers than when the warheads and missiles were kept at securely guarded missile sites. Transportation over great distances to temporary storage and dismantling facilities leaves these critical nuclear materials vulnerable to insider thefts and criminal organiza-tions. Security for the warheads and associated materials, as well as nuclear products from civilian research institutes and commercial power reactors, is grossly inadequate in Russia.

In the years since the collapse of the Soviet Union, there have been hundreds of alleged or reported incidents of nuclear assets spilling out of the former USSR. The German government alone has reported more than 700 cases of attempted nuclear sales between 1991 and 1994. Many such cases turn out to be frauds, but roughly half, 350 cases, are believed by Bonn, Germany to be true instances of attempted nuclear smuggling. In the last three years alone, there have been 60 instances that involved seizure of nuclear materials.

According to another source, there were over 100 reported instances of nuclear smuggling from the Soviet Union during just the first nine months of 1994. One Russian report states that in Russia in 1993, there were 11 attempted thefts of uranium, 900 attempts at illegal entry at nuclear facilities, and over 700 instances in which workers attempted to steal secret documents.

Americans and the world rejoice that the likelihood of all-out nuclear war has declined as a result of the end of the Cold War. But the risk of a nuclear detonation in the United States will be much higher now if terrorists gain access to Russian nuclear materials. The potential consequences of nuclear leakage need to be clearly understood because the stakes are simply enormous.

Let's look at the problem head-on. In December 1994, just last December, six pounds of highly enriched uranium were seized in Prague. The uranium was found in two plastic-wrapped metal containers in the backseat of an old Saab parked on a side street in Prague. A Czech nuclear scientist, a Russian, and a Belorussian were arrested in connection with the seizure. Russian documents were found along with the nuclear material. Scientific analyses of the material indicate that it had been irradiated prior to enrichment, a common practice in the former Soviet Union's fissile material production pipeline.

In August 1994, almost a pound of plutonium was seized by German police at the Munich airport. The plutonium had been carried in a suitcase on a flight from Moscow to Munich. Two passengers on the flight were arrested, as was a third man in Munich who was identified as the buyer. This came about as a result of a sting operation by German law enforcement agencies.

One of the two men arrested after debarking from the plane had earlier met with German undercover police operatives who paid him for a much smaller sample of plutonium. This man returned to Russia, where the German agencies lost track of him until he boarded the flight from Moscow with the plutonium that led to his arrest.

The available facts and anecdotal evidence are grounds for grave concern for at least four reasons. First, the large number of real or fraudulent efforts to sell things nuclear suggests a widespread appreciation within Russia that the material has market value. Second, these facts indicate there is a considerable effort within Russia to fill the supply side of an emerging, if not yet formed, black market for nuclear materials. Third, the fact that there are a large number of failed or false attempts to move nuclear materials across international borders is less important than the reality that even a tiny number of successes in transferring these materials would have disastrous consequences. And, fourth, it's unlikely that every attempt at smuggling has been detected or reported.

The culprits in some of these cases were not members of terrorist networks, organized crime groups, or a purchasing operation for states like Iran and Iraq. Rather, they seem to be rank amateurs, yet they succeeded in getting their hands on nuclear materials and getting these materials out of Russia. Organized smuggling efforts clearly would have been more successful.

The material control and accounting systems at Russian nuclear installations are almost universally inadequate. Why was this not a problem in the past? Well, in the past, the Soviet Union was a prison. The people and the nuclear materials were locked up. Now the prison bars have been lifted.

I will cite but one example that indicates the character of the control and accounting systems inherited from the Soviet days. When the United States was asked by the government of Kazakhstan last year to remove and to store highly enriched uranium from that country – the so-called Project Sapphire – the United States recovered 104 percent of the declared inventory. Consider the implications of a 4 percent error margin in Russian inventory accuracy.

The nuclear material I am talking about can be used to make simple, but effective, weapons which could be transported by hand, car trunk, or truck bed. The most simple gun-type weapon can produce a 15 to 20 kiloton blast with a little over a hundred pounds of highly enriched uranium. Slightly more challenging but very simple implosion weapons can be constructed with about 20 pounds of plutonium or about 40 pounds of the highly enriched uranium.

According to the National Resources Defense Council, a nuclear explosion can be created with as little as 2.2 pounds of plutonium or about 5.5 pounds of highly enriched uranium. These are weights that could be physically carried by a single human being.

A quantity of plutonium the size of a golf ball is enough to make a nuclear explosive. A quantity the size of a grapefruit is enough to build a conservatively designed nuclear weapon. Nuclear smuggling becomes an especially serious matter when it involves a few pounds of material that can fit in an airline luggage bag or even the pocket of a smuggler.

Who is trying to acquire this fissile material? There is a small but dangerous and highly motivated group of aspiring states, including Iran, Iraq, and North Korea, who have made strenuous efforts to obtain fissile materials and for whom access to the Russian stockpiles would be a catastrophe for the world.

A planeload of Russian nuclear experts, for example, were arrested shortly before taking off for North Korea, where they had been hired to work in the North Korean program. Iran is reported to have sent nuclear "buying teams" into the former Soviet Union in search of nuclear materials for its incipient nuclear weapons program. States willing to invest years of effort and billions of dollars in their quest for fissile material would be willing, if not eager, to buy what they can from the offerings produced by the nuclear leakage from materials from Russia.

The United States has already experienced how a covert nuclear deal might come about. Project Sapphire began this last year with a phone call from Kazakhstan to the United States. The Kazakh authorities reported they had found a large quantity of unprotected highly enriched uranium, and they asked the United States Government for advice on how to dispose of this material. This phone call led to the purchase and the removal of these materials by the United States and their transportation to a secure storage facility at Oak Ridge, Tennessee where the U.S. stockpile is located – another victory for the Nunn-Lugar Act.

But what if it had not been the United States on the other end of the phone call line? For a Russian engineer, guard, or scientist, the opportunity to steal and sell a cache of fissile materials could be irresistible, as it could be for some American under similar circumstances.

Just as we enter a new world of peaceful opportunity, vital American interests are in jeopardy. Forces hostile to the United States, whether it is states, terrorists, or criminals, could bring these materials into the United States by unconventional means and threaten to destroy targets on our territory. And nuclear smuggling from Russia can raise the risk of nuclear detonations and nuclear blackmail in the United States.

Once we confirm the loss of nuclear material, how many false alarms and evacuations will our cities endure? Nuclear weapons in the hands of extremists willing to use them would produce terrorism of a entirely new magnitude because the central logic of terrorism is to maximize horror and shock and to create a blaze of publicity and attention for the cause it represents. By that measure, the crudest of fission bombs set off in a modern American city would vaporize entire blocks.

For these reasons, the proliferation of nuclear material must be considered the greatest threat to the national security of the United States. I repeat, the proliferation of nuclear material must be considered the greatest threat to the national security of the United States. Nothing threatens our lives more than unsecured materials and weaponry in the hands of Third World fanatics and terrorist groups.

The White House is aware of the problem, but the transfer of modest funds from one account to another in order to beef up security at a few locations in Russia will not solve the problem.

The President must be willing to move the nuclear material security issue to the top of the Russian-American agenda. And this will require the President of the United States and the President of Russia to raise the level of public awareness of the threat of smuggling and destruction in both countries.

The current approach focused on funneling limited amounts of United States assistance to U.S. contractors for work at Russian installations holds little hope of persuading Russian military and nuclear leaders to undertake comprehensive reforms. Making the prevention of nuclear smuggling a common United States-Russian interest and a joint responsibility is the priority for the safety of the United States and Russia.

Its success depends on a U.S. financial commitment that is both larger and more flexible. New funds allocated by Congress cannot be constrained in the way that the current Nunn-Lugar program has been. These monies should not be treated as foreign aid or defense procurement. They should be conceived as performance contracts that motivate a foreign government to take actions that otherwise would not be taken and that serve the United States national security interest.

Senator Sam Nunn of Georgia and I have attempted to address these problems in the Cooperative Threat Reduction Act, the so-called Nunn-Lugar program. And we have been successful in assisting the Russian people in elimination of some of their nuclear inventories, their weapons of mass destruction, and military production lines. But the Nunn-Lugar program was not created to deal with the immense size and scope of the nuclear smuggling problem. The awesome dimensions of this problem were certainly not clear in 1991.

But what should be done now? First of all, since the Russian government does not know exactly how much or what types of nuclear materials and components are now held at its installations, it cannot reliably detect an insider theft or diversion after it's occurred. Therefore, I propose that Russia and the United States immediately begin a comprehensive, joint, and completely reciprocal inventory of their total fissile material stockpiles.

Such an inventory would allow the Russian government to determine exactly how much of which types of nuclear material are being stored at all of its nuclear installations. It would improve deterrence against insider theft, since an accurate inventory of existing stocks would increase the likelihood that a theft would be promptly detected.

A joint inventory could also lead to a mutual effort to reduce the number of installations containing special nuclear materials in both countries as both governments reevaluated which of their installations really must contain nuclear material.

Two, a glaring deficiency of Russia's current nuclear security and accounting system is the near total absence of technical equipment designed to prevent insider theft. Under the Department of Energy's lab-to-lab program, however, the United States and Russia have already jointly developed a model security and material control system that consists primarily of equipment designed and produced by Russian laboratories and enterprises. This system should be put into mass production immediately and distributed to all installations in the former Soviet Union.

Third, the United States ought to devise a program to encourage the Russian government to transfer all of its dismantled weapons components, excess weapons-grade plutonium, and highly enriched uranium stockpiles, from the storage facilities at the dismantlement sites to converted Ministry of Defense bunkers. This improves significantly the security of the maximum amount of weapons-grade nuclear material.

And, fourth, in 1992, the U.S. government agreed to purchase highly enriched uranium from dismantled warheads for use as reactor fuel over 20 years. There are problems with the current deal that should be dealt with quickly and decisively by the White House.

No American citizen can feel completely safe until this material has been accounted for. Senator Nunn and I will be holding hearings on August 22 and 23 to find a solution.

The immediate major challenge is to gain the attention of the people of the United States and Russia who must demand that their leaders take bold and timely measures to protect our future.

I am prepared to lead that effort. I believe the safety of my family and my countrymen depends upon my success. I am eager to start as soon as possible. I ask for your complete understanding of this awesome challenge and for your vigorous support in building a timely solution. In a very real sense, our lives depend upon it.

I thank you very much.

Senator
Arlen Specter

ROSS PEROT: Senator Arlen Specter of Pennsylvania is a Republican presidential candidate.

He is the son of immigrant parents. Senator Specter was born in Wichita, Kansas, in 1930. Coincidentally, he, like Senator Dole, grew up in the small town of Russell, Kansas.

His father, Harry, was a Russian immigrant who sold cantaloupes door-to-door. As a boy, Senator Specter worked as a farmhand. Because the family pulled together and worked together, he graduated as a Phi Beta Kappa honor student from the University of Pennsylvania. Isn't that the story we want to keep alive for the 21st Century? Absolutely.

Senator Specter served in the Air Force Office of Special Investigation during the Korean War. After the war, he entered Yale Law School where he became the editor of the Yale Law Review. He graduated from Yale Law School in 1956. Senator Specter began his public service career as Assistant District Attorney of Philadelphia. He was appointed Assistant Counsel to the Warren Commission in 1964 to investigate the assassination of President Kennedy.

He was elected District Attorney of Philadelphia in 1965 and served two terms.

In 1980, Senator Specter was elected to the U.S. Senate. He has established himself as a legislative leader on issues such as crime, drugs and terrorism. He is a member of the Appropriations Committee, Judiciary Committee, and Veterans Affairs Committee. He also serves as Chairman of the Select Committee on Intelligence.

Senator Specter and his wife, Joan, live in Philadelphia. They have two sons and one granddaughter.

Please join me in welcoming Senator Arlen Specter, a man who has lived the American Dream..

Thank you. Thank you, Ross Perot, for that extraordinary introduction. It is the Horatio Alger story of a son of immigrants who worked hard, studied hard, and fought hard. And now I want to be the next President of the United States.

I want to thank Ross Perot for convening this extraordinary group. Ross and I had a tough negotiation. I worked it out to speak right ahead of Ross. I thought the crowd would be big and the spotlight would be hardy, so I am delighted to be here right ahead of his final presentation.

I know you want change, and I also think there has to be change in America, and I ask you to look at Arlen Specter's record for change. As an independent Republican; as a populist; as a district attorney, born and raised in Kansas who then moved to a big city like Philadelphia; I offer you my ideas and my experience and my energy to lead this country into the 21st Century.

I begin by a comparison between an Arlen Specter presidency and a Bill Clinton presidency, and I begin with the simplicity of the Flat Tax. I am the only Presidential aspirant to have introduced this into the Congress, and here it is – you can file it on a postcard. It is 20 percent. It is pro-growth. It will increase the gross national product. It lowers the interest rate. Let us not talk about cutting the capital gains tax. Let us talk about the Flat Tax which eliminates the capital gains tax. Let us talk about the Flat Tax which is not regressive. It has a large exemption for a family of four and no taxes at all up to $25,500. My Flat Tax is modeled after the Hall-Rabushka formula that Congressman Dick Armey, the House Majority Leader, has introduced. It will be tremendous for America.

The dollar is in trouble because we do not have a discipline of savings in the United States. The dollar is in trouble because Germany and Japan do not have a capital gains tax. This Flat Tax will be a tremendous support to the economy, creating more jobs and better jobs. It eliminates 12,000 pages of Internal Revenue Service regulations, and perhaps best of all, it will eliminate 5 billion hours a year for American taxpayers who have to fill out these monstrous forms.

The Flat Tax tax return form would be only ten lines long; one page, one postcard, 15 minutes. Now, contrast that with Bill Clinton's idea of America. He and Hillary's health care proposal created 105 new agency boards or commissions and many of the existing bureaus or agencies had their power and scope increased.

Ladies and gentlemen, I am a fiscal economic conservative and a social Libertarian. I think Barry Goldwater had it right when he said, "Let us keep the government off our backs, out of our pocketbooks and out of our bedrooms." That is what is selling so well in New Hampshire where we have a great organization under their state motto, "Live free or die."

I know one of the big items on your agenda is the line item veto and it is a big item on my agenda, too. It is one of the first proposals I introduced when I came to the United States Senate, and right now it is bogged down. I will tell you what Arlen Specter would do as President; Arlen Specter would not wait for the Congress. I would exercise the line-item veto because I have studied the United States Constitution, and I know that today the President has the authority to use the line-item veto.

I took this idea to President Bush, and I said, "Mr. President, the U.S. Constitution is like the Massachusetts Constitution where the governor exercises it, and you ought to use the line-item veto too." And President Bush said to me, true story, "Arlen, my lawyer tells me I can't do it." I said, "Mr. President, change lawyers." And then I, of course, immediately said to him, "but don't tell the Bar Association." I told him that I may have to practice law again someday.

Then I took the idea to President Clinton. I talked with him about the line-item veto because it is so important to me that I would like to see President Clinton exercise it, even if he got some credit for it. I think there is too much bickering and too much politicking in Washington between the parties. I think it is high time for some of us to look to America's interest over a partisan political interest.

I said, "Mr. President, you have the authority, do it." A short time later I received a letter from him saying, "I am sorry, I cannot do that because the Congressional leaders would not like it." At that time Senator Byrd was chairman of the Appropriations Committee. I knew why President Clinton was not going to exercise the line-item veto and anger Senator Byrd. And I can understand Senator Byrd's point of view, because so far only half of West Virginia is paved. The other issue that I have pushed hard in my entire career in the Senate is the constitutional amendment for a balanced budget. It is time we stop building up debts for future generations, and I have always thought that. A year-and-a-half ago Joan and I were blessed with our first grandchild, Silvi Specter. And when you see that beautiful toddler, it is just unthinkable that we ought to be building up debts and charging them to her account.

And right now, ladies and gentlemen, we are on target to balance the budget in seven years. I would like to see a constitutional amendment, but I also have to tell you that Congress ought to have the restraint and willpower to do it on our own without a Constitutional amendment.

I also want to say to you that we have to do it with a scalpel and not a meat ax. When the House sent over to us a rescission package, we had to make some changes. I am the Chairman of the Subcommittee of Appropriations which deals with education, and I did not like the cuts on scholarship loans. I thought those cuts ought not to be made. Education is a capital investment for the future, and we ought to see to it that the capital investments are taken care of. It ought to be cut very prudently with a scalpel and not a meat ax.

I think the Contract with America is a real blueprint for America. We Republicans were elected on the strength of that Contract with America in 1994. We have to focus on those core values. Those core values are smaller government, less spending, reduced taxes, effective crime control, and a strong national defense.

I hope that many of you will join us Republicans – no, I hope that all of you will join us in 1996 – if we can do the job. We let up in 1992 on our political convention. Dan Quayle wrote in his book that the convention was very harmful to the Bush/Quayle ticket and that it turned many people off and hurt the ticket very badly. Pat Buchanan is a friend of mine. You may have seen us on *Meet the Press* a few weeks ago. But we disagree now and then. I said eyeball-to-eyeball to Pat that he was wrong on the divisive 1992 convention. I believe that the Republican party – and I invite you to be with us – has to be as you are, United We Stand America. I think we have to be a party of tolerance and I think we have to be a party of inclusion.

Right here in Dallas, Texas, June of 1984, at the Republican convention they held up big placards, "A vote for our candidate is a vote for God," and I found it offensive, frankly. I do not think God participates in political campaigns. I am personally very much opposed to abortion, and I have proved that with my support for tax breaks for adopting children and my work on abstinence to try and cut down on teen-aged pregnancies. But I agree with Barry Goldwater that the government ought to stay out of our bedrooms.

I just checked my applause meter, and that got the most applause. I think I am going to talk about that at other places, too.

There is nothing in the Contract with America about the abortion issue, and I am very much concerned if we elevate abortion to that kind of attention. I want to take it off the political table.

I do not mind being interrupted for applause, and I even like being interrupted for applause, but that was almost a standing ovation with a few people standing in the hall.

I am not looking for a pro-choice plank. I am looking for a plank that says we respect human life, but we all respect diversity of opinion because that is what America is all about.

I want to talk to you about some other subjects. I want to talk to you about crime control. That is something that I have spent much time on. I was an assistant DA for four years and then District Attorney of Philadelphia for eight years, and I personally have been in the pit. I have tried rape cases, robbery cases, and murder cases, and I think we can cut violent crime tremendously if we really get down to business and make some changes.

It is no surprise if a functional illiterate leaves jail without a trade or a high school education and that person goes back to a life of crime. That is why one of the first bills I introduced was realistic rehabilitation, with job training and literacy training.

But if that individual becomes a career criminal, I think they ought to have life sentences. That is why I wrote the armed career criminal bill in 1984 which has been a very effective tool against career criminals.

From my experience as a district attorney, I believe that the death penalty is an effective deterrent against violent crime. But in order to be an effective deterrent, it has to be swift and it has to be certain. Right now there are cases that have been in the federal courts for up to 20 years. That is why I have introduced legislation, the Specter-Hatch bill, and have gotten it past the Senate. This bill will limit appeals time to two years, giving the defendant a fair chance but saying to the judge, "You ought to put this as a priority item and you ought to hear that matter first."

Along with crime control for domestic protection on our streets is the issue of security from foreign attack. We have a President in the White House today who is inexperienced, inattentive, and indecisive; and right now we have given North Korea a window of opportunity for five years to develop the nuclear bomb, and I do not like it.

What I see from my position as Chairman of the Senate Intelligence Committee – and I wish I could tell you what I see – is a major threat out there on weapons of mass destruction, and we have to protect our vital interests, but we have to do it in a sound way. I disagree with President Clinton, who vetoed yesterday the bills passed overwhelmingly by the House and Senate to lift the arms embargo and to let the Bosnian Muslims defend themselves. The UN peace keepers have a "mission impossible" because there is no peace to keep. If the UN peace keepers are withdrawn, we could subject the Bosnian Serbs to the most pronounced air attack since World War II and teach them not to commit atrocities against other people and teach them not to thumb their nose at the world.

We are going to be looking at some very important aspects of women's issues as we move ahead. I am delighted to see that Mrs. Margot Perot is on the advisory council of Planned Parenthood in Texas. I was very shocked to see the House Appropriations Committee eliminate the funding for family planning. The full House has restored it, and as chairman of that committee, I can tell you we are going to keep funding there for family planning.

We have so many teenage pregnancies – perhaps the biggest social problem in the country – and we have so many people on welfare. An important item of welfare reform is to curtail the amount of children born out of wedlock. And in that same bill with family planning, we also have the funding for the Office of Surgeon General, a very important office as Dr. Koop demonstrated with his very strong activities. Right now there is an effort to eliminate the Office of Surgeon General because Henry Foster committed one crime – he performed medical procedures authorized by the United States Constitution. The man was practically run out of town on a rail without being given a hearing by the United States Senate, and I am going to see to it that that office is preserved. I think we need a Surgeon General.

Ladies and gentlemen, I have great admiration for the underlying principle of your organization, the principle of United We Stand America. And I think that is the America which has grown to be the greatest nation in the history of the world. I am very concerned when I see our campaigns degenerating to scapegoating, to attacks on minorities or to attacks on women, and changes of position by major political candidates who have a decade-long record of voting one way. They suddenly take a look at the polls, put their finger up to the political winds, and change positions.

And you may not like some of the positions of Arlen Specter, but I am consistent on what I stand for. I am not trimming my sails to blow with the political winds.

Ronald Reagan was a great President because he had principles and he stayed the course, and that is what is necessary for leadership in America. Leadership is a matter of strength, a matter of competency, a matter of confidence, a matter of consistency, and that is what I offer.

I am very concerned when I see the political attacks on immigrants. I say that to you because both of my parents were immigrants. My mother came to this country at the age of five with her parents from a small town on the Russian-Polish border. My father came at the age of 18 from Ukraine. He literally walked across Europe with barely a ruble in his pocket. He sailed steerage – that is in the bottom of a boat – to come to America for greater opportunity. And he did not know that he had a return trip ticket to France. It was not to Paris, but it was to the Argonne Forest with the American Expeditionary Force. He was very proud to be an American doughboy.

The government promised the World War I veterans a bonus, and they reneged on it. My father was very angry. I think I have been on my way to Washington to get my father's bonus for my entire career. It is really more than that, it is to create justice and fairness and equity for the American people.

On my way here today, I stopped in Des Moines to talk to Randy Weaver, who was part of a great tragedy at Ruby Ridge – a great tragedy where a United States marshal was killed; Weaver's young son Sammy was killed; and Randy Weaver's wife, Vicki, was killed holding their infant daughter. I believe there has to be accountability at the highest level of government.

I know we need strong law enforcement because I have devoted a large part of my professional life to law enforcement. It is no coincidence that we have the most stable government in the history of the world. It is because we have a Bill of Rights and we have a Constitution.

And when you have FBI special agents giving contradictory stories, and where you have the Number Two man in the Justice Department first demoted and then suspended, I think that is the time for Congressional oversight. I will chair that judiciary subcommittee, and I promise you that we will follow the facts wherever they lead. We will find justice in that case, wherever the facts fall. Let the chips fall where they may.

So, ladies and gentlemen, as an independent Republican – some might call a maverick here in Texas – with a rather unusual background from the state of Kansas to the state of Pennsylvania, I ask you to look at my qualifications – a background in law enforcement, a background in community service, a background in foreign policy which is so important to our future security, and an understanding of the line item veto and the balanced budget.

We Republicans were given a great opportunity with the Congressional elections in 1994, and I think if we stick with core values, with limited government, less spending, reduced taxes, effective crime control and a strong national defense, that we can persuade you fine men and women of United We Stand America to stand with us in the next election. Ladies and gentlemen, we owe it to the next generation to win the next election.

Thank you and God bless you.

Thank you all.

Morry Taylor

ROSS PEROT: Our next speaker is Morry Taylor. Mr. Taylor is a 1996 Republican candidate for President. He is the President of Titan Wheel International. His company makes wheels for tractors, tanks, and other off-road vehicles. It is headquartered in Quincy, Illinois.

He grew up in Michigan and he attended Michigan Technological University. He served in the Army Reserves until 1969.

After college he worked for General Motors as an engineer. He also worked as a marketing and engineering consultant and a sales representative for a wheel manufacturer.

He and a partner purchased Titan Wheel from Firestone in 1983.

Under his leadership Titan became a publicly traded company on the New York Stock Exchange in 1994. The company has more than 3,000 employees nationwide.

Mr. Taylor and his wife, Michelle, have three children and one granddaughter. They live in Quincy, Illinois.

Please join me in welcoming presidential candidate Morry Taylor.

Thank you, Ross. Good evening, ladies and gentlemen. It is an honor to be here with you tonight. I have enjoyed being the candidate who has spent the whole conference with you.

I would like to give a special thank you to Ross Perot for making this all possible and for making it possible for a businessman like myself to run for President.

Your conference is about issues. Well, I will give you issues. To begin, good-paying jobs must come back to America. We need to put Americans first.

To balance the budget in 18 months, we need to cut one-third of the federal bureaucracy. To simplify our tax system, we need to be sure that everyone pays something. We need to rewrite our lobbying laws and get rid of the PACs forever.

I am not a politician and I am not a lawyer, so excuse me if I do not talk as smoothly as the other guys. I have been campaigning hard for the past few months, and everywhere I go I get asked the same questions, "Who is Morry Taylor, why is he running for President, and why does he possibly think he can win?"

First, let me tell you about Morry Taylor. I was born in Detroit fifty years ago. When I was eight my father moved the family to a small farming town of 300 in Northern Michigan where I attended school.

I am the oldest of four children. I have a sister and two brothers. I served an apprenticeship as a tool and die maker and a welder. I went to college. After that, I went in the service in the Army Reserves; I was honorably discharged.

I was hired by General Motors right out of college, but I left them after six months to go on my own. I agree with Ross, General Motors was not running very well back then either.

I am married to a little Irish lady, Michelle Callahan. She is the backbone of our family. We have three children. Our son Tony is 26, for any of you ladies, he is a bachelor and he looks good. I have a daughter, Mauren, who is 25 and married to Mike. They have just blessed us with our first grandchild, Meagan Marie. I have one other little daughter, she is not little, she is quite a lady. She is 17, but she is at that stage where she is going on 25.

I am the President and CEO of Titan Wheel International, headquartered in an old factory in Quincy, Illinois. For 40 years that factory boomed. They made steel wheels, the best in the world, with skilled men and women who worked for an honest day's pay at a good wage. Then things began to change. As layers of management grew, the company became filled with bureaucracy.

Our government passed laws making it more economical to move good-paying jobs overseas. Like many companies in America, the government closed the company's doors when it seemed its problems could not be solved.

Twelve years ago we bought that shuttered factory and reopened the plant. We brushed aside the former executives, rehired the real work force and began to rebuild from the bottom. Today, Titan Wheel owns 20 plants, and is in the top one-half of 1 percent of all the New York Stock Exchange companies in sales and earnings growth. The American Dream is still possible.

Why am I running for president? I ask myself that every day, because I am not a politician; I am a businessman. When will we learn as a nation that politicians are the absolute worst people to manage our government? They are too busy to listen, and they have no experience whatsoever in managing anything.

Why is it so hard for them to understand that our government with income, expenses and personnel, is the largest business on earth? Our government should really be held to an even higher standard than business, because elected officials are responsible for our tax dollars.

Many folks I meet think that the problems in our country are so bad they cannot be solved. That is not true. It is just that we keep sending those same wrong people to solve them. Would you hire a politician to run your farm or your company? I would want an experienced business person. When you have a business in trouble, you hire a president from outside the political club. Our government will never change unless we elect a president from outside the political club.

Ross Perot shook up the world with his campaign for President in 1992. He identified many problems with today's political system. Morry Taylor brings the same experienced, can-do approach, the same fresh perspective to solving the problems, the same independence from Washington, and the same commitment to getting government under control as Ross Perot did.

There is a difference, though. I believe the only way we are going to effect real change in our country is to work within the existing two-party system. I also believe that the only party that is truly home to the Ross Perot voter is the Republican Party.

Here is what we need to do to get our country back on track. We begin by balancing the budget in 18 months.

Bill Clinton says he needs 10 years to balance it. He is not going to be there that long. Republicans in Congress say they need seven. Well, if it is going to take them seven years, they should not be there either. Neither approach is good enough.

Morry Taylor is the only candidate running for president who can balance the budget in 18 months and tells you how. I would lay off one-third of the bureaucrats.

Our government has nearly three million federal bureaucrats. It is costing American working men and women nearly two hundred billion dollars a year in salaries and benefits alone. That is $3,200 a year for every American family.

When I start to cut, I cut at the top. You do not lay off the mailman, it is the six to seven layers of management above him you cut. This saves over $60 billion in wages and fringes immediately. You will pick up at least $120 billion in administrative costs. That balances the budget, and we have not even begun to cut any of the foolish government programs.

American families and businesses make cuts and balance their own budgets every day, they have to. Many Americans have already had to go through the pain of corporate downsizing. Why should government bureaucrats be exempt?

The next thing we need to do is create jobs, good-paying jobs. There is a straightforward way to do this – look out for Americans first. Let's get tough and get rid of the ridiculous laws that have made it cheaper for American companies to build their products overseas.

Morry Taylor is tough with our trading partners like Japan and China. It is one thing to say we should all play by the same rules. I will make sure they do. If the Japanese continue to place layer after layer of barriers on American goods entering their country, I will tell you what I will do in ours. I will put customs officials in an old closed military base out in Sidney, Nebraska and make their products enter customs there. The message is simple – open your markets. That is fair trade.

Most politicians do not like to talk about taxes. Don't you think any of us could have invented a better system? Morry Taylor's solution is that everyone pays something. Two percent on the first $20,000 of income, even if you are on welfare; then 10 percent on the income over $20,000; and, 17 percent over $35,000. If you make $20,000, you pay $400 in taxes. If you make a million dollars, you are going to pay about $170,000. That is it. Fair for everyone because it is a free ride for no one, everyone pays.

Finally, let us look at how politicians keep getting elected and how their actions are influenced once they are in office. If money is the mother's milk of politics, then PACs are the crack cocaine of political campaigns. Politicians find them addicting. PACs corrupt the political system; they are wrong, so let us get rid of them.

Every Presidential candidate you hear today will say that it is time we get serious about our deficit and start running our country and government more efficiently. You need to ask – if they really believe that – why are they spending your tax dollars to run their political campaigns? Morry Taylor is the only candidate who is refusing to take PAC money and the only candidate who is refusing to take government-matching funds. If the other candidates are serious about changing the way we conduct public business in Washington, ask them to practice what they preach and give the money back. Put it in the Treasury.

We all know General MacArthur once said, "Old soldiers never die, they just fade away." If you look at Washington, you will see that old politicians do not die either, they become lobbyists.

A Taylor presidency will see reform of all domestic lobbying and elimination of foreign lobbyists. If foreign governments want to get the message to Washington, let them use the embassies. We need to get them out of our cloakrooms.

The question I am asked more than any is, "How can you win?" The answer is simple. If Bill Clinton can be elected, so can I. The challenge for me is to convince folks that I have the right experience and the real solutions for the problems this country faces.

Look at each candidate and consider these vital differences. Who has never been on a government payroll except for serving in the military? Only one, Morry Taylor.

Who is the only candidate who has turned around losing businesses? Only one, Morry Taylor.

Who has created thousands of good-paying jobs? Not minimum-wage jobs. Only one, Morry Taylor.

This is an easy one. Whose pension plan is the same as his employees'? Who has worked and traded worldwide and understands how to deal in the American workers' best interests? Again, me.

Who has the experience to cut the bureaucracy from the top and has a proven record of doing it? I win that one again.

Who is the only presidential candidate not taking taxpayers' money and PAC money? Morry Taylor.

Who is the only candidate who is not a member of the Washington club? Morry Taylor.

Politicians have gotten America into this financial mess, and no matter what they say, we know they can never get us out. Our only hope is to elect someone from outside the political club to guarantee the real change that America needs.

Our government is too big, too bloated, and too intrusive. It uses half-measures that do not get the job done. I am the only candidate with the right background and the right ideas for the times.

I hope you will join us in this campaign. With your help, we can win and I will be a President Americans can be proud of.

God bless all of you, God bless America, and thank you all.

Governor Pete Wilson

ROSS PEROT: *Our next speaker is Governor Pete Wilson of California. He is a Republican presidential candidate.*

Governor Wilson was born in Lake Forest, Illinois and raised in Missouri. Governor Wilson graduated from Yale University on a Naval ROTC scholarship. He then served three years as a Marine Corps infantry officer.

He earned his law degree from the University of California. He was elected to the California assembly in 1966 and later served as Mayor of San Diego for more than ten years. As a United States Senator he was a fiscal conservative, winning the Watchdog of the Treasury Award eight years in a row.

He was elected governor of California in 1990 and reelected in 1994, receiving more votes than any other governor in the history of California.

As governor, Pete Wilson has been a national leader on the issues that most affect the American people including Affirmative Action, crime, illegal immigration, tax and regulatory reforms, and welfare reform.

He has held the line on out-of-control state spending. He has actually reduced the state's budget by $1.6 billion since his first year in office.

California's welfare program has been called a model for the nation. Governor Wilson and his wife, Gayle, who is with him today,

have two sons. We are delighted to have him with us today.
Let's give Governor Wilson a big welcome.

———————

Thank you very much, Ross. Thank you, ladies and gentlemen. It is wonderful to see so many patriots, eager to put our nation back on track. Our task is great. We must undo decades of substituting big government for personal responsibility. But we will succeed. We will repeal the welfare state, and in its place demand and get an America of individual freedom and opportunity.

We are the most energetic, most creative, most entrepreneurial people on earth. Anyone who saw Apollo 13 this summer was reminded once again of what Americans can accomplish with lots of ingenuity and a little duct tape.

Americans deserve to feel optimistic about themselves, but their future is being undermined by their lack of confidence in a federal government that is out of touch, out of step, and out of control. Washington not only overtaxes us, it misspends too many of our tax dollars in ways that violate common sense and fairness.

America can and will have a great future, but only if we start to make it work again for people who work hard, pay their taxes, and raise their children to obey the law. To do that, we must renew the basic principles on which this nation was built: By rewarding hard work and individual merit; by holding individuals personally responsible for their actions; and, by shrinking government to expand your opportunities and your freedoms.

We must remember that even the best preventative government program is only a poor substitute for America's most important institution, the family, which I define as having both a mother and a father. Let us honor and preserve the family as the very foundation of our civilized society.

These are the values that have guided you and me, but today the federal government has lost touch with these values. It has lost touch with the people who get up every morning, work all day, and struggle to raise their kids. It is these Americans who will turn our nation around, but only if Washington gives them the chance, and only if it cuts their taxes and stops the deficit spending that is mortgaging their children's future. We must stop Washington from spending our children's inheritance now. It will not be easy. It is tough to break big spenders of their habit of spending your money.

As governor, I have had to fight to get California's fiscal house back in order. It was hazardous work, but in California we have proven that it can be done.

Since Ross is our host today, I thought what better way to show you what we have accomplished than with a few charts. I do not have Ross' famous voodoo pointer, but I think you will get the picture. This was the estimate for state spending five years ago when I first ran for governor. The independent commission on state finance predicted that by this year our budget would be $64 billion.

Cutting Spending
Projected vs. Actual Spending
(in billions of dollars)

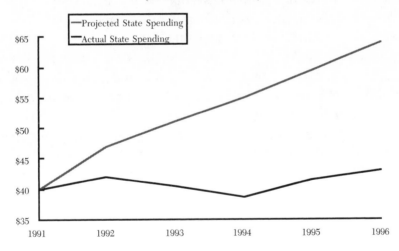

Like the federal government, California was simply living beyond its means. So I cut spending deeply, almost across the board, including entitlements. In fact, we cut everything except public safety and public education, not just slowing the growth in spending as they do in Washington, but making real cuts.

The result was that instead of letting spending increase by more than 50 percent in five years, we held spending flat. We held spending flat, and, of course, it raised howls of outrage from the special interests. This year alone, it saved nearly $2,500 for every family of four in the state of California.

That is the kind of spending discipline we need in Washington. My friends, if we can do it in America's largest state, why can't they do it in Washington?

If the federal government had shown the same spending discipline as California over the past four years and just held spending flat, instead of allowing the deficit to grow, our nation would actually have a budget surplus today.

Bringing that discipline to Washington requires fundamental change – like a line item veto, like a balanced budget – and a President who actually controls spending instead of just talking about it.

If you are satisfied with the status quo in Washington, I am not your candidate. We must change the way Washington has done the public's business for the past 30 years. We need term limits for Congress. Term limits will bring new ideas and fresh leadership to Washington, and they will break the ties that bind Congress to special interests.

People are understandably fed up with an arrogant, out-of-touch government that talks endlessly about the nation's problems, but never acts to solve them. There is no better example than welfare. It is downright irresponsible. It penalizes work. It discourages marriage, and it rewards unwed teenage pregnancy. A foreign power bent on ruining America could not have designed a more destructive system than the one that Washington has imposed on the American people. Bill Clinton declared that, "We must end welfare as we know it." But instead of ending welfare as we know it, he is perpetuating welfare as he loves it.

By contrast, the House of Representatives has passed real welfare reform. It proposes many of the reforms that we have already put in place in California. In California, I ended the practice of giving children who have children a welfare check to move out on their own. Some of these girls are not old enough to get a driver's license, and yet the federal government wants to give them a welfare check to get their own apartment and raise a child. In California, I ended the absurd practice of giving women bigger welfare checks for having more children on welfare. Why should a young couple working and saving to have a child be taxed to subsidize the promiscuity of that welfare mother? We did not think it was fair to California, not to the child, not to the taxpayers; and it is not fair for America.

This needed reform, so critical for change, is stalled in the Senate.

So we are stuck. We are stuck with roadblocks to welfare reform at both ends of Pennsylvania Avenue, at the White House and in the Senate. While they dither and debate, desperately needed reform is in peril. More and more children, now one in three, are born out of wedlock. The explosion in out-of-wedlock births is the greatest threat I can think of to America's future. Today's unwed 14-year-old mothers will give birth to daughters who will be the next generation of unwed teen mothers and sons who will be the next generation of teen trigger men for their drug gangs..

We are building too many prisons all over America because too many absent fathers are failing to prevent the brutalizing of their sons. That is why welfare reform is so urgent, and yet the Clinton Administration is actually blocking the states that are trying to end welfare as we know it.

Last week at a meeting of the nation's governors, President Clinton promised to fast-track federal approval for state reforms. Well, in California we have been waiting more than a year for one such approval, a delay that costs my state nearly $3 million a week. Only in Washington could they call that fast track. They must think O.J.'s trial is on fast track.

Governors who have the good sense to reform welfare should not have to go to Washington and kiss some bureaucrat's ring to get a waiver for reform. The states are not colonies of the federal government. The people of Texas and California and every other state deserve to set their own course and their own priorities.

Instead of micromanaging the affairs of the states, the federal government should begin doing its job discharging those responsibilities that are clearly federal. Everywhere I go in America, I find people outraged by the federal government's failure to secure our nation's borders against massive illegal immigration. I find folks who are outraged that Washington actually mandates the states to provide costly services to illegal immigrants rewarding them for breaking the law. It is like requiring free room service for anyone who breaks into a hotel room.

Here in Texas alone, state taxpayers are forced to spend nearly $500 million per year providing services to illegal immigrants. This is not just a problem affecting border states. Nearly one of every four inmates in federal prisons across the country are deportable aliens.

There is a right way to come to America and a wrong way, and illegal immigration is not the American way. That is why I have sued the federal government and led the people of California in sending Washington the clearest protest against tyrannical oppression of the states since the Boston Tea Party.

With a great deal of help from a lot of United We Stand America people in this room, we passed Proposition 187 to demand an end to the unfair burden of illegal immigration. We are a nation of laws. We must respect the law, and we must enforce it. Unlike Bill Clinton, I will not pretend that we have secured our borders against illegal immigration. I will not pretend as President. I will do it. As president I will never use your tax dollars to fight you in court when your state, like Texas, sues to be reimbursed for the cost of illegal immigration. Instead, I will use the money to beef up the border patrol and lift the mandates so that your state will never have to sue.

We must also start rewarding individuals based not only on the group that they belong to, but on the only basis that can be fair, individual merit. That is why in California I have removed Affirmative Action preferences based on race or gender. These special preferences undermine the basic American belief that anyone who works hard and plays by the rules will have an equal chance to succeed based on determination, self-reliance, and individual merit.

Since I raised these basic issues of fairness and responsibility, other candidates for President have started talking about them as well. Good. But there is a difference here. I have not only been the first to publicly address these issues, I am the only one who has dealt with them as a chief executive.

I shake my head at the debate on Capitol Hill as to whether the federal budget can be balanced in seven years or ten. I have to balance my state's budget in one year and do it every year.

I am really amused that Senators who have been in Congress for 15, 20, even 30 years have suddenly in this year of our Lord, 1995, discovered states rights and the Tenth Amendment. Suddenly they are outraged by federal mandates on the states for which they have been voting for years. They are shocked to learn of the unfair costs imposed on states by long years of federal failure to deal with illegal immigration. While they have been talking about welfare reform in Washington for the past four weeks, without much action, I have been making welfare reform in California for the past four years. That is the difference, and it is important. While the other candidates have talked about these issues, I have actually done something about them.

Most of these good men, through no fault of their own, have no executive experience. Most of them are experienced legislators. I have been a legislator twice. I have also been a chief executive twice, and there is a world of difference. A legislator talks and votes. A chief executive acts and leads. I am the first governor in America to sign into law a *Three Strikes and You're Out* measure to turn career criminals into career inmates.

I have led what is becoming a national movement demanding fairness and reform of the federal failure to deal with illegal immigration. I am the first chief executive to sign an executive order and take legal action to dismantle unfair racial and gender preferences in government hiring, contract, and university admissions. My state has provided a model for the nation on welfare reform in an effort that I began my first year in office in 1991.

I have made deep spending cuts that Washington has never had the guts to make, the kind required to turn a deficit into a surplus. I have acted. I have made change. That is what our nation needs today, not just talk, but action.

America was built on hard work, individual responsibility, and respect for the law. When the federal government abandons those principles, it puts our nation's future at risk. We must restore those values. We must reward those virtues.

My friends, it seems as if there is a new political poll every day, so why don't we just take one of our own right here and now. Is there anyone who thinks that we need a bigger deficit? Is there anyone who thinks Washington is not too arrogant? Is there anyone here who thinks that government is not out of touch and out of control?

Well, if you agree with me that it is time to take back control of our lives, then stand up. If you think leaders should quit talking and start acting, then please get up out of your chairs and stand up and be counted. If you think it is time to really end welfare, to really control spending, and really shrink government, then stand up and be prepared for the 21st Century. We can march with our voices, march with our hearts, and stand up for freedom and our future and make this nation great again.

Thank you. God bless you, and count on me to be standing with you. Thank you.

Closing
Remarks

Ross Perot

Preparing Our Country for the 21st Century

Closing Remarks to the Conference

I cannot express how much it means to me personally, and I know to millions of others across the country, that you would spend your money, take your time and make the sacrifices necessary to come here.

I cannot tell you how much it means to me that you would be so dignified and respectful to all of our guest speakers.

You have worked so hard.

You have done so much for this country.

You have received nothing.

Rarely are you even thanked.

You do it for noble reasons, and I do not have the words to describe to the American people how great you are.

I have asked Julie to express my feelings for you with this song.

["Wind Beneath My Wings" performed by Julie Hill]

Isn't she great? This young lady is an opera singer who just happened to be in the audience. Thank you, Julie.

Let me make it very clear that I would be nothing in this effort without you, the members of United We Stand America.

I want to thank every guest speaker. They came at their own expense. These policy experts were terrific.

Again and again this weekend, people kept saying, "Ross, this is incredible." People who have been to conventions said, "We have never seen anything so well organized; we have never seen so many speakers speak on time and provide so much information."

Everyone who organized this meeting is an unsung hero.

To all the volunteers that worked night and day for nothing except their country, God bless you and thank you.

All of the United We Stand America staff that has worked on this for weeks, God bless you and thank you.

We could not have pulled this off without the convention center team. In their spare time they could be on the Delta Team as far as I'm concerned.

The Dallas police have done a super job.

People say, "Well, this is almost as big and complex as a political convention. What did it cost?" It cost 3 percent of the amount spent on political conventions.

I hope that you have had a great day in the workshops. The feedback was terrific. The workshops gave you an opportunity to speak out.

Thank you for staying late this afternoon. You ought to be on your way home to get back to work, but you are here because you love this great country. Because of people like you, it will have a bright future.

All of us were thrilled last Friday night when the leaders of both parties said, "We've got to stop the bipartisan sniping, we've got to come together, and we've got to reform government."

We said to the leaders of both parties, "You would honor us all if you would give us a second *Contract With America* that implements all these reforms in a bipartisan way. It would be the nicest Christmas present that you could give the American people, and you still have more than a hundred days."

The next hundred days could be thrilling. We must reestablish confidence in our government. We must set the highest ethical standards in the White House and Congress. Our elected representatives are good people. They are operating in an ineffective system.

Reform means no more gifts, no more cash, no more junkets, no more meals, no more nothing.

Let me make it very clear. In your workshops today, you said you were not interested in having House and Senate rules passed about ethical standards. You want laws with penalties.

You also want election reform and campaign finance reform. You want everybody running for Congress to raise the money in his or her district. If they are running for Senate, they must raise their money in their state. The last thing you want is some person from a rural district in Congress that gets on the banking committee and gets money from big banks all over the world. You want to eliminate soft money.

One of the congressional leaders said that we should shorten the election cycle. That is a brilliant idea. God created the heavens and earth in six days. Surely we can elect a senator or congressman in two or three months. This will slash campaign costs.

Why don't we vote on Saturday and Sunday instead of Tuesday, so that working people can vote? Voting on weekends lets people vote on a day that is not a holy day no matter what their religion may be.

Exit polls should not be announced until the polls close in Hawaii.

Campaign finance reform should be passed in the next hundred days, and it should be a bipartisan team effort. We do not believe a commission is needed to study the problem. We know what the problem is. Special interests now buy influence with money.

We feel strongly that term limits should be passed. It is in the best interest of our country to keep a citizen congress – not make it a career.

You have expressed strong views on lobbying. Our speakers have acknowledged that it is wrong. They acknowledge it should be stopped. Both party leaders say we must clean it up.

We want lobbyists to stop writing the bills that Congress passes. We would like for the folks who we elect to write those bills.

It must be illegal for foreign companies and foreign countries to hire Americans at six and seven figures that have just come from senior U.S. government offices to represent their interests in Congress.

We do not have any problem with a domestic lobbyist presenting a good idea if he cannot give money, trips, junkets, or gifts, and cannot even take them to lunch.

We feel strongly that former presidents, vice-presidents, cabinet members, speakers of the House, leaders of the Senate, members of Congress, CIA Directors, the National Security Council members, and other senior officials for the rest of their lives must never take gifts, trips, or money for libraries from foreign interests or a foreign nation.

If they are determined to be domestic lobbyists – and that is all they could be under this plan – they would have to wait five years and let their influence cool off a little bit.

But wait, if we put in term limits, and they cannot lobby, what are these people going to do? Watch my lips – *GET A JOB! GO TO WORK!*

We asked for a detailed blueprint to balance the United States budget. Why? For the same reason if you said, "Let's build a building taller than the World Trade Center." The first questions would be: "Do you have a blueprint? Can you tell me what it's going to cost? How it's going to work?" We want a blueprint – a specific, realistic plan to balance the budget.

We also want a balanced budget amendment. We said Friday night, "Give us a balanced budget amendment that looks like the mouth of an alligator – it's got real teeth." The reason we said that is the Gramm-Rudman bill should have taken care of the deficit problem, but it did not. The Balanced Budget Amendment is essential.

There should be no off-budget programs. We want to have all programs included in the budget because you and I are stuck with paying for the programs. Eliminate the budget games. Include everything. The taxpayers are going to have to pick up the bill.

In connection with a balanced budget, we want an annual financial report for the United States of America.

We are within one vote in the Senate on the Balanced Budget Amendment. It is time to hit the wall and climb the cliffs.

Americans can do anything.

We can get this done.

We have got to go out and get that vote.

We must have a new tax system. It must be fair, and it must pay our bills. Every tax program starts out small. Social Security started out with a two percent payroll deduction, but the maximum that could be withheld from your check was $30 per year. Our first income tax was one percent of our paycheck. These percentages skyrocketed over time.

We propose that in the new tax system, if Congress wants to raise the rates, they must put it on the next federal election ballot for the people to approve it.

We have to pay for it.

Why shouldn't we have to approve it?

We will have a balanced budget amendment with alligator teeth.

We will have a new tax system. The voters must approve tax increases. Finally, we will impose discipline on spending. That is a new experience in our country.

After studying all these different tax systems, your first impression is that the national sales tax may be the best alternative. We need to study each plan carefully. We need to build computer models to test them carefully and rationally. Taxes are relatively easy to evaluate. Social programs are much more difficult.

We have problems with Medicare, Medicaid, and Social Security. Pretending we don't is not in the best interest of the recipients of those programs. We are not recommending that these programs be eliminated.

They must be overhauled carefully before they destroy themselves.

A bell is no bell until you ring it. You have rung the bell this weekend. A song is no song until you sing it. You have been singing the song of the American people since 1992, but you just packed the concert hall this weekend. All of America got to see our leaders and the policy makers here.

Finally and most importantly, you, among all the people in this country, have been a shining example that love in your heart is not put there to stay. You have been generously giving your love away, yet your hearts are still filled with love. The more love you give away, the more you seem to have.

Starting now, across America, take care of your neighbors, take care of the people down the street.

Do not say, "Oh, a government program will do it." Your hearts are filled with love, and you have given and given and given. Yet, your hearts are still overflowing with love. Your love and your devotion and your pure spirit is an example to this country.

All of you keep asking, "Where's Margot?" She has been here all weekend.

God bless her. She is a soldier like the rest of you.

I have asked Julie to come up to sing a song that I would like to dedicate to both Margot and you.

Keep in mind, this song is for Margot and for you because we consider all of you part of our family.

["You Light Up My Life" performed by Julie Hill]

MARGOT PEROT: Thank you very much, Julie. I have loved getting to know so many of you this weekend. It has been a wonderful experience for all of us and certainly for Ross and me. Thank you again.

ROSS PEROT: Everybody says, "Ross, why in the world did Margot ever marry you?" I don't know, but in the words of a western song, "I got her boys, and that makes me the winner."

We have our mission. We have work to do.

You have always stood and delivered.

You have never flinched.

You get it done.

In closing, there is one song that really explains to America who you are. I have asked the band to light up the hall playing it as you leave, and that song is "When the Saints Go Marching In."

Thank you very much for coming to Dallas. Thank you for being here. Thank you for the workshops.

["When the Saints Go Marching In" performed by the band]

ROSS PEROT: One last good-bye. Good-bye and God bless you all. You are the greatest.

Acknowledgments

I want to thank our distinguished speakers and their staffs for arranging their busy schedules to participate in this conference. Their presence during a hot Texas August while most of them were supposed to be on vacation says much about their dedication to their country.

The staff members of United We Stand America and many volunteers worked tirelessly for three months to put this conference together. Anyone who has ever been involved in a project of this size can appreciate the amount of work required to make things happen flawlessly. The staff of the City of Dallas Convention Center did a remarkable job of hosting this event.

This book was made possible with the assistance of several people. I want to thank Mike Poss, Marvin Singleton, Ralph Perkins, Cone Johnson, Bobbie Van Pelt, C. J. Barthelenghi, Pauline Neuhoff, Bill Fisher, Todd Sharp, Shari Guthrie, Cordelia Spicer, Becky Bates, and Paul Nichols.

Ross Perot

Intensive Care:
We Must Save Medicare
and Medicaid Now
by Ross Perot

Medicare costs are skyrocketing. Millions of Americans, near or past retirement have valid concerns that Medicare and Medicaid will be unable to service their health care needs. Ross Perot offers a straightforward, thorough analysis of this problem and proposes workable solutions that everyone can understand. Cost of $9.99 ($10.65 for Texas residents) includes shipping & handling.

United We Stand America Order Form
or call 1-800-925-1300 to order by phone

NAME (Please print)

_____

PHONE

_____

ADDRESS

_____

CITY   STATE   ZIP

                                            Total

___ Total number   X   Cost of $9.99 $ _____
    of books   *($10.65 for TX residents)*

Method of payment:

_____Enclosed is my check or money order made payable to:
      UWSA Books, P.O. Box 6, Dallas, Texas 75221

_____Please charge to my credit card:

_____

Card Number & Type (Visa, MasterCard, Discover, AMEX)

_____

Expiration Date   Signature

UNITED WE STAND AMERICA
ENROLLMENT FORM

_____ Yes! I want to JOIN UNITED WE STAND AMERICA.

_____ Yes! I want to RENEW my UWSA membership.

_____ Yes! I want to GIVE A GIFT UWSA membership to the person listed below. *Please print your name, address and membership number in the space provided on the next page.*

Name _____

First   Middle Initial   Last

There is no additional cost for family members residing at the address listed below. Please provide their names on the next page.

Address _____ Apt. # _____

City/State/Zip _____

Day Phone   (   ) _____

Evening Phone   (   ) _____

Fax #   (   ) _____

E-Mail Address _____

Membership # _____

(for renewing members only)

___ Enclosed is my $20 annual fee. $ _____

___ I would like to make the following contribution to United We Stand America.

     __ $250 __ $100 __ $50 __ Other $ _____

                        TOTAL $ _____

___ Enclosed is a check for the total made payable to: UWSA Mail to: UWSA, P.O. Box 6, Dallas, TX 75221-0006

___ Please charge the total to the credit card below.

Number _ _ _ _ _ _ _ _ _ _ _ _ _ _ _ Expiration Date _ _ - _ _

Type of card: __ Amer. Exp. __ Discover __ MasterCard __ VISA

Signature _____

Contributions and membership fees are not tax deductible.

Please list additional family members who reside at your address to be included on your Family Membership:

Please Print		
Name _____		
First	Middle Initial	Last
Name _____		
First	Middle Initial	Last
Name _____		
First	Middle Initial	Last
Name _____		
First	Middle Initial	Last

Gift Membership Sponsor:

Please Print
Sponsor's Name _____
Address _____
City/State/Zip _____
Membership # _____
___ I am not a member, but wish to give a gift membership.

For more information about United We Stand America, call (214)960-9100.